CORRIDOS IN MIGRANT MEMORY

Corridos IN Migrant MEMORY

MARTHA I. CHEW SÁNCHEZ

UNIVERSITY OF NEW MEXICO PRESS
ALBUQUERQUE

© 2006 by the University of New Mexico Press
All rights reserved. Published 2006
Printed in the United States of America

YEAR   PRINTING
11 10 09 08 07 06   1 2 3 4 5 6

Library of Congress Cataloging-in-Publication Data

Sánchez, Martha I. Chew, 1968–
   Corridos in migrant memory / Martha I. Chew Sánchez.— 1st ed.
      p. cm.
   Includes bibliographical references (p.   ) and index.
   ISBN-13: 978-0-8263-3478-7 (pbk. : alk. paper)
   ISBN-10: 0-8263-3478-4 (pbk. : alk. paper)
   1. Folk songs, Spanish—Mexico—History and criticism. 2. Corridos—
Mexico—History and criticism. 3. Alien labor, Mexican—New
Mexico—Songs and music—History and criticism. 4. Alien labor,
Mexican—Texas—Songs and music—History and criticism. I. Title.
   ML3570.S26 2006
   782.42162'6872073—dc22

                                          2006002273

Book design and composition by Damien Shay
Body type is Columbus MT 10.5/14
Display is Meistersinger and ATSackers

Contents

Acknowledgments

To my mother, Selfa Sánchez Cisneros, whose sense of responsibility and hard work were crucial to my studies. To the memory of my father, Manuel Chew, whose love for corridos and *conjunto norteño* music and fascination with migrant experiences inspired me to carry out this work. To my uncle Dr. Rodolfo Sánchez Cisneros, my guardian angel throughout my childhood, who has been very generous in his support, understanding, and love for me. I want to express my deepest gratitude to my sister Selfa Alejandra for her unconditional support in this project; she was my constant companion while I was doing my fieldwork and in every single phase of the writing process. Alejandra has been my best support and greatest critic and, more importantly, the photographer for this work. To my brother Pedro for his generous heart, sharp mind, and support. To my sister Mariana for encouraging me to continue studying. To my nephew and *ahijado* Pedro and to my *sobrinitas*, Ximena, Nolí, and Thelma. To my uncles Hermilo Sánchez Cisneros, Alberto Sánchez Cisneros, Francisco Sánchez Cisneros, and Mario Sánchez Cisneros and my cousins Virginia Sánchez Landeros, Rosa Elia Sánchez Gómez, and Alberto Sánchez Gómez for their love and constant presence in my childhood; they taught me to appreciate and love various genres of Mexican music. To my aunts Hortencia Chew and Irma Chew and my uncle Pedro Chew, the sisters and brother of my father, who, like him, taught me very patiently and with great love the wonderful gifts of being a migrant. To Alberto Esquinca and Zulma Méndez, *mis hermanos*, for their generosity, companionship, wisdom, and care. To David Venn, *mi compañero*, for his love during these years.

I am very grateful to Hortencia Vitela and her family, El Pasoans who became part of my family by providing me with great support and care while I was studying on the border. I am most thankful to my very dear friend Rosamaría Tabuenca and to the memory of John Moyer, wonderful mentors. My warm thanks to my friend and partner in crime, Yolanda Olivas, whose wisdom, wit, and laughter made my life as a student in Albuquerque so enjoyable. To my *comadre* Bidisha Barnejee, a wonderful colleague and friend, for her great understanding, support, and love, and also to her daughter, *mi ahijadita* Arushi Gosh. I am especially grateful to *la familia* Prieto Barrera for their incredible love, support, understanding, and help while I was doing this work. To Dr. Margaret Bass, *mi hermana*, for her invaluable mentorship and care, in particular for her unflagging commitment fairness in the academia. To Dr. Judith DeGroat whose work and activism has been quite inspirational to me. Both Margaret and Judith have woven a creative and fertile space for academic women and for that I am immensely grateful. To Dr. Marina Llorente, Dr. Ron Flores, Florence Molk, Dr. Marcella Salvi, and *La Familia* Hernández: Daniel, Traci, Miguelito, and Helenita, for their unvaluable support and friendship.

To the memory of Dr. Everett Rogers, for his invaluable guidance and tremendous commitment toward me as a student. Dr Enrique Lamadrid's creative, artistic, visionary, and acute way of approaching social phenomena has been an inspiration to me; his mentorship has been invaluable. I am deeply grateful to Miguel Gandert for his visionary, unique, caring, and respectful way of studying and representing the every day experiences of *la raza*. To Dr. Henry T. Ingle, for this mentorship. To Dr. Juan Flores, whose wonderful work and collegiality has been inspirational to me. To Dr. Steven White, for being such a caring colleague and providing me with endless hours of guidance and advice that allowed me to explore the relationship between my work and myself. Without Steven's help, I would not have dared to write about what the work and the corridos mean for me. To Dr. William H. Walters, for being incredibly accessible and always ready with insightful advice. Bill was kind enough to read all the drafts of this manuscript. Thanks to Dr. Mehretab Assefa, Dr. Victor Ortíz, Marta Albert and Dr. Eve Stoddard who provided insights to make this work more fluid and clear.

I want to express my deepest gratitude to the participants in this study, who are key collaborators in this research. Without their gracious and kind willingness to help me, it would have been impossible to learn about the meaning of corridos and *música norteña* to Mexican migrants. I am specially grateful to the musicians of *conjuntos norteños* who kindly agreed to participate in this project: Los Misioneros de Chihuahua, from Chihuahua City; Los Campeones del Valle, from el Valle de Zaragoza, Chihuahua; Los Ciclones de Manny Márquez, from Dumas, Texas; Los Diamantes, from Albuquerque, New Mexico; and Grupo Bego, from Ciudad Juárez. I would also like to thank Roberto Martínez and Al Hurricane, both from Albuquerque. I feel fortunate to have had the opportunity to hear their views of the world and expressions of their values and the way they position themselves within the communities for which they perform. It was extremely touching to witness their love for Mexican music and the extraordinary sense of aesthetics they as artists are continuously creating, reshaping, and transmitting. My heartfelt thanks go to *los hermanos* Hernández of Los Tigres del Norte, a conjunto norteño of San José, California, particularly to Jorge Hernández, who was very gracious in allowing me to interview him despite his tight schedule whenever I attended their concerts on both sides of the border.

I want to thank all the Mexican migrants and vaqueros who participated in this work. Their life experiences and practices, as well as their insistence in re-creating their culture in the United States, were a constant source of inspiration, strength, celebration, and admiration. I also want to express my sincere thanks to the students from the Universidad Autónoma de Ciudad Juárez, who participated in the focus groups and personal interviews for this study. Thanks to Alfredo Baca, CEO of KABQ and La Super X radio stations, based in Albuquerque; Victor El Gato, DJ of La Super X; Manuel Pineda from XEBU, La Norteñita, from Chihuahua City; the late Abuelo Chabelo of Radio Cañón, in Ciudad Juárez, Chihuahua; and Elias Herrera, a promoter of conjuntos norteños in Albuquerque. To my friends and colleagues from Universidad Autónoma de Ciudad Juárez, Alfredo Limas and Manuel Arroyo, who helped me carry out part of my fieldwork in Juárez.

I want to express my gratitude to the Smithsonian Center for Latino Initiatives for the fellowship that encouraged me to pursue this project. To my students, who have enriched my research and teaching and who have constantly given me great gratification. To St. Lawrence University, for providing me with a small grant to complete this project and for their institutional support. Thanks to Jim Forney for his technical assistance and Carol Cady for drawing the maps.

Acknowledgments

As the African proverb says, "It takes a village to raise a child." I feel that this project would not have been completed without all of the many people with whom I crossed paths. My thanks to the people who have helped me to make my life journey meaningful, enjoyable, and exciting. I am extremely grateful for such a gift. Some of the countless other kind people who have helped me along the way are Dr. Victor Acosta, Dr. Alfredo Aranda, Dr. Rodolfo Acuña, María Eugenia Ashcroft, Dr. Clara Chu, Dr. Yoko Chiba, Cecilia Cisneros, Irela Cisneros, and *mi padrino* Ing. Manuel Cisneros, Modesta Cisneros, Orfelinda Cisneros, Dr. John Condon, Karen Cortéz and family, Rance Davis, Lic. Adriana Díaz, Jackie Fleisher, Conchita Heywood, Lic. Miriam Posada García, Dr. Ning Gao, Rubén García, Dr. Bob Gassway, Esther Gómez, Josefina Gómez, Lic. Salomé Gómez Robles, Fernando Ham, Geet Goa Ham, Dr. Randall Hill, Mariam Jiménez, Dr. Abraham Katz, Rosita Kim and family, Dr. Valery Lehr, Celia Landeros, Alicia Larios, Velia Licón, Dr. Assiss Malaquias, David Mendoza, Dr. Evelyn Powell Jennings, Young Min Moon, Marimar and *mi ahijadita* Briana Mendoza Prieto, Luis Mora, Josefina Nakamura, Cristine Nelson, Melissane Parm, Dr. Kathryn Poethig, Gaspar, Graciela, Homar, Mary, Don Nicolás, Rosa, and Victor Prieto, George Rodríguez, Patricia Rodríguez, Dr. Bazán Romero, Joyce Sheridan, Dr. María Soldatenko, Rafael Torres, Dr. Obiora Udechukwu, Edwin and Mónica Vera, Dr. Roberto Villarreal, Rosa Vitela, and Dominque Watts.

Preface

In the winter of 1974, my family and I spent a four-week holiday in the Mexican state of Jalisco. I was five years old, and I remember my family relaxing on the beach of Barra de Navidad. My brother and sisters were playing with me in the sand on the beach near a *palapa*, a wooden table with a big umbrella made of palm fronds. My mother murmured in a sad way, "Lucio Cabañas has died." Cabañas was a guerrilla leader who commanded the military arm of the Partido de los Pobres, the Party of the Poor, known as the PDLP, based in the state of Guerrero.

My father said that it wasn't possible, that he had heard the previous night that Cabañas was still alive. My mother replied softly, in what seemed to me a slight state of trance, as if she were deciphering something very delicate: "I can hear his corrido in the distance." I remember vaguely hearing music and lyrics sung by male voices. Although I can't remember how the musicians were dressed or the words to their song, I remember that their voices were like a softly spreading breeze and that the feeling of their music was very sad, almost like a funeral dirge. I didn't have a clear idea of who Lucio Cabañas was, but I could feel that the local people were grieving his death, and that made me think he had been an important man to them.

The image of the corrido, a topical ballad form characteristic of Mexican popular music, as a means to spread news has stayed very vividly in my mind. It was perplexing to me that we learned about the death of a guerrilla leader through a song and not through more formal mechanisms of communication. It was also fascinating to me that my mother had the "training" to hear news this way, that it was quite natural for her to pay attention to a specific musical genre, and that she believed what was said in the corrido without hesitation or doubt. The details of the death of Lucio Cabañas and his career as a guerrilla leader were recounted in the corrido. Amazingly, we found out later that he was killed only about twelve hours before we heard a corrido about him.

Corridos have been part and parcel of family gatherings for me, and it was there that I learned some of these ballads by heart. There were corridos about horses, heroes, and love that my parents, aunts, uncles, and cousins liked to hear or sing. We used to have family gatherings every Sunday, and these reunions always involved plenty of food and lively music (especially *música de la Costa Chica* and *Chilenas*) from the states of Guerrero and Oaxaca and occasionally from Jalisco and the north of Mexico. Sometimes musicians came to play at our home when there was something special to celebrate, such as a birthday or visits by special family members from out of town.

Later I became familiar with other types of corridos, those about revolutionary heroes and heroines. In my elementary school days, during the festivities celebrating the Mexican Revolution, students commonly played out scenes from the war and sang *corridos revolucionarios* (corridos of the revolution). In first grade I learned "La muerte de Emiliano Zapata" (The Death of Emiliano Zapata) and "El Corrido de Benito Canales." These corridos made me want to know more about Mexican history than the textbooks offered.

My father bought us a collection of records with the lyrics of corridos recited by the actor Ignacio López Tarso. López Tarso interpreted his recitation of some verses of a corrido with others of the same corrido sung by musicians. Listening to this combined recitation and singing was much like listening to a radio story with alternating voices, sound effects, and dramatic elements. López Tarso powerfully dramatized the roles of all the characters of the corridos (the naive peasant, the good wife, the strong and courageous Zapata, the corrupt politicians, the famous horses that gained heroic reputations in the revolution). When one hears López Tarso's performance, it is very easy to imagine snapshots of some of the battles of the Mexican Revolution, to feel the love of the soldiers for their wives, to experience the admiration that people had for leaders who were intelligent and wanted to change social conditions, and to imagine the everyday life of peasants in that period.

From 1973 to 1980, I lived in Ciudad Juárez, Chihuahua, and there I was exposed to *música norteña* (northern music), particularly the first hits by the group Los Tigres del Norte. *Contrabando y traición* (Contraband

and Betrayal), their first hit record, was heard in every neighborhood, and the corridos were sung even in schools. Los Tigres del Norte were the main pioneers of transforming classical corridos about rural heroes, race-horses, and national caudillos into popular culture artifacts that reflected the experiences of marginalized groups that were no longer exclusively rural. Thus the content of corridos came to reflect issues of the urban proletariat, their migration to the United States, and associated activities, such as drug smuggling.

My father's generation liked to listen to Los Alegres de Terán, Los Montañeses del Alamo, and Eulalio González—"El Piporro." Most of these bands were from the states of Nuevo León and Tamaulipas, and in many ways they were the pioneers of modern conjunto norteño music.[1] These conjuntos norteños performed corridos differently from what I heard in central and southern Mexico. Their voices were higher and more nasal, and they used the accordion. Their corridos were danceable and lively. On my eighth birthday, my father gave me an album of Eulalio González that included some songs about the experiences of *braceros*—temporary Mexican workers under contract in agriculture and on the railways in the United States after World War II. When I moved back to Mexico City, I almost lost contact with popular música norteña, because radio stations that played traditional music played mainly the *música ranchera* genre and also because at that time música norteña was not valued in the capital city.

In 1986 I moved to England, where I studied applied linguistics and taught Spanish as a second language. Before I left for England, the migrant experience of many Mexicans in the United States was a remote reality that I didn't understand very well. My sojourner experience in England, however, made me understand the struggle of trying to get along in a culture where the weather, seasons, laws, customs, and values of the host society are unfamiliar. While abroad, I gathered with other Mexicans who also were sojourners or migrants; listening to and singing corridos was a key aspect of such gatherings. Thanks to social contacts with Mexican sojourners in various parts of Europe, I realized that the corridos are a very important part of the cultural memory of many of us. My Mexican friends and I tended to make references to the narratives, the moral lessons, and the wisdom of certain corridos in our everyday con-versations, jokes, poetry, essays, and other forms of oral and written expression. During dinners and at other social gatherings while in

England, we inevitably sang some classic Mexican songs, including *canciones rancheras* and corridos.

At the end of 1992, I moved back to the Ciudad Juárez–El Paso border area to study. The atmosphere then was quite different from the one I had known when I was a child. The border was quite tense, and people were fearful, distressed, and divided. On September 19, 1993, the U.S. Border Patrol in El Paso, under Silvestre Reyes, closed the breaches in the border fence that had been major entry points for illegal immigrants. Simultaneously the patrol instituted a strategic reform and redeployment of its forces. There was a concentration of agents along the border itself, including the downtown El Paso area. The agents were stationed each within sight of the other. Shortly after the start of the operation, Reyes announced that the new approach would continue indefinitely as Operation Hold the Line. This operation created a clear-cut division between residents of El Paso and those of Ciudad Juárez, between some Mexican Americans and Mexicans, and within the Mexican American community in El Paso. Crossing the border became tenser even for people who were entering the United States legally. Reactions toward this military blockade of the border varied. The Roman Catholic bishop of El Paso and some other El Pasoans in nongovernmental organizations opposed it. The Ciudad Juárez Chambers of Commerce and Industry called for a boycott of El Paso businesses. On the other hand, Silvestre Reyes, the grandson of a Mexican revolutionary soldier under Pancho Villa, who had worked in the fields of southern New Mexico and was the border patrol's first Hispanic sector chief, had enthusiastic supporters who made him a symbol of national self-determination for his planning and implementation of Operation Hold the Line.

Reyes left his post at the border patrol to become a U.S. congressman in 1996. Ironically, this grandson of a revolutionary soldier who participated in a social and anti-imperialist movement is the current congressional Hispanic Caucus Chair and a state representative for Texas due to his anti-immigration proposals.

The increased policing of the border began to affect the way people separated by the border interacted with one another. Some Mexican-descendant friends who had been very kind and incredibly hospitable to me strongly supported measures to cut Mexican immigration into the United States; they supported the militarization of the border. Other friends opposed it and even participated in protests at the University of Texas at El Paso and some that blocked the international bridge. The result was division and anger among border residents.

While I was studying at the University of Texas at El Paso, I found myself in the middle of an anti-immigrant hysteria and witnessed increasing terror among undocumented Mexicans living in El Paso. I observed displays of hatred toward such a disfranchised group. I knew of families who went into hiding and could not carry on their everyday life activities. Some of them so feared arrest and deportation by the border patrol that they would not even leave their homes to buy groceries, depending on friends or relatives to shop for them; they would not report abuses and crimes committed against them; their children stopped going to school; they stopped going to mass and to social gatherings. They were even afraid to visit doctors. If they became sick, they asked friends to provide them with the medicines they needed. Gradually, such anti-immigrant measures made undocumented Mexicans the most vulnerable population of El Paso. Their situation reminded me of stories about Jews living in hiding during World War II.

In May 1997, local radio and TV stations announced a fiesta to celebrate the Mexican national holiday Cinco de Mayo, May Fifth, taking place in Sunland Park, New Mexico. The event was attended mainly by Mexicans of different classes and backgrounds from the border area. Among the participants were many undocumented Mexicans who worked in the dairy farms close to the area. The celebration mostly involved dances and performances by mariachi and norteño bands, but it included other events, such as horse racing, as well. When the dancing was at its peak, I saw two tanks, several border patrol vans, and other vehicles surrounding the racetrack. Border patrol officials started asking people they evidently took to be Mexicans for proof of legal status. All of us were subject to inspection. Most people looked tense and some seemed truly terrified.

Although I had my passport with me and I was not asked to show it, I felt vulnerable because the people who were detained looked like me, had the same skin color, spoke my language, and danced like me. I had feelings of impotence, harassment, sadness, and disbelief. The distinction between supposedly "legal" and "illegal" Mexicans was sometimes blurred, but at other times it seemed quite clear, particularly in the matter of class and race. Most people who appeared to be better dressed or European, even if they might have been Mexicans, were not asked for their passports. The migrant experience of many Mexicans, confronting all the negative stereotypes so prevalent among Americans of European descent, was no longer a remote and unfamiliar reality for me.

I have seen quite unfair treatment imposed on people with a Mexican accent or other physical and social traits of Mexican culture—even in academic settings. The everyday experiences and cultural expressions of Mexican Americans and Mexican immigrants have not found their way into textbooks either in Mexico or in the United States; they seem to be misunderstood by the elite and middle classes on both sides of the border.

I have been impressed by the courageous spirits of the many Mexican immigrants I met in El Paso. I have seen disenfranchised Mexican migrants who cross the border with almost everything against them: separating themselves from their families, facing the possibility of dying during their crossing, enduring persecution while they are working, fearing arrest and detention for long periods, living under inhumane working and living conditions, and becoming the scapegoats of social, economic, and political problems in the host country. Add to these stresses the lack of knowledge of the dominant language, education, and political and economical influence. Every Christmas, I have seen thousands of vehicles from different parts of the United States, driven by Mexicans crossing the border on their way home to visit their families. It has been very moving to see their proud, happy faces and their trucks and cars full of gifts for their families in Mexico. The long queues of vehicles on Interstate 10 that head toward Mexico every Christmas season have made me want to capture the plans these people have for when they are in their hometowns. Unfortunately, these immigrants are also a very vulnerable group even in Mexico, particularly at the hands of Mexican customs officials and the federal judicial police, who make part of their living by confiscating migrants' hard-earned gifts, vehicles, and money. I have come to admire the creativity of these embattled people, which applies not only to their physical survival but also to their cultural survival, the preservation of their language, and the maintenance of family links in Mexico. They find sustenance in their music, traditional celebrations, food, parties with piñatas, *matlachines* dances, and celebrations of holidays such as the day of the Virgin of Guadalupe.

The longer I have been in the United States, the more meaningful corridos about immigration have become to me and the more I have wanted to know about the different migrant experiences of Mexicans in the United States. But when I decided to research the role of corridos among Mexican migrants, I faced a major problem of accessibility. During my more than two years at the university, I was for the most part out of touch with the Mexican and Mexican American communities.

By late fall of 2000, I was about to abandon my proposed research on the music most consumed by Mexican immigrants, due to my lack of ties with the Mexican community outside the university. I simply didn't know where to begin. Fortunately a friend introduced me to Louie Pérez, the son of the owner of Cristy Records, a local Mexican and New Mexican music store. He then introduced me to a musician and gave me important clues about the social networks related to the performance and production of corridos. From there, I began to find the social pathways that have led me to more musicians, their recording studios, record stores, fans, dances, and parties, where corridos provide the links connecting Mexican immigrants and New Mexicans and Texans of Mexican descent. Along the way, I have found evidence that certain kinds of music—especially the corridos and canciones rancheras—help link many Mexican Americans and immigrants, both documented and undocumented, to their "Mexicanness." Many of the most popular corridos express what it means to be an immigrant, vulnerable to the exploitation, surveillance, and dehumanization stemming from the racism and classism of the host country. The corrido is a cultural lens that has helped focus on one mechanism of communication created and re-created by Mexican migrants in the United States, a medium that helps to humanize, dignify, and make sense of their often traumatic experiences.

Introduction

Paso del Norte, ¡qué lejos te estás quedando!:
MUSIC ALONG EL CAMINO REAL

> We should have to study not only the history of space, but
> also the history of representations, along with that of their
> relationships—with each other, with practice and ideology.
> — H. Lefebvre, *The Production of Space*

> Survival is not an academic skill...it is learning how to take
> our differences and make them strengths. For the master's tools
> will never dismantle the master's house. They may allow us
> temporarily to beat him at his own game, but they will
> never enable us to bring about genuine change.
> — A. Lorde, *Sister Outsider: Essays and Speeches*

Some of my fondest childhood memories greet me as I pass through
Waterfill and Zaragoza, Chihuahua, to the towns of Ysleta, Texas,
and the Mesilla Valley of New Mexico, where I used to go with my
parents to visit friends when we were living in Ciudad Juárez. These towns
were strikingly similar to towns in Mexico that lay along part of El Camino
Real de [Tierra] Adentro,[1] known as the Chihuahua Trail— particularly the
cities of Delicias, Saucillo, Cuahutémoc, and Jiménez. To my child's eye, the
Chihuahuan lands north and south of the Río Bravo were part of a self-
contained region, and the border was an inconvenience that got in our

El Camino Real de Tierra Adentro.
Map drawn by Carol Cady.

way of freely visiting our relatives and friends on the other side. What made me think this way was the many similarities I saw among people from both sides of the border: the accent and the particular local idioms; the cooking specialties, techniques, and ingredients; the type and ways of celebrating family and community gatherings; the adobe house, which is central to the landscape of the area; and even the family names.

Later in life, I realized that those points of reference and the vernacular knowledge of buildings, the land, and its use were not only quite different from those of white people living on the U.S. side of the border but were either nonexistent or dismissed in the United States, as if the two groups were living in different states of consciousness. I also realized that although borderlanders who inhabit the northern part of El Camino Real are far from being a cohesive and monolithic group, they do share some everyday life practices and frames of reference. In his work *The Production of Space*, Lefebvre (1991) suggests that space should be conceptualized in terms of the signifying practices that occur in a particular space and that construct and change the meaning of the space as well as of the practices. The meaning of space depends on the community's collective memory, values, and concepts. In other words, the practices and representations related to space are inseparable from its meanings. Despite lack of acknowledgment and knowledge of the Mexican presence and Mexicans' cultural practices in New Mexico and northern and western Texas, the cultural landscape of the northern part of El Camino Real retains its Mexican imprint.

This book examines the role of corridos in shaping the cultural memories and identities of transnational Mexican groups. These narrative songs, dating from the earliest colonial times and heavily influenced by the Spanish epic *romancero*, recount the historical circumstances surrounding a protagonist whose history embodies the everyday experiences and values of the community (Hernández 1999; Herrera-Sobek 1993; Maciel and Herrera-Sobek 1998; Mendoza 1939, 1964, 1974).

This study focuses on transnational communities from northern and central Chihuahua through northern Texas and New Mexico for two main reasons. First, one of the most important cattle trails developed in this corridor and with it a new vaquero culture that has been a crucial part of regional identity for centuries.[2] More importantly, most of the members of this transnational community have excellent horsemanship skills and knowledge about cattle ranching, and most of the important rituals where they play corridos are related to the performance of vaquero skills. The strong cultural links between New Mexico, west Texas, and Chihuahua can be explained by the region's very limited cultural, economic, and political ties to central Mexico, as well as by its remoteness that marked a consolidation of specific cultural social and economic practices and identity.

The second reason for studying this region is that academics in Mexico and the United States have neglected the social analysis of this transnational group, particularly the cultural practices of current mestizo populations in the area.[3] New Mexicans and western Texans not only share part of the Chihuahuan desert but also a vast common history and culture that the new political border and the new policies and legacies of conquest and colonization could not completely erase. Chihuahuenses in New Mexico are part of this transnational community that has survived centuries of threatened cultural erasure. In many ways, Chihuahua is the other half of New Mexico, and the racialized post–Mexico-U.S. war border created serious displacements, instabilities, and interruptions to this community.

Although música norteña[4] plays a significant role among Mexican migrants, very little is known about such cultural expressions outside the migrants' communities. Even in the restricted field of Mexican cultural and folklore studies, the contemporary corridos performed by conjuntos norteños are still perceived as lacking the sophistication of those of central and southern Mexico.

Diaspora and Transnational Communities

The term *diaspora* derives from a Greek root meaning to scatter seeds. As it is employed in postcolonial theory, it has been very useful in offering new possibilities for understanding identity politics because it disrupts absolutisms that have been key in articulating nationalism and racism. This theoretical viewpoint has allowed us to recognize that the so-called new concepts of hybridity and creolization are in fact part and parcel of human history: we have all been subject to contact with and influence from other people.

In the particular case of Mexicans in the United States, diaspora implies that there were no Mexicans in the country before 1848, thereby erasing the history of American colonization of the Southwest. In the words of a popular Mexican saying, "Nosotros no cruzamos la frontera, la frontera nos cruzó" (We didn't cross the border; the border crossed us).

Transnational communities have been able to use the loopholes that the border offers to challenge the political borders (for example, when people cross the U.S.-Mexico border without a visa and face persecution and stigmatization because of it). The border divides families, but at the same time, thanks to transnational support networks, family members are able to cross borders and survive in both countries. Corridos narrate the specificities of the lives of transnational groups.

Américo Paredes's concept of *El México de afuera* (Mexico outside Mexico) organically defies notions of current political boundaries and occupies the ever-expanding spaces of intertwined histories of displacements.[5] Pushed by economic necessity, Mexicans are daring to settle in places where, until recently, there was no historic Mexican presence.

Now You see It, Now You Don't:
Images of the U.S.-Mexico Border

There has been a tendency among academics and politicians to homogenize all Southwestern border towns and to overuse the metaphor of the

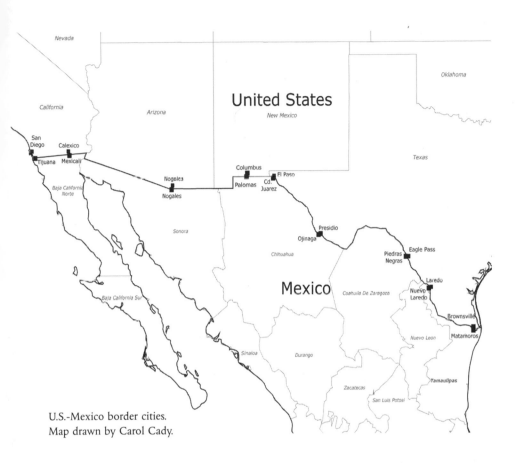

U.S.-Mexico border cities.
Map drawn by Carol Cady.

border in multiple contexts. The border in the everyday life of the U.S.-Mexico borderlanders, however, is not a metaphor—it is a complex, emergent reality. Five hundred migrants die every year crossing the U.S.-Mexico border—that is far more than the number killed during the twenty-eight years of the Berlin Wall.[6] Borderlanders endure intense police and migration scrutiny every time they cross, particularly in times of war. The border seems to be in an almost eternal state of emergence. It is central to drug smuggling and to all the violence and displacement that narcotraffic brings. It is also the main crossing point for people from all over the world into the United States, the division between Latin America and Euro-America, the border between first and third worlds.

Border theory was born in the U.S.-Mexico geographical space, out of a necessity to rethink and transform borderlanders as political subjects

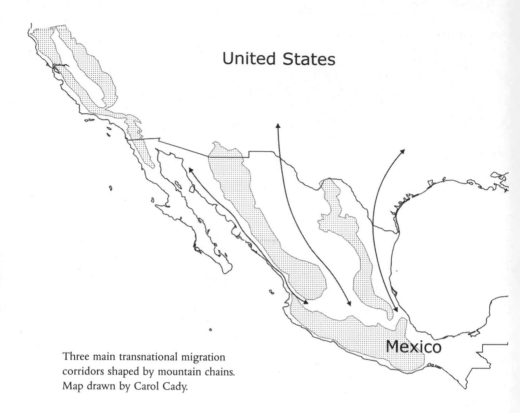

United States

Mexico

Three main transnational migration
corridors shaped by mountain chains.
Map drawn by Carol Cady.

with critical sensibilities that will explain and eventually resist oppression. The social conditions of borderlanders cannot be changed unless specific economic, cultural, social, and geographical realities are recognized. Fregoso (1999) argues that the border is a militarized line that has witnessed a history of conquest, racism, and genocide. It is from this assumption about the border that I analyze the ways in which migrants negotiate their lifestyles and reconstruct their cultural memory, particularly the ways in which music shapes cultural identity through listening to, dancing, and singing corridos.

The three main corridors of transnational movements between Mexico and the United States are clearly shaped by the two Mexican mountain ranges.[7] The histories of these corridors are quite distinct, and consequently the economic and cultural dynamics that take place in each border city demand close attention to the specificities of local conditions. One of the objectives of this work is to avoid generalizations about border communities by focusing on the central corridor, the route of El Camino Real.

With this study, I hope to bring forth some engaged questions about the politics of representation and identity. The politics of representation is an arena where power struggles take place and where dominant groups produce and reproduce representations of themselves and of "others" that justify their position at the apex of the racial/spatial order. Under Western racialized colonial discourse of representation, stereotypes play a crucial role in the exercise of symbolic violence toward marginalized groups, fixing them in disadvantageous positions within the social hierarchy (Hall 1997).

In general, Mexicans in the United States have been stereotyped as a problematic minority. Mexican and Mexican American men have been portrayed as backward, corrupt, dishonest, incompetent, dirty, and lazy. According to O. J. Martínez (2001), the "greaser" character was present in U.S. films as early as 1908 (for instance, *The Greaser's Gauntlet*, 1908, *Tony and the Greaser*, 1911; *Bronco Billy and the Greaser*, 1914). For the most part, Mexican and Mexican American women in American movies have been portrayed as ignorant cantina dancers and prostitutes. The general representation of Mexico, moreover, is characterized by political scandals, corruption, and violence, in the land of lawlessness and no accountability, where white college students can be wild and get drunk on tequila during spring break. Mexico is blamed for many of the social and economic problems the United States is experiencing (such as drug consumption and economic crisis) and sometimes for what has been perceived as a "cultural crisis of Western civilization" due to the strong presence of Mexicans and Mexican cultural expressions in the United States.

Music and Migration

As a cultural artifact, music expresses the substance and style of group and/or individual experiences, because it blends personal, social, and cultural meanings (Lull 1997). Music plays an important role in shaping identity through the experience of listening, dancing, or singing within certain group contexts. Such contexts enable people to place themselves in specific cultural narratives. Identity, of course, does not exist autonomously or in isolation; it is always based on relationships between individuals in the contexts of these relationships (Hall 1997). In this sense, music can provide a sense of the self and of others, the subjective and the collective.

The relationship between music and identity has been conceptualized as mobile and constantly emerging—as a process rather than an object. Music shapes our identity because it fuses mental fantasy and body engagement through the integration of shared aesthetics, ethics, social roles, relationships with nature, and relationships with others. It provides the means by which ethnic, gender, and class identities are constructed, negotiated, and transformed (Stokes 1994). Music powerfully conveys, in the simplest way, certain narrative rules, an ideal world, and more generally the whole range of human emotions (Gilroy 1993).

Music can take our subjectivity infinite places and so crosses spatial and temporal borders (Frith 1990). This quality of music might explain why music is a cultural expression that migrants take with them in their uncertain journeys to unfamiliar geographical settings. Although migrants cannot always carry their material possessions with them as they move, they do carry those intangible cultural expressions that are harder to leave behind, such as language, habits, and music. The insistent evocation of place in Mexican canciones rancheras and corridos heard in radio stations, dancing halls, and fiestas in the United States helps define a community in relation to the world in which they find themselves. In this particular process of relocation, the places, boundaries, and identities involved are of a large collective order. As Fiske (1996) points out, people can use music to locate themselves in quite idiosyncratic and plural ways. A private collection of tapes may evoke highly idiosyncratic places and boundaries.

Frith (1996) states that lyrics can be analyzed at three levels: words, rhetoric, and voices. Most research on songs has been limited to the analysis of the words and has not included rhythmic structure or the performance and reception of songs. Without music, Frith asserts, the words of songs are "unmemorable" words that by themselves do not determine or articulate the feelings, beliefs, or values of the performers or the audience. The melodies and rhythmic structures are not necessarily in harmony with the words, nor do they convey the words' meaning. According to Frith, the lyrics of a song should not be treated as poetry because poetry is intended to be read without music, whereas lyrics have their own musical protocol that determines how they are performed.

Musicians' voices perform, change, pretend, and articulate identities. In general, performance is a process that requires interpretation by an audience who can understand and participate in the meaning of the interpretation. Such competence is derived from the fact that a public performance is a crystallized version of the values and beliefs of everyday life. In this context, a performance is not a singular act but part of a process with a specific historical, social, political, and economic context (Frith 1996). Hetcher (1975, 1978) suggests that marginalized groups use their own cultures to resist oppressive circumstances. Each group develops an oppositional culture or a culture of resistance that embodies a coherent set of values, beliefs, and practices that mitigates the effects of oppression and reaffirms what is distinct from the dominant culture. Marginalized groups create resistant cultural expressions that are a product of the "transvaluation of all values" precipitated by historical colonial circumstances such as the experience of racial terror in the New World as experienced by African Americans (Gilroy 1993, 133).

Studies of oppositional culture have tended to focus on dichotomies such as the idea that cultural expressions must be either directly and totally counterhegemonic or else entirely integrated into the system. The negotiations that occur in this continual and very wide spectrum are for the most part disregarded. However, those cultural expressions that have survived the passage of time and geographies tend to be located at neither pole. Instead, they are part of the lengthy and sophisticated archive based on embodied, negotiated knowledge passed down through generations.

Popular culture and folk culture, such as dance, drama, folktales, and religious beliefs, are examples of cultural expressions that can encode the experiences and values of subordinate groups (Scott 1990). The ambivalence of meaning lends itself to many audiences negotiating the meaning in different ways. The oppositional cultural expressions of marginalized groups may take the form of extended kinship networks that function in the face of harsh economic circumstances, for example, or of artistic and cultural expressions that voice or visualize cultural pride or protest/critique of the dominant culture (Gilroy 1993). Many marginalized groups have made oppositional culture their own form of art.

Oral culture is an important part of folk culture and resistance because there is more control over the interaction between the communicators and the audience, place, and circumstances than over written communication (Scott 1990). Oral performances are very flexible and can be readily adjusted to particular settings, places, and audiences. For instance, oral performances can be abbreviated, enlarged, substituted for, and used in different regionalism. They are also more difficult to monitor and regulate because they tend to be decentralized (Scott 1990).

Music is part of the collective historical memory and the continuing social dialogue. According to Gilroy (1990), the destruction of collective memory causes the most problems of identity for individuals. When the collective memory of displaced people is in fragments or almost completely destroyed, members resort to creative forms of "re-creating" their collective memory. For instance, they may look elsewhere for new images to fill the gaps where the original collective memory was destroyed. Because we recall these memories as members of social groups, individual recollections can be traced in social contexts by linking them with the memories of others (Halbwachz 1980). Although remembering does not require the physical presence of others, individual remembrances are the meeting point of manifold networks of solidarity to which an individual may belong. Halbwachz (1980) states that the process of recalling a group memory is very complex and contradictory. On the one hand, community memory responds to the needs of the present. The present acts as a filter because memories and traditions change in accordance with circumstances and demands (Pérez 1999). On the other hand, communities need stable supports and frames of reference.

Corridos are an important archive and outlet of the cultural memory of Mexicans, New Mexicans, and Texans along El Camino Real. Since the end of the Mexican-American War, Mexicans who remained north of the Rio Grande have experienced a dialectical process of resistance and affirmation that shapes their understanding of what it is to be an American of Mexican descent. Corridos played by conjunto norteño, as well as other cultural expressions along El Camino Real, are reminders that El Camino Real has been the homeland of Mexicanos, Tejanos, and Nuevo Mexicanos for more than four hundred years and that they developed a cultural identity that has evolved and endured over time. A complicated dialogue seems to exist between the geography of the Chihuahua Trail and the cultural practices of Mexicans and Mexican Americans from Chihuahua, New Mexico, and Texas in which corridos and música norteña are very much part of the cultural landscape.

Corridos about migration keep insisting that Mexicanos in the United States are still struggling to be acknowledged and are seen as entitled to their space. Anzaldúa (1987, 6) uses a Mexican saying to illustrate this point: "El Chicano, sí, el Chicano que anda como un ladrón en su propia casa." (The Chicano, yes, the Chicano who walks around as if he was a thief, silently, apprehensive, with no rights, and worried, in his own home.) These contradictions and tensions in regard to Mexicans' perceptions not only of the space but the cultural landscape reminded me of the following incident I experienced while I was living in Albuquerque.

Most of the time I arrived at my office quite early, before the janitor assigned to the building had finished his work and left the building. I felt very much at ease with David, a Nuevo Mexicano from Tierra Amarilla, because he was always polite and dignified and spoke Spanish. After some months we established our daily ritual of greeting each other and having short conversations about the music we liked, my travels to the border, and our work. His accent and his way of walking and carrying himself reminded me very much of Chihuahua. He told me that his grandfather was in a photograph that was going to be part of a book by a well-known Chicano photographer from northern New Mexico. In the photo, David's grandfather carried a cross for an Easter ritual that takes place in northern New Mexico. David told me very casually that his family was from northern New Mexico and that they had been there for many generations (see the description of the land grants struggle in Tierra Amarilla in chapter 3). Since the economic situation in northern New Mexico wasn't good, he had taken a job in Albuquerque, although he traveled frequently to northern New Mexico to visit his relatives. I realized, deeply moved, that I was talking to a person whose family not long ago were owners of a part of what are now national parks and other tourist places. His family had lived in adobe houses in the New Mexican landscape that were now occupied by white Americans. (Before it became fashionable to live in adobe houses, they were stigmatized because Mexican people lived there.)

I found it ironic to be talking to somebody who had enormous vernacular knowledge of New Mexico and a deep attachment to the landscape but had been dispossessed of the land—someone whose cultural practices were either ignored, appropriated, or misrepresented. The longer I lived in New Mexico, the more people like David I met. Although most people who worked in that building were studying cultural relations, David was at best an invisible entity to them and at worst an unwelcome foreigner. In fact, one of the attractions of living in New Mexico for some white Americans is the opportunity to have a firsthand experience in this tricultural state that is the epitome of "multiculturalism." People can live in adobe houses with antique doors, view Spanish colonial artwork, and enjoy the vast "empty" land. In this construction of the "enchanted land," the Mexican memory is obscured. The experience of living in Santa Fe or any other town that has displaced Mexican people from their plazas, adobe houses, and way of life seems to offer the privilege of being close to the objects that "represent" that culture without dealing with questions of colonization and power. As I walk into the plazas of La Mesilla, Santa Fe, and Albuquerque that once were the political, economic, and cultural centers of those towns, I see that most of such areas has been converted into art and craft shops for tourists, where one can find items from Peru, Bolivia, Central America, Mexico, Texas, and New Mexico. All indigenous artwork from the continent is almost indistinguishable. In this capitalist system where one can buy everything, one can also buy multicultural sensitivity that is mostly limited to interactions with "ethnic" and often colorful objects. The new "theme park" of multiculturalism has not managed to completely erase inequalities based on race. The new uses of such adobe buildings are a reminder of the colonization and dismissal of Native Americans and Mexicans within that landscape.

Chapter One

COLLECTING THE DEBRIS OF HISTORY AND RESHAPING IDENTITY

> The task of interpretation is...to go beyond one's own
> individual experiences...to transform oneself from a unitary identity
> to an identity that includes the "other" without suppressing the difference.
> — Edward Said, cited in S. Jhally, *Edward Said on Orientalism*

I have taught intercultural studies courses for the last six years, first while a graduate student in Albuquerque, New Mexico, then as a professor at a liberal arts college in upstate New York. In all my classes, only four students have had some knowledge of the Mexican-American War and the general consequences for Mexicans in both countries. The past continues to speak to us in the way we interact with the "other"; in this sense, how we think about our past influences how we think about others and ourselves. This dialectical interplay between past, present, and vision of the future is frequently overlooked.

Mexican American history, literary work, folklore, and cultural expressions have been systematically excluded from the basic educational curriculum in the United States and, for the most part, silenced from the national consciousness. The corrido has been one of the only oral archives that have documented such experiences. The corrido is the precursor of Chicano literature in that it is a form of resistance, critique, and denunciation of cultural, historical, and physical erasure under the occupation of the

Southwest after the Mexican-American War, in particular, the corridos that recount the exploits of a hero who prevails against privileged groups with courage and dignity.

Cultural and Economic Repercussions
of the Mexican-American War

The Mexican-American War has had a tremendous impact on Mexican national consciousness. A Japanese friend who lived in Mexico for more than ten years often told me: "Mexicans see this war like it just happened yesterday. It is so vivid in your memory." The colossal northern neighbor invaded Mexico, creating mistrust and fear that is still present and reinforced by the subsequent political and economic treatment of Mexico. Even the term "war" (which assumes a declaration of war and two willing and equal opponents) is disputed. The memory of the "war" is present from the national anthem to references and jokes that reflect a sense of impotence and abuse. At first glance, the Mexican national anthem may seem very aggressive, but the song that we sing in primary and secondary school every Monday also reflects weakness, a sense of frustration and loss, *la visión de los vencidos:* "If a foreign enemy dares to profane your land with their soles, think, beloved patria, that heaven gave you a soldier in each son" *[Mas si osare un extraño enemigo, profanar con sus plantas tu suelo, piensa ¡oh! patria querida que el cielo, un soldado en cada hijo te dió].*

After the Mexican-U.S. war, Mexicans who remained in the conquered territory were considered foreigners and not entitled to the same civil rights as white Americans. The Treaty of Guadalupe Hidalgo, which guaranteed language, property, and citizenship rights to the Spanish-speaking residents after the war, has been ignored in practice and in spirit (Acuña 2000). Mexicans soon began to experience substandard living and working conditions with few opportunities for upward advancement. Their situation was so bad that many decided to move to Mexico. Of the one hundred thousand Mexicans who stayed in the newly acquired Southwest of the United States, sixty thousand were in New Mexico. The large population of Mexicans in New Mexico played a major role in the territory's late admission to statehood, and not coincidentally, New Mexico is now one of the poorest states in the nation (Rosales 1997).

The Southwest and its Mexican inhabitants became what Rodolfo Acuña (2000) calls an internal colony. Although Mexicans experienced

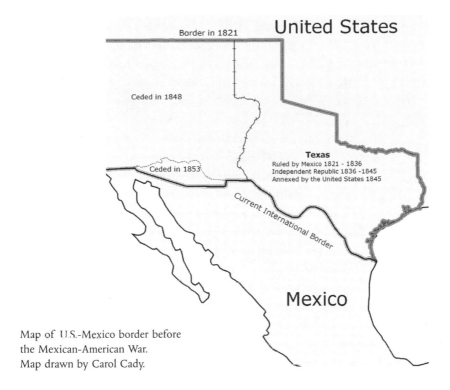

Map of U.S.-Mexico border before
the Mexican-American War.
Map drawn by Carol Cady.

subordination that varied with social class and race, few Mexicans escaped marginality from the war in which even the elite (which at some points made alliances with the invaders) lost economic and political power. The rapid conversion of Mexicans into a numerical minority made possible the creation of institutionalized white privilege that secured its advantages through policies aiming at the institutionalization and perpetuation of the existing stratification systems.

The contribution of the Mexican workforce to the development of the economy and prosperity of the United States started with the takeover of the Southwest. Mexicans have often performed strong and efficient work in the neighboring country in exchange for low wages, poor treatment, discrimination, and disdain. Despite the passage of years, negative perceptions of Mexicans have not yet been eradicated from the dominant white American mentality.

Colonization is not merely about physically exploiting people; it destroys and disfigures every part of the identity of the colonized, including their past (Fanon 1968). White historians have been active in justifying the takeover of Mexican lands by portraying colonizers as martyrs, such as in the Alamo battle, fighting for liberty and freedom, while portraying Mexicans as cruel in nature, villainous, treacherous, and led by a dictator. In this regard, Pérez (1999, 17) argues that

> once control of northern Mexico's land had been won in 1848, the next stage was to enforce a colonialist knowledge in order to erect the past as a pedestal on which the triumphs and glories of the colonizer and their instruments and the colonial state could be displayed. Building monuments and naming battlefields after those who had "won the West," the colonialists eulogize their victories. In the texts, the Alamo mission and San Jacinto battlefield continue to occupy firm spaces as they contribute to the production of colonial knowledge. In these spaces statutes and photographs of Anglo Texas or Texans, heroes such as Sam Houston and S. F. Austin come from the heads and minds of Texan nationalists who still celebrate the former Republic's history with a fervor.

Since the end of the nineteenth century, Mexicans and Mexican Americans have been represented in a decontextualized way, often as *bandidos* (bandits). Bandido images have been the staple of westerns that portray Mexicans as border outlaws, thieves, smugglers, and horse and cattle rustlers. Many of these portrayals are based on the legendary figures that appeared soon after the Mexican-American War (Elfego Baca, Juan Cortina, Gregorio Cortéz, and Tiburcio Vásquez), those who were present during the gold rush in California (e.g., Joaquín Murrieta), and, of course, Pancho Villa and other revolutionaries. Interestingly enough, a rich corpus of corridos is based on those social bandits who sought to defend Mexicans and Mexican Americans against the loss of lands, murders, lynchings, economic exploitation, and oppression that accompanied the rise of white American cultural, economic, and political ideals.

The bandido figure became even more prominent during the Mexican Revolution, due to the presence of *revolucionarios* along border states.

Francisco Villa was a very well-known "bandit" of El Camino Real de Tierra Adentro. During my childhood, it was still common to know people with firsthand memories of the Mexican Revolution, particularly of Francisco Villa and his División del Norte. Francisco Villa was godfather of innumerable children, mainly the children of revolutionary soldiers. Villa is probably one of the most beloved vaqueros and guerrilla leaders of the Chihuahua Trail of El Camino Real, as testified to in the thousands of corridos that describe his spirit, social consciousness, vision, horsemanship, and vaquero skills and lifestyle; his anti-imperialist stance; and his excellence as a military strategist. His military skills are narrated in various corridos of military battles that took place along El Camino Real, such as "Corrido de la toma de Ciudad Juárez," "Corrido de la toma de Ojinaga," "Corrido de la toma de Torreón," and "Corrido de la toma de Zacatecas." El Camino Real, particularly the Chihuahua Trail, was Villa's main space of action. While in exile, Villa lived in El Paso, Texas, in the Chihuahuita neighborhood, and worked for ASARCO (American Smelting and Refining Company), which processed lead and copper from mines in the state of Chihuahua. From El Paso, he plotted against Victoriano Huerta, the Mexican president, and organized his famous División del Norte. He often traveled to El Paso, as many Mexicans still do, to buy supplies and merchandise. Villa was governor of Chihuahua for a short time, and the list of this powerful figure's actions in the region is endless. As a result, Pancho Villa's presence in the history of El Camino Real de Tierra Adentro and in the vernacular knowledge of the people in this region is overwhelming. Everywhere he went, admirers and enemies witnessed his actions and passed on this knowledge to younger generations. Almost every family I know living along El Camino Real has an anecdote to tell about a specific moment of Villa in their lives or the places where they lived. In some ways, Villa's persona embodies the spirit of the transnational vaquero. Villa was and still is a very loved figure in this region. Part of his popularity results from Villa's awareness of the consequences of the Mexican-American War: Europe's economic and political dominance over Mexico. Such memories of Villa on the Mexican side of the border contrasts with the image still prevalent in the U.S. public arena of Villistas as irrational, cruel, and bizarre people without the vision or drive to improve conditions in their country. Not surprisingly, in the United States, very little is known about the Villistas' pleas for social justice or Villa's anti-imperialist stance.

Don Leandro Rodriguez, a musician and a fisherman from La Boquilla, Chihuahua, who was playing for a Christmas party in Satevó, Chihuahua, told me:

> I participated in a corrido contest organized here [Satevó] about General Francisco Villa. I got a third place at the state level. For many, a third place is nothing, but it is important to me because it was evaluated by people who really know about music, about corridos, people from Chihuahua City. I chose to write about [Francisco] Villa because...well, firstly, let me tell you and I do not know if you will believe me, but General Francisco Villa was the godfather of my mother. My mother is from El Valle de Zaragoza...and, well...I feel a great respect for the general and I was invited here in Satevó to the contest. The contest was promoted here. I was told in El Valle de Zaragoza that the Municipal Museum was organizing this event, and I was lucky enough to participate. I got third place with the corrido called "Recordando al general" [Remembering the General], in 1996.

To this day, Mexicans battle with the cultural representations forged in the aftermath of the Mexican-American War—the same cultural representations that brought racialized labor exploitation.

According to Pérez (1999), much of the history of Mexicans and Mexican Americans is like a faint shadow. Although the Mexican presence in the United States has not been well documented or recorded, it reveals itself in people's memories and cultural expressions. The tensions between, on the one hand, indifference, denial, and exploitation and, on the other hand, resilience, persistence, confusion, and the pain of being "other" have played an important role in reshaping transnational identities among Mexicans in the United States.

Not until 1972 did the first Chicano scholar challenge the colonialist historiographies that have long been a part of the harmful duet of power and knowledge proposed by Foucault (1980) that legitimizes interlocking systems of domination. Rosales (1997) argues that the history of the presence of Mexican Americans in the United States—particularly during the civil rights struggles of the 1960s and 1970s—is practically untold in the official history of the United States. This can be attributed at least partly to the relative prominence of African American social struggles and white Americans' focus on the "sin of slavery". Another reason is that the struggles of Mexican and Mexican descendants have been expressed mainly in Spanish rather than English. Perhaps the most important reason, however, is that Mexicans, citizens or not, continue to be viewed as "aliens" (Rosales 1997; Gómez-Quiñones and Maciel 1998).

Mexican Americans are part of the larger U.S. "Latino" group of thirty-two million people. Martínez (2001) states that "Latinos" are perhaps the most culturally diverse population in the United States, representing seventeen nationalities of Latin Americans. Today, el *México de afuera* constitutes approximately 7 percent of the total U.S. population. They are concentrated in the Southwest, particularly in California and Texas, but can be found in every state of the United States (Martínez 2001). Because of geographic proximity, a unique characteristic of el México de afuera is that some Mexican cultural expressions are continuously reinforced by constant transnational contact. Mexican Americans and Mexican migrants are always categories within every gender, class, geographical origin, and host city. Although Mexicans and Mexican Americans in the United States share common characteristics such as language, religion, origins, and identification with Mexico, both populations are very heterogeneous. Differences among members of this group can be traced to several factors: how long they and their families have been in the United States, which may date to the sixteenth century or only a few days ago; the specific cultural, social, economic, and political characteristics of their origin and destination communities; the extent of intermarriage; and the level of contact with Mexico, a country that is itself heterogeneous.

To understand Mexican Americans and Mexicans in the United States, we need to be very specific about the social and geographical locations of the social analysis we carry. Mexicans in the United States are far from a unified and internally homogenous group. Our social identities and practices are continuously being forged. As a result, our histories do not necessarily have a definite beginning, middle, and end because fragments of different groups are intertwined and coexist in the same histories. It is a challenging task to place all Mexican and Mexican American people in the same category or in binary and/or oppositional groups and even more challenging to cover the multiple histories and analyses of those histories in a limited space. Here I will provide only a brief overview of el México de afuera and the main points of contention that are related to the corridos.

Mexican Immigration to the United States

Migration laws are created in response to the particular moment of the economic cycle of capitalism and are enforced not necessarily to inhibit movements of people but rather to make them "illegal" to regulate their level of political, social, and economic participation. Policing the border and investing a spectacular infrastructure in the border is a form of labor discipline and labor division. The migrant identities produced by the state have literally dehumanized "illegal" immigrants, who although very useful to agriculture, construction, hotels, restaurants, and domestic services, function as an invisible and disposable labor force with no rights to a dignified life. "Illegal" immigration is part of a political contradiction. On the one hand, migrants are encouraged to work in jobs that U.S. workers would never do for such poor wages and under such poor labor conditions. On the other hand, migrants are criminalized for crossing the border and forced to risk their lives. Those who manage to cross are subject to intense surveillance and harassment.

The United States used Mexican workers to fill labor needs created by the expansion of cattle ranches in Texas and New Mexico, agriculture in California, and the post–Civil War industrial expansion. The enactment of the different Exclusion Acts targeted at Chinese, Japanese, and other Asian groups made the demand for Mexican labor in the United States higher. Now Mexicans and other migrants of color sustain labor-intensive industries, such as garment manufacturing and agriculture, and serve as a constant supply of the cheap labor needed to maintain a standard of living that would otherwise be unattainable for most white Americans. Regardless of whether Mexicans were in the United States before the Mexican-American War, they have been constructed as eternal migrants, those who "suck" the system and are a cultural threat.

Mexican immigration to the United States is a very complex phenomenon and has been the main point of contention between the two countries. Pressure groups range from armed ranchers in southern Arizona who apprehend and have killed undocumented immigrants to human rights organizations and religion-based shelters for migrants. Politicians from both sides of the border have used Mexican migration as a topic for gaining electorate votes. Migrants have been the targets of xenophobia and racism and the ideal scapegoats for economic and social problems in the United States.

Discourses of hate are heterogeneous and change in accordance with historical specificities. Van Dijk (1995) shows in studies based on discourse analysis how the socioeconomic and political elite enacts hate speech that takes the form of "modern," "symbolic," and even "tolerant" discourse. Hate speech from the elite is hardly ever blatant, and it ultimately culminates in fundamental policies that are hard to oppose because they are constructed in a context where the elites position themselves very positively (Van Dijk 1995). In this regard, the state has been very successful in producing migrant identities that distinguish between those who are entitled to basic human rights and those who are not, most often on the basis of citizenship, color, and national origin.

According to Muñoz (2000, 1),

> the dramatic increase of the Latino population has generated a racist anti-Latino immigrant politics in the United States that has resulted in perhaps the most repressive immigration policy in the nation's history. One of President Clinton's proud accomplishments has been the militarization of the U.S.-Mexico border. Anti-Latino immigrant politics has also resulted in increased violence against Latinos in border cities and throughout the United States. In Arizona, white vigilantes have terrorized scores of immigrants....Latino immigrants have also become the targets of white politicians who have spearheaded anti-immigrant electoral campaigns. In California, the majority of white voters passed Proposition 187...to cut all state benefits to immigrants in the areas of public health and public education.

The differentiation of migrants (and therefore labor) on the basis of status and race has been very important for the growth of capitalism. All migrants, regardless of their education, nationality, and color, are fulfilling a particular role needed in the global capitalist machinery depending on the legal status that is assigned to them. However, migration has recently been portrayed as a relatively new cause-and-effect phenomenon in which poor people leave their countries due to the unstable economic and political situations created by inept third world governments. In this simplistic model, third world people are responsible for mending their situation, and migration will stop the moment economic opportunities are available in their countries, as if the nation is a "sealed-off" system.

In her work on migration, Saskia Sassen (1998) argues that liberal and conservative politicians have the same assumptions about the causes of migration: they just disagree on the level of strictness of migration laws. Sassen states that migration laws have failed because the West, in particular the United States, has failed to acknowledge its own crucial role in the global economic system, the impact of its military operations, and its consequent position of cultural dominance in the world. The current globalization of the economy has transformed labor conditions and lifestyles by increasing the number of low-wage, temporary, and part-time jobs and by fostering the feminization of poverty. The current political debates on migration are inadequate because it is not simply poverty, overpopulation, or economic stagnation that causes migration. Migration arises in response to the internationalization of labor, the displacements and disruptions caused by the military activities of the United States and other nations, and the need for the transnational exchange of goods and people in a global economy. The parties involved in these developments need to take responsibility for their actions.

Migrant Women

Social analysis of immigration to the United States has tended to privilege European migration. In the national memories "settlers" are white Americans and "aliens" are nonwhites. During the 1980s, Chicana feminist scholars questioned androcentric and heterosexual normativity by male academics, including Chicanos and liberal humanists. As Chandra Talpade Mohanty explains, "Histories of slavery, indentured servitude, contract labor, self-employment, and wage-work are also simultaneously histories of gender, race, and (hetero)sexuality, nested within the context of the development of capitalism" (1997, 9).

Mexican women's participation in the economy of the United States and Mexico has been neglected even in Mexican cultural expressions about migration. Female labor migration is a very recent topic of social analysis, and much still needs to be done to address the social, economic, and cultural impacts of this phenomenon on the U.S. and Mexican economies and on the migrants' own lives, families, and communities. Studies of female migration have partly resulted from a desire to understand the complexities of the rapid growth in international migration in the 1990s and the changes in its nature.

Migrant women have been present since the very early periods of migration that helped to develop the southwestern United States (Ruiz 1998). Officially, migration policies have encouraged male migration to the United States. However, according to Hondagneu-Sotelo (1994), since 1940 the majority of legal immigrants to the United States have been women and children, particularly Mexican women. The presence of women has been stronger after the changes in 1965 of U.S. migration policies on family reunification (Hondagneu-Sotelo 1994). There is a notable silence, though, on gender inquiry and gender issues regarding migration and transnational studies.

Mexican female migrants, like most women of color, are at greater risk of suffering human rights abuses from the moment they decide to migrate. On their way to the United States, women have a relatively high risk of being sexually abused by coyotes, people who cross the border with them, border patrol agents, and their employers. As Anzaldúa (1999, 34, 35) states: "*La mojada, la mujer indocumentada*, is doubly threatened in this country. Not only does she have to contend with sexual violence, but like all women, she is prey to a sense of physical helplessness. As a refuge, she leaves the familiar and safe home-ground to venture into unknown and possible dangerous terrain."

It has often been assumed in the West that women will be liberated from patriarchy once they migrate to western countries. However, migrant women, particularly from third world countries, are subjected to new forms of control and quite often find themselves in a more disadvantageous gender situation in their new homes. Migrant women, documented and undocumented, tend to work mostly in unregulated sectors

harvesting food, sewing clothing, cleaning offices, and raising other people's children. These jobs make it difficult to complain about abuses,
especially when the employees are undocumented workers. Many women
did not have to work in their country of origin before they migrated.
Once they migrate, they lack the social network they had at home and
institutional support to take care of the family and work at the same
time. Migrant women often find themselves more dependent on men in
the United States than they were in Mexico, particularly the undocumented ones (from the crossing of the border to transportation), who
often work in male-dominated areas such as farming.

Migration studies often do not take into account the ways migration
is planned in the households. Families, not individual members, study carefully the factors that are going to affect the family and extended family the
most; for example, who is going to take care of the children at home, who
is going to work at home and where, who is going to migrate and where
she/he is going to live abroad, and how much money is going to be sent
home and when. Migration affects the whole household: those who leave
and those who stay. Hondagneu-Sotelo (1994) states that gender relations
prior to migration affect migration, settlement patterns, and the everyday
life of the family in the new country. Women who stay in Mexico are left
alone and face new challenges, such as taking responsibility for family
and community affairs. At the same time, these women are heavily monitored by their and their husbands' families to remain loyal to their husbands and to perform their duties as mothers, sisters, daughters, and
daughters-in-law. In the best of the scenarios, couples who live apart
endure maintaining a long-distance relationship under economic and legal
conditions that do not allow for frequent visits. In addition, women who
remain in their home country take the chance that their husbands will
abandon them and start a new family in the United States.

The current economic globalization characterized mainly by capital
flows and technological advances requires new economic policies and production systems that have serious repercussions for national economies
and migratory flows. Developing countries have undergone drastic structural adjustment policies aimed at balancing budgets and increasing com-
petitiveness through trade and price liberalization. Some of the structural
adjustments include reduction of the public-sector wage bill, the growth
of the private sector, the privatization of social services, the encouragement

of foreign investment, and the production of goods and services for export ("tradables"), for which "flexible" labor markets are a necessary condition for efficient markets.

In general, Mexican women have faced a paradox: they have gained an increasing share in the labor market while at the same time experiencing inequality (either at home or in the United States) in terms of wages, training, and occupational segregation. Women's participation in the labor market has not been translated into a redistribution of domestic, household, and child-care responsibilities. Women are disproportionately involved in forms of employment increasingly used to maximize profits, such as temporary, part-time, casual, and home-based work. Most migrant women have obligations to their families back home, and even though their living and working conditions are meager, they are a reliable source of income for their families.

Migration to the United States has hurt a disproportionate number of women because women tend to assume (and are expected to assume) extra productive and reproductive activities to survive the austerities of adjustment while they are left behind in Mexico when their partners leave or when they are reunited with their nuclear families. The declining cost of labor in real terms over the years has encouraged demand for female migrant labor. At the same time, declining household budgets have led to an increase in the supply of job-seeking women.

Corridos make visible the human migrant, impoverished and displaced back home, who is seeking El Norte, facing hardship, danger, and rejection and yet so indispensable to the American way of life and the national economy. Few people engage in a conscious struggle regarding their participation in the global economy and the way it reinforces global hierarchies of domination. Our participation ranges from the cup of coffee we drink in the morning to the clothes we wear, the computers we use, and everyday economic and political decisions. After all, we need to make a living.

Despite the fact that the extensive lands of the Southwest were conquered by white Americans and that Mexican Americans constitute around 7 percent of the U.S. population, many Americans seem to know relatively little about Mexican cultural expressions and Mexico itself—aside from the consistent representation of Mexicans as a threat to the economy, culture, and society of the United States. The topics most likely to be found

In relation to Mexicans and Mexican descendants in the U.S. mass media are ethnic relations, cultural differences, and immigration as well as violence, crime, riots, and other forms of deviance. Although the mainstream arena denies a space to acknowledge the experiences of Mexican immigrants, Mexicans have insisted on recording their history through the main medium at their disposal: folk songs (Herrera-Sobek 1993).

Most of the people I talked to from the transnational community told me in various ways that corridos about immigration not only analyze certain events that are worth keeping in the collective memory but also represent a space to record the feelings that emerge during such events. Since the corridos integrate the subjective and objective parts of certain events, they express the collective hopes, suffering, happiness, and disappointments of the community. The strength of the corridos about immigration seems to be their holistic approach toward the immigrant experience. The corridos about immigration have the capacity of talking about real events in such a way that listeners cannot pretend to dissociate from the phenomena that affect the lives of people like them. Corridos dissolve the pretense of objectivity and distance. As Rosa Mendoza, who is from Chihuahua but lives in Dumas and travels frequently to Chihuahua, told me, "You really have to have a heart of stone not to feel those corridos. I feel pain, I feel a link to the people. I feel like something related to me is being mistreated, like if it is about something about me."

The people I talked to often referred to very specific corridos about immigration to describe the important elements of their personal lives. For instance, they made reference to relatives or close friends being close to death or even dying when they attempted to cross the border. The corridos about immigration were not by any means a distant or fictional narrative. Immigrants could decipher very clearly the meaning of the corridos because many immigrants were in some respects involved in the tragic events described by the corridos. The most emotive moments were when immigrants shared their experiences and perceptions about corridos. The narratives about death, going into hiding, being blackmailed, and not being able to see their relatives brought up feelings of sadness. In these moments I often felt like an intruder. What right did I have to talk about issues that were so very sensitive to them? Nubia, a niece of my extended family who migrated to the United States when she was in primary school, was visiting her grandfather in Satevó, Chihuahua, when we talked about her migrant experience. She told me about the importance of this visit, and she started to remember the impossibility of visiting her beloved relatives in Chihuahua as well as the harassment she went through in elementary school. Suddenly she broke down in tears, and so did I. I knew Nubia shared her experiences with me because she trusted me and felt comfortable talking in her grandfather's home with her mother and uncle present.

People from this transnational community do not treat immigration, politics, and Mexican cultural expressions separately. Even musicians and *corridistas* (those who write corridos) who were not immigrant themselves, such as Roberto Martínez (a musician and corridista from Albuquerque), spoke in great detail about their feelings about immigration and the corridos:

> In my opinion, there are not enough corridos that talk about immigration. There is not enough information, positive information that advocates for the immigrants. My heart goes to them. The only thing that separates Mexicans from here and the United States is a line. The Rio Grande is a beautiful river, it is a beautiful thing, it gives water, gives life to humans and, unfortunately, it also divides Mexico and the United States. Instead of giving life, it takes life. Many people die when they cross the Rio Grande. I put myself in their situation and I think, "Good Lord, I hope I never go through the same things immigrants go through in the United States." I love my family very much and I would not like to leave them. I can imagine when a father or a son leaves his country and does not know if he is going to come back. Every day people die. The border with Canada is not the same as the one with Mexico. Many Canadians enter the United States through that border and they are not treated in the same manner.

Because the "debris" of migrants' histories is ignored in the mainstream United States, corridos about migration become almost like collective biographies. When Manuel Márquez, a musician in northern Texas, tried to explain his long road to becoming a U.S. citizen, he often referred to corridos or songs about migration: "Have you heard 'De paisano a paisano'? The one that Los Tigres del Norte sing?" Then he recited the words that were especially relevant to his own situation: "De paisano a paisano, yo le pregunto al patrón, ¿quien trabaja en la limpieza, en la cosecha, hoteles, y restaurants? y ¿quien se mata trabajando en construcción? mientras el patrón regaña, tejiendo la telaraña su lujusa mansión, muchas veces ni nos pagan...nos echan la migración. Si con mi canto pudiera derrumbar las fronteras para que el mundo viviera con una sola bandera, en una sola nación." [From a countryman/woman to a countryman/woman, I ask the employee who works in the harvest, hotels, and restaurants and who kills himself in construction while the employer slacks off, knitting a web in his luxurious mansion. Very often we are not even paid; they sic immigration officials on us. If I could do it with my singing...I would demolish the borders so that the world would live under only one flag and in only one nation.] Manuel told me, "This happens often when the employers do not need you anymore. They themselves call to 'la migra' [immigration officers] and they dispose of you, like a thing." To Manuel and most of the people I spoke with, the almost autobiographical narratives about their migrant experiences served several purposes—as vehicles for diffusing knowledge, as catalysts for critical analysis, and as forms of resistance. Corridos attempt to promote self-affirmation and to grant access to emancipatory possibilities.

Like some other scholars of color, I often find myself navigating a double consciousness that has at least two layers. The first layer consists of transnational spaces and the people who travel within them, with all the contradictions and ambiguous positions that such spaces and communities embody. The second layer is found in privileged institutions, where many are unable to understand the pain of being the "other"—in particular, the conditions of the Mexican experience and presence in the United States. The dialectic relation between the personal struggles and the collective ones provides a space for critical consciousness that continuously reshapes our collective and individual identities. I will discuss this further in the next chapters.

Chapter Two

Romper con el canto la frontera:
NARRATIVE ANALYSIS OF CORRIDOS
ABOUT MIGRATION

We know, of course, there's really no such thing as the "voiceless."
There are only the deliberately silenced, or the preferably unheard.
— Arundhati Roy in her speech on accepting the Sydney Peace Prize, 2004

I met Octavio Fernández in Santa Fe at a concert performed by Los Tigres del Norte in March 2001, and we had a long conversation about corridos some days after we met. A devoted and knowledgeable fan of Los Tigres del Norte, he interrupted me when he realized that I was focusing my research on corridos about migration. He told me,

> Oiga, quería decirle que no todas las canciones y cor-
> ridos de Los Trigres son de migración. Hay muchas
> historias de ranchos, de niños, de amor de todo. De
> todo tienen ellos y ojalá salga eso en su reporte, que no
> solamente salga de migración. [Listen, I want to tell
> you that not all the songs and corridos of Los Tigres
> are about migration. There are so many stories about
> the ranches, about children, about love, and everything.
> They have songs about everything, and I hope that
> comes out in your report, not only about migration.]

Octavio told me that by choosing to focus only on migration, I was imposing a too restrictive order on the corrido genre and simplifying complex issues related to the human spirit, human agency, the power of the human will, and the wittiness and struggles that are part of the corrido repertoire.

Octavio kept questioning my focus on corridos about migration and demanded a more thorough study of the elements of the performance of the corridos: "Si usted quiere entender bien esta música tiene que saber que en realidad se tiene que saber todo lo que hacen, no nada más las palabras o la historia. También tiene que saber la música misma, el sonido, el acordión. La música del acordión es una cosa que entra adentro del corazón, es todo." [If you want to understand this music, you need to know that in reality, it's everything you need to know, not only the words or the story. You also need to know the very music, the sounds, the accordion. The accordion music is a thing that enters right here in the heart. That is all I want to say.] By the same token, Mr. Manuel Granillo, a musician from Albuquerque, told me that although corridos about migration are very popular and sell well, they are not meant for dancing: "¿Los corridos de migración? No nos los piden mucho para bailar, no fíjese, la verdad. Los corridos de migración son mas bien para escucharlos, para bailar se usan corridos y música más bien alegre. [Corridos about migration? No, people do not ask for them to dance. No, not really. Corridos about migration are more to be listened to. For dancing people like happy upbeat corridos and music that is happy.]

Octavio's and Mr. Granillo's comments are important to clarify that as a researcher, I am imposing an arbitrary order and focus on the corpus of corridos that are listened to and danced by this transnational community. One consequence of this is that my analysis is very specific but at the same time does not reflect the whole experience of the community.

What Are the Corridos?

Although corridos have been sung for over five hundred years in Mexico and are an important cultural expression of Mexicans and Mexican Americans, the meaning of the corridos to those who perform them, dance them, and listen to them has not been thoroughly researched. In part, this situation can be explained by the fact that the study of corridos presents such challenges as the need to decipher the very specific local, regional, and time-frame conventions and meanings embodied in the corridos.

Researchers who are not part of the communities where corridos flourish find this a special problem. Corridos provide a point of view of marginalized groups, which very often is different from or in opposition to the official views of key events. Since corridos are created, listened to, and performed by rural and urban working classes, they are normally seen as in opposition to the cultural expressions of the dominant culture and as unworthy of serious study.

Corridos play a very important role in the oral tradition of Mexican and Mexican American communities. The corrido transcends space and time because although some aspects of the corridos may change through generations or vary according to geographic regions, the main content of the corrido remains the same. Past events are transformed into present consciousness despite changes in society. Epic corridos might be popular because the community values and folklore are normally packaged or put into a one-man (normally male) narrative. In Mexican culture, the function of the corridos is not equivalent to that of the newspapers: in order to interpret the corridos, people have to be already informed of the major important events and characteristics of the main protagonists (McDowell 1972). The corrido is more comparable to a newspaper editorial: it takes a position in the analysis of an event and does not pretend to be an impartial medium for the delivery of news (McDowell 1981).

There is common agreement among corrido scholars that the antecedents of the corrido are found in the epic romancero, or ballad, that developed in Spain, particularly in the Andalucía region. Although scholars generally agree that corridos have a Spanish legacy, some disagree that the corrido developed in Mexico and what is now part of el México de afuera. Paredes (1990, 1) states that "the word *corrido* comes from *correr*, which means 'to run' or 'to flow,'" for the corrido tells a story simply and swiftly, without embellishment. Corridos are a popular source of entertainment for Mexican and Mexican American communities, perhaps because they are easy to memorize, they use locally meaningful language, and they narrate events in which the community is invested. The themes of the corridos express the entire range of human experience and feelings: love, war, nostalgia, homesickness, humor, natural disasters, criminals and their activities, folk heroes of various persuasions, miracles and miraculous events, violent deaths, hometowns and regions, smuggling, migration, and social and political events.

Mendoza (1939), Hernández (1999), and Herrera-Sobek (1993) have pointed out that corridos have several elements, presented in a more or less consistent order: (1) the singer's initial address to the audience; (2) the place, the time, and the name of the main character; (3) antecedents to the arguments of the main character; (4) a message; (5) the main character's farewell; and (6) the songwriter's farewell. Most corridistas agree that not every element is found in every corrido. The definition of the corrido is limited not by aesthetic characteristics so much as by cultural representativity: whether the people who listen to and perform corridos perceive them as corridos. The basic formula is a guideline to identify corridos but should not be taken as a strict standard or model.

Corrido scholars have resisted accepting the transformations that corridos have gone through over the years. Often, we are entangled in academic discussions about the authenticity, degeneration, corruption, and even the death of this genre. As scholars of everyday cultural practices, we tend to be prescriptive and normative about cultural expressions that we do not ourselves practice. The classic corridos that are often used as a standard against which to measure the current corridos are the ones that were created during the Mexican Revolution. In their time, they were judged and sung mainly by poor, rural revolutionaries. The development of the corridos follows a common cycle in which the Mexican national sociopolitical elite appropriate cultural expressions that formerly were stigmatized. The national elite thereby manage to continuously position themselves as the arbiters of taste—as the "customs officers" who judge the quality and authenticity of the corridos.

Cultural expressions created by marginalized groups are often romanticized as innocent and independent from the capitalism, patriarchy, heteronormativity, and sexism that pervade other areas of society. Rosaldo (1989) tells us that the perception of the "others" as innocent and naive is part of the imperialist nostalgia that adopts a paternal and humanitarian imperialist position toward the "others." Imperialist nostalgia serves at least three purposes. First, it allows us to deny responsibility for the destructive disruptions caused by colonization processes. This denial in turn allows us to feel guiltless about the "ugly" face of displacements and the social, economic, and political problems caused by imperialist projects. Second, imperialist nostalgia allows us to position ourselves in a paternalistic and condescending role in which we assume we know what is best for the "other" and tell them what they need to preserve and how changes should occur. Keeping the noble savages "noble" is a way of keeping them more manageable and less threatening and a way of keeping ourselves more comfortable and unconfronted. Third, imperialist nostalgia allows us to use the "original" customs of the "other" to retreat to "nature" according to our needs. We can experience this "unchanged" culture as a theme park or a spa so that we can detoxify ourselves from the evils of the West through close contact with nature: the uncivilized noble savage and the unspoiled landscape. We can purify ourselves in this unchanged heaven that does have things that remind us of "home," such as electricity, television, radio, and western clothing.

In her book *The Bracero Experience: Folklore versus Elitelore*, Herrera-Sobeck (1979) asserts that researchers assume a paternalistic assumption regarding cultural expressions of migrants; specifically, that there is a tendency to portray them as lacking a sense of agency or creative capacity and of being always vulnerable. Herrera-Sobek argues that although the corridos express the undignified circumstances of the immigrants, they also present migration as a complex and multidimensional phenomenon where there is irony, humor, love, intelligence, and the capacity for survival. The corridos illustrate ways of coping with adversarial situations as well as the very real positive aspects of migration to the United States.

There is no doubt that corridos play a key role in constructing the cultural memory of transnational communities. Since the early 1970s, however, corridos have gone through an important transformation. They are now an important artifact of the cultural industries, with special ties to Fonovisa, a division of the Mexican monopoly that dominates the media in Spanish-speaking countries.

Televisa is the world's most profitable producer, exporter, and distributor of Spanish-speaking television broadcasting, film, publishing, and music recordings (Chew Sánchez et al. 2003). Corridos are available to transnational communities at many commercial outlets, from flea markets to major U.S. companies with Mexican customers (Wal-Mart and Kmart, for example).

Since the corridos are supposed to reflect people's perspectives and feelings, authorship was considered *de dominio público*: the corridos were anonymously written by common people, and performers had some liberty in changing certain parts of the lyrics according to their own circumstances. Capitalism requires specificity in authorship for royalty purposes, and even scholars on corridos are finding a new academic niche in highlighting the importance of certain contemporary authors of corridos. As part of the vertical integration of media industries, since the 1980s, stories of corridos created by Los Tigres del Norte have also been part of movies that are made and distributed by Televisa.

Corridos created during the Mexican Revolution were very much a part of the postrevolutionary national project. They were mainly about the qualities of those who fought for social justice and on behalf of the poor, like Emiliano Zapata and Francisco Villa. In a way, these corridos, which were created by *campesinos revolucionarios*, were appropriated as part of the national discourse and officialized. The lyrics and performance of the corridos before the 1970s were quite long. Contemporary corridos are shorter due to the imposition of commercial formats in the recording industries, and some are being transformed into what scholars call *corrido-canción* (corrido-song).[1]

In the 1980s, revolutionary corridos were widely played in the schools, and other kinds of corridos—those about horse races and rural life, for example—did not have the same popularity among the youth of the time. Los Tigres del Norte were pioneers in the resurgence of corridos in a time of crisis when young people were becoming uninterested in the genre. Their corridos were more about marginalized people, but in urban settings and with different problems, such as migration, drug smuggling, and the displacements caused by globalization. These new corridos met with astonishing success and acceptance, not only because of the format and content but also because of the style of the performances. Conjuntos norteños incorporated elements of rock and roll, and their stages and tours were very similar to those of pop music. Although corridos have changed from folklore to popular culture, many corridos fall between these two genres.

Chicano scholars such as Paredes (1990), Limón (1992), Peña (1999), and Herrera-Sobek (1993) have made a crucial contribution in the study of corridos as a form of symbolic expression that resists economic exploitation and racial prejudice. The most prominent work illustrating their approach is Américo Paredes's (1958) book *With His Pistol in His Hand*, a model for an in-depth, multidisciplinary study of the corridos. Paredes describes the historical, cultural, political, and social context of the mid-nineteenth-century lower Rio Grande Valley in which "El corrido de Gregorio Cortez" was created (Limón 1992).

Corridos can be performed in various ways: recited or sung or performed with one or two guitars, a mariachi band, or a conjunto norteño. Specific genres of music and corridos are very distinctive of specific regions, for example, *los corridos de la Costa Chica*, Mexico's southern Pacific coast, or *los corridos del bajío*, or horse race corridos from central Mexico. I chose to focus on the corridos sung by conjuntos norteños.

Conjunto Norteño

Conjunto norteño is a musical expression that is unique to the U.S.-Mexican border and came out of people's persistent crisscrossing of that national and highly sensitized boundary (see chapter 1 for a definition of conjunto norteño and Peña 1982 for a thorough study of conjunto). The conjunto norteño has evolved and incorporated sound amplification with the electric bass, electric pickup for the bajo sexto, and electric guitar. According to Peña (1985), one characteristic of conjunto norteño singers is their pinched, shrill, nasal style. In contrast, *canción ranchera* singers have an open, full-voiced style of singing.

La canción ranchera is a subgenre that first emerged in the late nineteenth century. The literal translation of canción ranchera is "ranch songs," referring to songs from rural Mexico. According to Mendoza (1998), la canción ranchera expresses ideas or "strong feelings written in two or more stanzas.... The *ranchera* song has an undeniable influence of the Italian opera, particularly regarding the chanting of lamentations" (Mendoza 1998, 28). La canción ranchera originated in rural haciendas (a large farm or state) and was incorporated in stylized form into urban theater music, especially in Mexico City (Mendoza 1998). La canción ranchera is sung at a slow tempo and tends to be quite sentimental and often amatory.

The dramatic immigration from rural areas to cities that took place in the 1930s made the canción ranchera very popular because such migration coincided with its incorporation into the mass media: radio, records, and, especially, the cinema of the 1930s. The canción ranchera continued to be one of the most vital aspects of Mexican music. Its distinctive character lies in its virile, melodramatic vocal style and in the accompanying ensembles, usually consisting of a mariachi band. Música ranchera tends to romanticize *lo ranchero*. As Manuel Peña (2001) has said, Mexican romantic nationalism has been a unifying influence that appeals to the nation's "unique" heritage. As components of this nationalism, la música ranchera is supposed to elicit lo ranchero, the agrarian way of life, which is "presumed unspoiled by the pretensions of social snobbery" (47). Música ranchera has long been a symbol of nationalism, particularly during the construction of "Mexicanness," one of the main political projects that took place after the Mexican Revolution. According to Peña (2001), Mexican people, whether in Mexico or in el México de afuera, tend to respond quite enthusiastically to la música ranchera, regardless of who interprets it: a conjunto, an orquesta, or a mariachi.

La música norteña has not enjoyed the status or recognition granted to other genres of national music, such as música ranchera, mariachi music, and other types of mestizo and nonmestizo musical expressions (Reyna 1996; Peña 1985, 1996; Manuel 1988; Geijerstam 1976). As Reyna (1996, 82) says, "The conjunto is the unwanted stepchild of Mexican folkloric and popular music."

The northern part of Mexico has developed a sense of regional identity in reaction to the highly centralized and hierarchical political and economic structure, perhaps because the region has historically had only limited cultural, economic, and political ties to central Mexico. The remoteness of the inhabitants led them to adopt distinctive cultural features.

The key characteristic of the conjunto norteño is the use of the accordion. The accordion has such a symbolic value for conjuntos norteños that if a band plays all the instruments characteristic of a conjunto except an accordion, it ceases to be considered a conjunto (Reyna 1996). Thus, to determine the origin of the conjunto, it is important to explore the appearance of the accordion in Mexico and in the Mexican communities in Texas (Peña 1985). The accordion was used in Mexico by the mid-nineteenth century in European instrumental forms such as the schottishe, redowa, waltz, mazurka, and especially the polka. Although these instrumental forms were first popular among the Mexican elite, they eventually became part of the repertoire of the Mexican lower classes (Peña 1982).

According to Peña (1999), the settlements established by Germans in the northern Mexican industrial town of Monterrey in the mid-nineteenth century were crucial to the incorporation of the accordion in northern Mexican music. Monterrey became an important commercial and industrial center after the end of the Mexican-American War. Because of

Los Tigres del Norte, the most popular and commercially successful conjunto norteño that performs corridos about migration (2001). Courtesy of Los Tigres del Norte.

its geographic position, it became a link between the border towns and the ports of Tamaulipas that facilitated commerce in European goods and cotton between Texas, Tamaulipas, and Nuevo León. Monterrey consolidated its leading position in the brewing industry of Mexico, an industry in which Germans contributed greatly (Peña 1999).

During the early decades after the Mexico-U.S. war of 1848, Mexican families who remained in Texas perceived that Mexican prestige came from Mexico and saw Monterrey as an important source of culture and prestige. For example, some social rituals, such as weddings or christenings, had more meaning if they were done in Mexico, and the finest musicians hired to play in Texas by Mexican families were those from Monterrey. The migratory waves of northern Mexicans to Texas and the geographical proximity of Nuevo León and Tamaulipas to Texas made possible the diffusion of the use of accordion among Mexicans living in Texas (Peña 1982). Several authors have argued that the use of [the] accordion by Mexicans in Texas was due to the influence of [the] Germans and Bohemian settlers in Texas (Peña 1982). No doubt such interaction occurred and had a major impact on the development of the conjunto. However, many ethnomusicologist studies have ignored the interaction that Germans had in Nuevo León, specifically Monterrey, and even more the lesser racial tensions that

Conjunto norteño Bego plays along the El Camino Real corridor on both sides of the border (2004). Courtesy of Brupo Bego.

prevailed in Mexico compared to the ethnic conflicts that were prominent in Texas after the Mexican-U.S. war.

Peña (1985) divides the evolution of the conjunto into three main stages. First, from the mid-nineteenth century to the 1920s, the ensemble was improvisational and the accordion "was still played either solo, with guitar or bajo sexto, or drum, the *tambora de rancho* (ranch drum)" (Peña 1985, 208). Second, from the late 1920s to the mid-1930s, the combination of the accordion and bajo sexto was settled. Conjunto accordion technique also diverged from German practice at this time in that the left hand was rarely used. Third, after World War II, when the modern trap drum and the canción ranchera were introduced, the redowa and schottishe were often left out. In recent years, conjuntos norteños have incorporated *cumbias, boleros,* and *baladas románticas.*[2] The conjuntos now play polkas at a much slower tempo than in earlier eras (Peña 1985).

Peña's work is particularly significant for this study because the conjunto norteño and the Texas-Mexican conjunto are quite similar and have mutually influenced each other. However, the particular social and political conditions of Mexican Americans in Texas have influenced the lyrics, style, and performance of conjunto norteño music performed by Mexican Americans in Texas in such a way that Tex-Mex music is very similar to the conjunto norteño. Nonetheless, the two genres are not entirely the same.

Conjunto norteño music is now enjoying a period of great success and expansion that started in the early 1990s. This popularity may be due to the current waves of internal migration within Mexico, the urbanization of northern Mexico, and the creation of a niche market serving the needs of people with rural backgrounds as well as those who want to reinforce their norteño identity. Mexican migrants who live in the United States have been able to promote música norteña not only in northern Mexico and the southwestern United States but also in the places that working-class Mexican migrants have passed through or originated from—the northeastern and northwestern United States, for example, as well as central and southern Mexico. For these reasons, conjunto norteño and Tex-Mex music cannot be confined to the Mexico-U.S. border region. Cultural industries have played a decisive role in the popularity of conjunto norteño music, as explained in chapter 6.

Narrative Analysis

Narrative analysis assesses how people make sense of events and actions in their lives. According to Potter (1996, 139), narrative analysis is an "analytical technique that seeks to fit messages into a pattern of storytelling. The storyteller uses characters and events as symbols to tell his or her interpretations about how things in the world behave and change over time." Narrative analysis is appropriate in this case because it allows us to see how people impose their order on experiences and environments in the corridos by narrating their relationships between events and actions through stories. Narrative analysis enables us to identify the transitional stages leading to a given situation and to identify similarities and differences between groups of respondents.

Narrative analysis focuses on the relationships that exist within the stories: the plot structure, the spheres of action commanded by different characters, the control of information through point of view, the relationship between the storyteller and the story world, and the interaction between the reader and the physical world (Potter 1996). Each narrative has formal properties that inform us about time, place, situation, participants, sequence of events, significance and meaning of the action, attitude of the narrator, resolution, and perspective of the event to the present (Langellier 2004). I conducted my analysis with an eye to the main elements of corridos as defined by Hernández (1999): characters, values, time and setting of the main narrative, and language. "Without their presence, especially the sections of challenge, confrontation, and defeat, corridos lack the emotional power characteristic of the genre and may be excluded from its corpus" (Hernández 1999, 81).

Frith (1996) warns us, just as Octavio Fernández explained to me, that lyrical analysis should not be confined to words but rather to words in performance in order to open up various possibilities of meaning and uses of the lyrics. In Frith's opinion, songs cannot be treated as "literary objects which can be analyzed entirely and separately from music, or as speech acts... because a song doesn't exist to convey the meaning of words; rather the words exist to convey the meaning of the song" (Frith 1996, 158). Although my study deals with many different aspects of corridos, the following sections focus especially on the lyrics. Specifically, I present a narrative analysis of six corridos that are commonly performed by conjunto norteños in the border region.

Corridos about Immigration

Herrera-Sobek (1993) points out that the corridos are representative of the political, economic, and social context of the different immigration waves of Mexicans to the United States. In her book *Northward Bound* (1993), she carries out an excellent analysis of corridos that deal specifically with migration to the United States. Such corridos began to flourish after the Mexican-American War of 1848, when Mexicans participated in the construction and maintenance of major railroads crisscrossing the Southwest. These corridos provide rich data about the railroads, the stations and cities they served, the landscape they crossed, and the experience of traveling in the border region. Herrera-Sobek (1993) analyzed the most popular corridos written and performed during the U.S. economic depression, when over five hundred thousand Mexicans were deported to Mexico—even those who were born in the United States. Her analysis includes corridos written during the bracero program, after the bracero program, and during the Chicano movement.

My analysis focuses on the corridos about migration that were written during the 1980s and 1990s. Many of these corridos illustrate the radical economic and political changes during those decades and how such changes have further impoverished the south and enriched people in wealthy countries. These changes in the global economy have caused hostile feelings toward one of the most vulnerable sectors of the population: the migrants. Antimigration movements have crystallized in the militarization of the U.S.-Mexico border, welfare reforms, immigration reforms, and the emergence of civil organizations that chase immigrants in the border region.

I also chose relatively recent corridos because most of the participants in my study were between eighteen and thirty years old (with just a few as old as fifty). This audience is familiar with the new corridos-canción that deal with current topics and are widely broadcast in the United States and Mexico by radio stations, Spanish-language television in the United States, and Fonovisa. Some of the main clusters of themes that emerged from my narrative analysis of six corridos follows.

Corridos, Autobiography, and Self-definition

The corridos have an autobiographical element that refers to real events or stories. The characters that appear frequently in the corridos about immigration are the migrants; their wives or loved ones; their brothers, sisters, parents, and children; and people from their hometowns. When autobiographies or biographies are presented within a social and political context, they are integrated into the history of the community. Biographies are important not only because of the personal lives of the character or characters but also because they represent part of the community's experiences. In this way, the stories and histories complement each other. The individual dimension of the corrido is surpassed by the relevance the corrido has within the community. So, corridos are transformed into a collective treasure.

Mexican immigrants in the United States are labeled in ways that problematize their presence in the United States. One common derogatory term for undocumented immigrants is "wetback," which means that they crossed the border through the Rio Bravo/Rio Grande "illegally." In the public arena, "wetback" is synonymous with "criminal" or "parasite"—those who are a burden to society. Many corridos make use of transcodification, however. That is, they take a term such as "wetback" and reappropriate it with a new meaning. In the corridos, the concept of "wetback" goes through a transcodification that humanizes and dignifies the mainstream definition. "Wetback" becomes a source of ethnic pride that defines migrants as social, cultural, and economic actors, as people who cross the Rio Bravo and whose hard work makes a significant contribution to the U.S. economy. Wetbacks are presented in the corridos as people who make important contributions to U.S. society, culturally and economically. Wetbacks are presented with multiple subjectivities as parents, husbands/wives, sons and daughters, workers, and people who celebrate their culture; as survivors of racial scapegoating and low-intensity terrorism against them; and as people who have a joy for life, who possess great humor, and who try to empower themselves.

The subjectivities of the *mojados* (wetbacks), as mentioned in the corridos, are not presented unilaterally or unidimensionally but rather as conflicting, contradictory, ambiguous, and discontinuous. The corridos show the conflicts that migrants face regarding assimilation into the mainstream culture of the host country. On the one hand, the use of the Spanish language in the corridos might be read as a powerful rejection of assimilation, as an acknowledgment of the need for unity and solidarity in the face of a system that works against the interests of migrants or as a way to disguise the political content of the corridos. Corridos do incorporate cultural elements of the host country, however, especially in the way they are performed. The lyrics include words in English and often mention particular places in the United States as well as relationships with other migrant groups and with members of the host culture. This incorporation is not so much assimilation as the selective embracing of particular elements of the cultural context in which migrants are living. These external cultural elements are not always or necessarily part of mainstream society. In fact, they can be cultural elements of other migrations, such as the Central American migrations.

The corridos often analyze and lament losses. Migrants lose their families, their land, and their visibility and regret their children's loss of language and cultural pride. The protagonists often talk about losing their lovers. Although Mexican migrants send more than $10 billion to their families in Mexico every year, the corridos hardly ever mention these contributions except when explaining why the migrants left. In these instances, the main content of the corrido is sometimes more of a political analysis of the attitudes of middle-class Mexicans who are quick to criticize working-class migrants as sellouts or traitors yet do not work for the interests of poor people in Mexico. These corridos tend to reject and criticize the political projects of the economic and political elites—projects that create more poverty and therefore more migration.

The corrido about immigration is a cultural practice of self-definition. It is self-centered and performed in spaces where the corridistas, the performers, the audience, the dancers, the promoters, and all those involved in this cultural practice exercise control over the manner of dissemination, the place where the corridos are played, the content of the corridos, and the performative acts of the corridos. In this sense, the corrido is a cultural practice that can be heavily decentralized among participants. The corridos are constantly readjusted, revised, abbreviated, created, and even forgotten, depending on the immediate reality of the people who create, sing, listen to, and perform this kind of music.

The corridos about migration can be polyvalent and ambiguous. Quite often exact dates, names, or places are not provided by the corridista, perhaps to make the stories and the meaning more universal. Sometimes only subtle references are made to economic, political, or social problems, and the constant use of metaphors may disguise the true message of the corridista. Corridos provide different readings to different audiences. Through ambiguity and the use of metaphors, the core of the content of the corrido is often accessible only to the intended audience and becomes opaque to those audiences the corridistas do not want to include. Sometimes the excluded audience may consist of middle- and upper-class Mexicans and white Americans, monolingual English speakers, or people who are not familiar with this musical genre. Some may not identify the contrapunctual content of the corrido. These elements of the folk culture genre make it difficult for audiences to contest the potentially subversive messages of the corridos, since the existence of multiple meanings allows any performer to claim that the message was different due to its polivalency. For these reasons, the corrido as a transgressive genre has the capacity to take advantage of the loopholes and ambiguities available to the genre without attracting censure.

Narratives of Corridos and Space

The lyrics of the corridos invite us to read the spaces: the rural landscape of Mexico, the neighborhood, the border, the city, the home, the country.

The lyrics mark and create spaces that are in tension. That is, the spaces created in the corrido are often related not to the concept of nation-states but to the culturally and individually defined spaces in which migrants live and work. The migrant routes and el México de afuera are places defined more by their cultural borders than by political ones. The corridos also give ample descriptions of marginal or dominated spaces. Migrants are portrayed as people who are physically displaced, who live and work in the margins, and who therefore lead marginal lives. For undocumented migrants, public spaces in the United States can mean deprivation or liberty, vulnerability (the risk of being detected and deported, accused, monitored, rejected, mistreated), or invisibility (lack of acknowledgment). Paradoxically, the homes of immigrants can also be like jails where they are condemned to live in hiding. Social inequities in the home country, the host country, the border between the two countries, and the workplace also lead to confinement and limitation of movement. Migrants are confined by both geographical space and social space.

The border is another constant in the corridos about migration. The border is portrayed in real, concrete terms as well as metaphorically. In either case, it is a central part of the economic, social, and political hierarchy that keeps people separated from the center-periphery domains. Symbolic and concrete borders are monitored, policed, and militarized to keep people in their places within the established social and economic hierarchy. This is particularly the case with the low-intensity repatriation that exists in the United States, not to mention the massive repatriation of Mexicans that occurred during the U.S. depression (Hoffman 1974). People who transgress established borders are demonized, persecuted, and denied their human rights.

The Mexico-U.S. border marks one of the many racialized, economic boundaries between the European and non-European New World. The border is also expressed in the corridos as a reminder of the U.S. military conquest of the Mexican territory that is now the Southwest of the United States.

The political borders between Mexico and the United States are continuously challenged, deconstructed, and broken down by the physical movements and cultural expressions of Mexican migrants. Such transnational cultural expressions and performances indicate a certain level of autonomy among migrants. Música norteña and other Mexican cultural expressions accompany migrants wherever they go, regardless of immigration laws, political borders, geographical segregation, and symbolic and physical marginalization. Working-class Mexicans from both sides of the border reinforce, complement, and interact in the co-creation of cultural expressions such as música norteña.

Corridos about migration romanticize people's places of origin; they represent spaces of security, tenderness, support, and love, full of cultural symbolism related to religion, grief, departure, and return. The landscape of the hometowns of the migrants is also greatly romanticized and described in detail. The solitude, poor working conditions, lack of social support, labor exploitation, persecution, and other elements common within migrant communities generate longing for a hometown—either a real hometown or a utopian construction and reconstruction of the community of origin. The corridos about migration provide an account of the *campo*, the *ranchos*, and the *pueblos*, a rich information set that shows how migrants construct their world in the face of adversity.

The description of the landscape and the feelings attached to the hometown are part of the collective memory, knowledge, and identity of the migrants as well as an archive for future generations of the Mexican diaspora. The corridos address Mexico and the migrants' Mexican hometowns not as spaces inhabited by migrants but as symbols that are part of the Mexican identity that migrants construct outside Mexico. The corridos help to co-create new cultural and social spaces in the host country that serve as places for collectivity and mutuality outside the migrants' hometowns. Since the corridos about immigration describe not only rural settings but also migrants' new cultural contexts, they address issues of adaptation to urban areas and modernity. Corridos lament the loss of the idyllic garden that represents rural life in Mexico. In a sense, they lament not only the past but also the future—the loss of what society might be if not for the conditions of the present. The corridos are especially critical of the loss of cultural values, such as the loss of humanity in social interactions. Consequently, they are also critical of the possible negative future of society. Corridos about migration portray anxiety about what society might become if the trends toward dehumanization, the ghettoization of the working class, labor exploitation, crime, and racial hate continue.

The corridos often make only ambiguous reference to regions, perhaps so that audiences can identify individually with the corrido or perhaps to underscore the heterogeneity of the regions in order to create a collectivity based on solidarity of broad geographic spaces. In fact, corridos and songs about immigration tend to be inclusive of migrants' experiences in a general (not necessarily Mexican) context, and they often call for intercontinental solidarity among migrants of color, particularly among those from Latin America. This is especially true in corridos such as "Tres veces mojado" (Three Times a Wetback), "Cuando gime la raza" (When the Race [People] Cries), "America," and "El sueño de Bolivar" (The Dream of Bolivar).

It is noteworthy that corridos about immigration originally gained popularity within marginal spaces in both the United States and Mexico. As time passes, however, they are "gaining ground" in terms of both real and symbolic spaces. For example, audiences for this type of music are increasingly found in urban areas of the United States, Latin America, and Spain, including places where corridos about migration were previously stigmatized and dismissed.[3]

Inversion of Roles

The inversion of roles is a frequent tool that appears in the corridos to transgress and decenter existing economic and racial hierarchies. For example, in the corrido "Los hijos de Hernández," the main protagonist answers the INS (Immigration and Naturalization Services) officer on equal terms and informs him of the contributions that Mexicans have made to the U.S. armed forces. The terms of the conversation between the INS officer and the Mexican immigrant would hardly ever happen in real life because of the extreme power difference between the two protagonists. However, the inversion of roles and power has an important symbolic function in the corrido: to represent the wish of people for a more egalitarian society where such encounters can take place on equal terms, where people from different classes, races, and nationalities can inform each other with respect and humanity. Such inversions of power celebrate human subjectivities because they acknowledge that the current hierarchies are socially constructed and, therefore, that people can deconstruct them and make tangible changes based on other social constructions that the corridistas create.

Corridos provide an archive of events of society that might undercut, contradict, or contest the official interpretation of the event. In other words, the corrido becomes the unofficial version, analysis, critique, or editorial of an event, the point of view of the masses that encompasses people's everyday experience and values. In the case of corridos about immigration, they give an account, critique, and analysis of the uncovered experiences of Mexican and Latin American immigrants—the extreme economic and social asymmetries, family separations, work hazards, and exploitive labor conditions.

Women and Corridos about Migration

The narratives of contemporary corridos about migration privilege men's experiences and points of view. No single corrido has a female narrator or makes direct reference to female migrants. Despite the fact that women participate actively in transnational movements and are a significant part of undocumented migrants and workers, corridos about migration offer very little information and analysis of the effects of migration on women. Women are normally mentioned indirectly, if at all. However, in the corrido "Bajo el cielo de Morelia" (Under the Sky of Morelia) it was the migrant's wife and the hardship of being separated from her that makes this migrant change his mind and remain at home. In the corrido "Carrera contra la muerte" (Race against Death) (see the appendix), the wife dies of "love," the painful situation of not seeing her migrant husband for over three years. In "Pueblo querido" (Beloved Town), the migrant misses every family member but especially his mother in her nurturing and giving role. However, in most corridos the narrators construct their masculinities around the ethics of work (giving the impression that women do not work or it is not as important for them) and the freedom (or frustration for lacking it) of movement. In these corridos men construct themselves as benevolent patriarchs where they carry out important decisions and are protectors of their families, particularly the children. In "Sin fronteras" (Without Borders), the migrant is quite proud of his womanizing and chivalric qualities and migration is a sign of not being restrained or attached in a committed relationship. Another current representation of women is the young woman left back home who is a traitor for not waiting for the return of the migrant to get married. In reality, the opposite is true: more women are left by a migrant husband who forms a new family. In the corrido "Pedro y Pablo" (Pedro and Pablo; see the appendix), it is impossible not to judge Leticia, the girlfriend of the migrant, because of the added twist that she marries her ex-boyfriend's younger brother.

In the six corridos below, the lyrics of each corrido are followed by a narrative analysis.

"LA JAULA DE ORO" GOLDEN CAGE

Enrique Franco (1995). Performed by Los Tigres del Norte.

Aquí estoy establecido	I have established myself here
en los Estados Unidos	in the United States
diez años pasaron ya	Ten years have passed by
en que crucé de mojado	since I crossed here as a wetback
y papeles no he arreglado	I have not legalized my status
sigo siendo un ilegal	I am still an illegal alien
Tengo mi esposa y mis hijos	I have my wife and my children
que me los traje de chicos	I brought them when they were very young
y se han olvidado ya	and they have already forgotten
de mi México querido	my beloved Mexico—
del que yo nunca me olvido	the one I never forget
y al que no puedo regresar	and the one I cannot go back to
¿De qué me sirve el dinero	What is money good for
si estoy como prisionero	if I am living like a prisoner
dentro de esta gran nación?	inside this great nation?
Cuando me acuerdo hasta lloro	When I remember my country, I even cry
que aunque la jaula sea de oro	Even though the cage is made of gold
no deja de ser prisión	it is nothing but a prison

(hablado)	(spoken)
Escúchame m'ijo ¿te gustaría que	Listen, my son, would you like to go back to
regresáramos a México?	Mexico?
What are you talking about, Dad?	What are you talking about, Dad?
No way, I don't want to go back to Mexico.	No way, I don't want to go back to Mexico
No way, Dad.	No way, Dad.
Mis hijos no hablan conmigo	My children do not talk to me
otro idioma han aprendido	They have learned another language
y olvidado el español	and have forgotten Spanish

piensan como americanos	They really think like Americans
niegan que son mexicanos	They deny they are Mexicans
aunque tengan mi color	although they have my skin color
De mi trabajo a mi casa	From work to home
yo no sé lo que me pasa	I do not know what is going on with me
que aunque soy hombre de hogar	although I am a man that likes to be at home
casi no salgo a la calle	I rarely go out
pues tengo miedo que me hallen	because I am fearful that they will find me
y me puedan deportar	and can deport me
¿De qué me sirve el dinero	What is the money good for
si estoy como prisionero	if I am living like a prisoner
dentro de esta gran nación?	inside this great nation?
Cuando me acuerdo hasta lloro	When I remember my country, I even cry
que aunque la jaula sea de oro	even though the cage is made of gold
no deja de ser prisión	it is nothing but a prison

The narrator of this corrido gives an account of intergenerational conflicts exacerbated by his condition of dislocation and isolation as a migrant. This migrant mourns the loss of a relatively coherent earlier identity, that of a free man, and expresses anxiety and trauma due to his experience of being constantly persecuted because of his illegal status. This corrido has been the epitome of intergenerational conflicts experienced by migrants.

The characters of this corrido are the protagonist/narrator (an undocumented migrant living in the United States) and his wife and children. The implicit characters are the INS officers, who are a constant threat to this migrant. The places mentioned are Mexico, for which he expresses longing and nostalgia; the migrant's workplace; the streets, which he cannot walk freely for fear of being deported; and the United States, for which the protagonist expresses admiration and gratitude because he has a job that enables him to support his family. At the same time, the United States represents a prison for him because he cannot enjoy the basic human right of going out without feeling persecuted and risking deportation. His home is both a refuge and a prison.

The language of this corrido is direct and concise, although in the spoken section of the corrido, the migrant talks in a tender tone to his child and asks him if he will go back to Mexico with him, presumably if he is deported. His child answers by ruling out such a possibility and answers in English to his migrant father, revealing the child's assimilation into U.S. society. The moral values of this corrido are related to endurance, resilience, responsibility, love for family, and hard work. The most relevant feelings are nostalgia, gratefulness, and, above all, the migrant's fear of the consequences of making himself known to the authorities.

This character cannot go back to his country as frequently as he would like, given his "illegal" status in the United States. The main character says that he feels psychologically and physically trapped because he does not enjoy full human rights despite his relatively good economic situation. He has to live a hidden, invisible existence in a nation that claims to be democratic.

This corrido reflects on the gains and losses of migrating as an undocumented individual with his family. After ten years, his children are fully assimilated, and they feel alien to Mexican cultural practices. His children have been forced to choose between complete assimilation in the mainstream U.S. culture and the prejudice they would experience if they chose to maintain the language and culture of their parents. This migrant's children are victims of cultural erasure. His children learn that in order to be accepted by their host country, they must reject their heritage and become monolingual English speakers. They distance themselves from Mexican culture by choosing not to speak Spanish, a language that is linked in the United States to a nonwhite skin and that signals a third world homeland. The second generation is trapped in this false promise of "social mobility" and "social acceptance" by valuing the dominant culture positively over (and at the expense of) the "parent" culture. The main character expresses sadness at not being able to talk to his children in Spanish and not sharing cultural values with them. While he wants to provide his children with the best opportunities, he misses Mexico and wants to enjoy the basic human right of walking free. The narrator exposes the exploitive labor system of the United States, the land of freedom, which accepts his labor but denies him basic human rights. In the last part of the corrido, the migrant tells about his hard work and the fact that his masculine identity has been tarnished by the white patriarchy. The narrator does not challenge patriarchy; on the contrary, he regrets that one outcome of migration as an undocumented man of color has meant the loss of some of the privileges he enjoyed at home. A very important part of his masculine identity is his pride in his responsibility for his family and kin with regard to both decision making and the provision of food and shelter. This migrant's wife and her experience is secondary in the migration story.

"MIS DOS PATRIAS"   MY TWO COUNTRIES

Enrique Franco (1997). Performed by Los Tigres del Norte.

["I pledge allegiance to the flag of the United States of America and to the republic for which it stands, one nation under God, indivisible, with liberty and justice for all. Congratulations, you are now all American citizens."]

Para quien dice que soy un malinchista	For those who say that I am a traitor
y que traiciono a mi bandera y a mi nación	and that I betray my flag and my nation
para que rompa con mi canto las fronteras	I will open very wide my heart
les voy a abrir de par en par mi corazón	so that the borders can be broken by my heart singing
Dejé las tumbas de mis padres, mis abuelos	I left the tombs of my parents and grandparents
llegué llorando a tierra de anglosajón	I came crying to the land of the Anglo-Saxon
yo trabajaba, mis hijos iban creciendo	I was working while my children were growing up
todos nacieron en esta gran nación	All my children were born in this great nation
Y mis derechos los han ido pisoteando	My rights have been slowly taken away
van formulando leyes de constitución	They are formulating constitutional laws
que haré ya viejo si me quitan mi dinero	What am I going to do when I become old
yo solo quiero mi seguro de pensión	if they take away my pension
	I only want my social security pension
[Coro]	**[Chorus]**
Pero ¿qué importa	But does it matter
si soy nuevo ciudadano?	if I am a new citizen?
Sigo siendo mexicano	I am still Mexican
como el pulque y el nopal	like the pulque and the cactus
Y mis hermanos	and my brothers

centro y sudamericanos

caribeños o cubanos

traen la sangre tropical

Para que respeten

los derechos de mi raza

caben dos patrias

en el mismo corazón

[hablado]

El juez se paró en la corte

la tarde del juramento

de mi corazón brotaba

una lágrima salada

que me quemaba por dentro

Dos banderas me turbaban

una verde blanca y roja

con el águila estampada

y la otra con su azul lleno de estrellas,

con sus rayas roja bien grabadas

la bandera de mis hijos

que alegres la contemplaban

No me llamen traicionero

que a mi dos patrias las quiero

en la mia dejé a mis muertos

aqui, aqui mis hijos nacieron

por defender mis derechos

no puedo ser traicionero

[Coro]

Pero que importa

si soy nuevo ciudadano

sigo siendo mexicano

como el pulque y el nopal

Y mis hermanos

Central and South Americans

Caribbeans or Cubans

they all have the tropical blood

So that they respect

the rights of my people

two countries fit

in the same heart

[spoken]

The judge stands up in the court

the afternoon when pledging allegiance to the flag

From my heart a

tear was coming out

It was burning me inside

Two flags made me feel confused

One was green, white, and red

with an eagle printed in the middle

and the other was blue full of stars

with its red lines very well printed

That is the flag of my children

who were looking at it very happily

Do not call me a traitor

that I love my two countries

I left my dead family in my country

My children were born here

I cannot be accused of being a traitor

considering that I did it to defend my rights

[Chorus]

But it does not matter

if I am a new citizen

I am still Mexican

like the *pulque* and the cactus

and my brothers

centro y sudamericanos	Central and South Americans
caribeños o cubanos	Caribbeans or Cubans
traen la sangre tropical	they all have the tropical blood
Para que respeten	So that they respect
los derechos de mi raza	the rights of my people
caben dos patrias	two countries fit
en el mismo corazón	in the same heart

This corrido celebrates the fluidity of migrants' identities. The narrator destabilizes national identities by articulating an irreducible alterity that resists total assimilation to both Mexico and the United States. This transnational subject is in an impossible position where he cannot give up either Mexico or the United States. The narrator enacts resistance and intervention in the dominant culture of both countries, Mexico and the United States, even as he himself is being transformed in the process of becoming. The narrator problematizes binary constructs of cultural and national identities based on essentialist discourses of nationality. However, this migrant does not erase difference, deny, or reduce his "otherness." The narrator is simultaneously enacting as well as undermining the official procedure of naturalization. The ceremony of naturalization is necessary for practical purposes, but in reality the concept of nation-state is put into question. In the ceremony of naturalization this migrant has nostalgic memories of home, which overlap with his hope for a better life. Paradoxically, at some points in the corrido the narrator reinscribes essentialist notions and symbols of nation-states of both countries such as the flags.

This corrido addresses an audience of Mexican people who might criticize the narrator's decision to become a U.S. citizen. It does not specify the time at which the ceremony occurs. The characters involved in the corrido include the narrator, who is the main character; the Mexicans, who might not understand his migrant experience and might judge him as having sold out; the migrant's family (both the new generation in the United States and the old generation who died in Mexico); the judge at the naturalization ceremony; other Latin American immigrants who are in a similar situation as this Mexican immigrant; and, implicitly, those individuals who made legal reforms that deny education and other public services to immigrants who are not naturalized.

The values portrayed in this corrido include hard work to provide for one's family, cultural assertiveness and inclusiveness, the migrant's love and admiration for both countries, solidarity with other Latin Americans who have gone through the same migrant experience, the courage and assertiveness to make a decision to become a U.S. citizen, and confusion during the naturalization ceremony due to his dual allegiance. The narrator hopes to explain his decision to those Mexican nationals who do not understand the migrant experience and who might dismiss the naturalization process of Mexican nationals as proof of "*malinchismo*" (national treason).

This corrido does not provide the exact time of the events, but it can be inferred that the narrator's decision to become a U.S. citizen occurred after the passage of laws such as California's Proposition 187. Such laws stipulate that only U.S. citizens are eligible to receive public social services, publicly funded health care, and public education. Not only illegal workers but also legal alien residents in the United States saw their human rights diminished when Proposition 187 passed in California in 1994.

The narrative discourse of this corrido is about judgment. Throughout the corrido, the character provides arguments for becoming a U.S. citizen and reflects on the positive cultural, sentimental, and practical implications of such a decision. The narrator addresses his audience, which consists of those who think he is "a traitor," and he promises to explain from his heart (and with the hope that "borders can be broken") the reasons he chose to become a U.S. citizen. He seeks to make people understand more about the Mexican migrant experience.

This migrant hopes that his new citizenship will protect him from human rights violations. The legislative reforms of the 1990s affect him because he will not receive social security payments when he retires unless he is a U.S. citizen, even though he has worked hard for his retirement benefits. The chorus reassures the narrator's audience that it is not really important that he has become a U.S. citizen. After all, his love for Mexico has not been lost. The narrator establishes solidarity not only with Latin Americans but with all immigrants who face similar problems. He calls for the protection of their rights.

The narrator's cultural identity is being transformed by his experiences in the United States, yet he is heartened by the possibility of identifying himself with both cultures—of not yet having to choose between one or the other. As he says, "Two countries fit in the same heart." The narrator implicitly values cultural encounters because they provide vitality, validity, and hope to new generations and because they help people from both Mexico and the United States see cultural relations in a more favorable light.

The following corrido was identified by participants as significant for this study because of its major themes: migration and cultural pride.

"SIN FRONTERAS"   WITHOUT BORDERS

Enrique Franco (1986). Performed by Los Tigres del Norte.

Estoy orgulloso de tener la piel morena	I am proud of having my skin brown
hablar la lengua que Cervantes escribió	of speaking the language in which Cervantes wrote
desde hace tiempo se rompieron las cadenas	The chains that used to enslave
que esclavizaron al hombre por su color	humans because of their skin color have been broken since long ago
Yo me he paseado por los cinco continentes	I have traveled throughout the five continents
yo he disfrutado lo mejor	I have enjoyed the best of life
a las mujeres no les soy indiferente	I am not indifferent to women
soy descendiente del indio y el español	I am a descendent of the Indian and the Spaniard
Soy como el águila que vuela por el cielo	I am like an eagle that flies throughout the sky
libre su vuelo por donde es amo y señor	flying free where he is master and lord
arriba no está dividido como el suelo	The sky is not divided like the land
que la maldad de algunos hombres dividió	which the maliciousness of some has divided
Estoy dispuesto siempre a ayudar a los amigos	I am always willing to help my friends
y a ellos ayudo si necesitan un favor	I always help them if they need a favor
también me sé parar de frente al enemigo	I also know to stand up and confront my enemy
siempre defiendo de las damas del honor	I always defend the honor of women
Las que he tenido no han dejado de quererme	The girlfriends I have had have not stopped loving me
yo nunca olvido a las que me han dado su amor	I have never forgotten those who have given me their love
yo no me humillo nunca he bajado la frente	

soy exigente siempre busco lo mejor	I have never tolerated humiliations
	I am demanding, I am always looking for the best
Soy como el águila que vuela por el cielo	I am like an eagle that flies throughout the sky
libre su vuelo por donde es amo y señor	flying freely in the territory where she is a
	master and in command
arriba no esta dividido como el suelo	The sky is not divided like the land
que la maldad de algunos hombres dividió	which the maliciousness of some has divided

The narrator of this corrido challenges politically bounded and dichotomized identities and subverts them by providing a reinterpretation of his identity and reminder of the key historical facts related to national boundaries. The narrator crosses national borders regardless of the failed attempts to seal them. He expresses wittiness and astuteness when he underminies hierarchies of race, culture, or nationality and binary social orders by calling into question such boundaries. Temporal migration has become part of the masculine identities of many towns that have historically sent migrants. It has become almost a rite of passage based on hard work ethics and commitment to the migrants' community.

In this corrido the narrator is a male transnational migrant who continuously crosses borders. The implicit characters are the narrator's friends, girlfriends, and enemies. No particular date is implied by the narrator. The space in which the character develops his narrative is vast. The spaces he covers are the five continents, the vast sky, and the land, which has political, human-made borders. The values portrayed in this corrido are pride in the narrator's cultural roots and skin color and love and respect for freedom, resilience, courage, generosity, and competence. In this corrido, the character proudly signals his cultural heritage and challenges stereotypes about Mexicans. The narrative discourse of this corrido is about judgment of and reflection on Mexican immigrants' cultural heritage.

The narrator refers to literary history to praise the beauty of his language, Spanish, which has been so stigmatized in the United States for being spoken by large numbers of brown people. Although the character does not internalize racial oppression of Mexicans, he points out that social exclusion based on race, ethnicity, homeland, and economics is still with us, even when it is not openly acknowledged. In the second stanza, the narrator states that he is capable of sophistication through knowledge and extensive travel. He is a self-made, hardworking person, not bad looking, and proud of having the best of Spanish and Indian cultures. In the chorus, the character identifies himself with the eagle that travels freely and across borders. He states that a land without borders has the potential of being vital, happy, and enriched by the contributions of the people who live there—those who are creative and enjoy the eagle's freedom of spirit.

Implicitly, the main character reminds his audience that Mexican people previously traveled freely for centuries across the current Mexico-U.S. border. The political borders that resulted from the Mexican-American War are not natural or divine but products of "malicious" men who impose their will to limit the freedom of other humans.

This transnational subject expresses his cultural values in the way he sees human relations. Male friends are important to his masculine identity, as is the code of ethics appropriate to men and their unequal relation with women. The narrator states that his male friends are forever; they represent something precious, they are treated with generosity, and they are the people on whom he relies in times of need. To him, it is very important to challenge mistreatment and to fight to preserve his personal honor. The author states that part of his code of ethics is to protect women. He is quite explicit in stating that part of his masculine identity is based on the ability to provide shelter and food and to protect women's reputations. He also asserts that he is very popular with his current and former girlfriends.

"TRES VECES MOJADO"   THREE TIMES A WETBACK

Enrique Franco (1988). Performed by Los Tigres del Norte.

Cuando me vine de mi tierra El Salvador	When I came from my country, El Salvador
con la intención de llegar a Estados Unidos	with the intention to arrive in the United States
sabía que necesitaría más que valor	I knew I would need more than courage
sabía que a lo mejor quedaba en el camino	I knew that I could be dead on my way here
Son tres fronteras las que tuve que cruzar	I had to cross three borders
por tres países anduve indocumentado	I was undocumented in three countries
tres veces tuve yo la vida que arriesgar	I had to risk my life three times
por eso dicen que son tres veces mojado	That is why they say that I am three times a wetback

En Guatemala y México cuando crucé
dos veces me salvé me hicieran prisionero
el mismo idioma y el color reflexioné
¿Cómo es posible que me llamen extranjero?

When I crossed to Guatemala and Mexico
I managed not to be in prison twice
I thought, *The language and skin color are the same
How is it possible that they call me a foreigner?*

En centroamerica dada su situación
tanto política como económica
ya para muchos no hay otra solución
más que abandonar su patria
y tal vez para siempre

In Central America, given its
political and economical situation
for many people there is no other solution
but to abandon their country
and perhaps even for good

El Mexicano da dos pasos y aqui está
hoy lo echan y al siguiente dia está de regreso

Mexicans walk two steps and are here
They can be sent back today and they come
back the next day

eso es un lujo que no me puedo dar
sin que me maten o que me lleven preso

That is a luxury I cannot afford
without risking being killed or put into jail

Es lindo México pero cuanto sufrí
atravezarlo sin papeles es muy duro

Mexico is beautiful, but how much I suffered
crossing the country without documentation
it is very hard

los cinco mil kilómetros que recorrí
puedo decir que los recuerdo uno por uno

I can say that I remember each one of the
five thousand kilometers I crossed

Por Arizona me dijeron cruzarás
y que me aviento por enmedio del desierto
por suerte un Mexicano al que llamaban Juan
me dió la mano que si no me hubiera muerto

I was told that I should cross through Arizona
and so I went through the middle of the desert
Luckily, a Mexican whose name was Juan
gave me a hand; otherwise I would have been
dead by now

Ahora que al fin logre la legalización
lo que sufrí lo he recuperado con creces
a los mojados les dedico mi canción
y a lo que igual que yo son mojados tres veces

Now that I finally managed to legalize my residence
I have made up what I suffered
I dedicate my song to the wetbacks
and to those who just like me are
three times wetbacks

This corrido documents migration forced by the extreme violence that Central America experienced in the 1970s and 1980s. After the civil wars, Central Americans still face the prospects of further displacement and tremendous economic pressures to migrate. For this migrant the moment of displacement proves central to his historical consciousness. Part of his collective identity with other Central Americans is forged through the violence they experienced during the civil wars, the collective loss and trauma of exile, the outrage over the injustice of dispossession and misrecognition, the idea of return, and the concept and practice of resistance. The narrator provides a very detailed description of the relation between spatiality and the constitution of his identity in conditions of exile punctuated by extreme violence along the countries he had to cross in order to survive. However, the narrator also discovers that building a new life in a new country can be both invigorating and difficult.

In this corrido, this migrant was forced to leave due to the civil war. He is implicitly referring to Central America's longest war, in which seventy-five thousand people died and in which the guerrilla forces of the Farabundo Martí National Liberation Front (FMLN) battled the Salvadorian government. This civil war, the largest U.S.-backed counterinsurgency war since the Vietnam War, had an immense effect on the economic, social, and political situation in El Salvador. It caused a massive exodus of El Salvadorians. In the fifth stanza, the narrator states that his situation as an undocumented El Salvadorian migrant in the United States is very different from that of undocumented migrants from Mexico due to the fact that Mexico is geographically closer to the United States. In the event that Mexicans are deported, geographic proximity allows them to try to migrate again without facing the immense effort and mistreatment that Central Americans have to endure in Mexico and the other countries they pass through on their way to the United States.

This migrant states that while Mexico is a beautiful country, it is not enjoyable for everyone. (At the official level, Mexico maintains a very colonialist attitude toward Central Americans.) However, he expresses the class and migrant solidarity that a Mexican man showed to him when he was crossing the border. He expresses gratitude and solidarity to a presumably poor Mexican immigrant who, like him, was forced to leave his country.

"PUEBLO QUERIDO"

BELOVED TOWN

Ismael Armonte Fierro (1998). Performed by Los Tigres del Norte.

Hoy me encuentro muy lejos, muy lejos
de la tierra que me vió nacer
de mis padres y de mis hermanos
y del barrio que me vió crecer

La nostalgia me destroza el alma
y quisiera volverlos a ver
el recuerdo se me hace tristeza
la tristeza me hace llorar

Y entre llanto parece que miro
a mi pueblo y a mi dulce hogar
y también a mi madre bendita
que sin duda por mí ha de rezar

Yo ansío con todo mi ser
regresar a mi pueblo querido
y mi Diós me lo ha de conceder
para morirme allá con los míos

Es muy triste encontrarse ausente
de la tierra donde uno ha nacido
y más triste si no están presentes
los amigos y los seres queridos

El destino nos hizo dejarlos
más el alma jamás ha podido olvidarlos
yo he vagado por grandes ciudades
por sus calles retebien alumbradas
pero nunca he olvidado a mi pueblo
y ni pienso olvidarlo por nada
aunque tenga sus casas de adobe
y una que otra calleja empedrada

Today I find myself very, very far away
from the land that saw me born
from my parents and my brothers
from the barrio that saw me growing

The nostalgia is breaking my heart
I wish I could see them again
remembering them makes me sad
sadness makes me cry

And through my tears I can almost see
my town and my sweet home
and also my blessed mother
who without doubt is praying for me

I wish with all my heart to
go back to my beloved town
and my God shall grant it to me
to die over there with my people

It is very sad to find oneself far away
from the land where one was born
and it is even sadder if one does not have his
friends and beloved ones

Destiny made us leave them
but the soul has never been able to forget them
I have traveled through big cities
walking by their very well-lit towns
but I have never forgotten my hometown
and I do not intend to do so for anything
even though its houses are made of adobe
and some streets are paved with stones

Yo ansío con todo mi ser	I wish with all my heart to
regresar a mi pueblo querido	go back to my beloved town
y mi Diós me lo ha de conceder	and my God shall grant it to me
para morirme allá con los míos	to die over there with my people

This corrido portrays chronic homesickness, derived from the narrator's desire to belong and loss of social network. The narrator seems to be in a permanent state of disorientation due to migration. The pain of loss and isolation makes this migrant idealize the spaces where he was born and raised without much room for ambiguities.

The characters presented in this corrido are the immigrant, his parents, his brothers, his friends, and people from the town where he was born. This corrido does not provide an exact time frame. However, modern urban settings inform the audience that the story is contemporary. The spaces described in this corrido are the country to which the immigrant migrated, large cities, luxurious avenues, the town and neighborhood where he was born and grew up, the adobe houses of his homeland, streets paved with stones, and his home. The values of the corrido are gratitude, humility, work ethics, solidarity, and brotherhood. The discursive area of the narrative discourse is related to judgment. The character is reflecting on the hardships of migrating and on appreciating and missing his family and dear ones as much as the landscape of his homeland. He also appreciates the job that he has in the United States.

The character is in a deep state of sadness, nostalgia, and loneliness because he cannot be with the people he loves. In moments of deep sadness he visualizes his hometown, home, and mother, who he imagines is praying for him. The migrant explains that his reasons for migrating, international economic and political changes, were completely out of his control. Although "destiny" forced him to leave his country, he is not going to forget his family. He compares the poverty of his hometown and the greatness of the urban luxuries of the host country. However, his admiration for the metropolitan areas does not diminish his desire to return to where his family is.

The next corrido is about a Mexican man whose sons fought in the U.S. armed forces. In general, this corrido talks about Americans' failure to acknowledge the contributions of U.S. soldiers of Latin American descent.

"LOS HIJOS DE HERNÁNDEZ"   THE HERNÁNDEZES' CHILDREN

Enrique Franco (1988). Performed by Los Tigres del Norte.

Regresaba de mi tierra	I was coming from my country
y al cruzar por la frontera	and when I was crossing the border
me pregunta un oficial	the immigration officer asked me
que cumpliera mis deberes	to comply with my duties—
que si yo tenía papeles	that if I had documents to cross the border
se los tenía que enseñar	I had to show them to him
Y mientras los revisaba	And while he was checking them
escuché que murmuraba	I heard him saying something
algo que me hizo enojar:	that made me angry:
"Ya con tantos emigrados	"With so many immigrants
muchos norteamericanos	many North Americans
no pueden ni trabajar"	cannot even work"
Le dije muy enojado.	I said to him with anger
eso que usted ha murmurado	What you have murmured
tiene mucho de verdad	is very true
los latinoamericanos	Latin Americans
a muchos norteamericanos	have taken
le han quitado su lugar	the place of many North Americans
Sí, muy duro trabajamos.	Yes, we work very hard
tampoco no nos rajamos	We do not back out
si la vida hay que arriesgar	if we have to risk our lives
En los campos de combate	in the battlefields
nos han echado adelante	We have been placed in the front lines
porque sabemos pelear	because we know how to fight
Aquí nacieron mis hjos	My children were born here
que ignorando los prejuicios	Ignoring the prejudices
y la discriminación	and discrimination they responded
su patria los reclamanba	to their country's call for them
y en el campo de batalla	and in the battlefield
pusieron el corazón	they put their heart

Ahí nadie se fijaba	In that situation nobody paid attention
que Hernández ellos firmaban	to the fact that they signed as "Hernández"
eran carne de cañón	that they were human ammunition
quizá mis hijos tomaron	Maybe my children took
el lugar que no llenaron	the place that was not filled
los hijos de Anglosajón	by the children of the Anglo-Saxon
Si en la nomina de pago	If in the payroll
encuentras con desagrado	you find unpleasant
mi apellido en español	my surname in Spanish
lo verás en otra lista	you will see it in another list
que a la hora de hacer revista	when the roll is called
son perdidos en acción	of those lost in action
Mientras esto le gritaba	While I was saying this
el emigrante lloraba	the inspector felt touched
y dijo con emoción:	and said with emotion:
"Puedes cruzar la frontera	"You can cross the border
esta y las veces que quieras	this time and as many times as you want
tienes más valor que yo"	You are braver than I am"

This corrido gives an account of the overrepresentation of minorities in the U.S. armed forces and the lack of acknowledgment of their participation in nationalist endeavors. Historically, migrants, racial minorities, and working-class people have been overrepresented in the U.S. armed forces and have been the target of recruitment efforts. According to Mariscal (2004),

> New immigrants have yet to experience the disconnection between the promise of democracy and equality in this country and what the country has actually delivered to working people of color over time; many of them will adopt an uncritical view of current events.... Some will even join the armed forces or encourage their children to join. What better way, they ask, to show our gratitude to the United States? What better way to prove our patriotism and

show that we too are real Americans?...Add to this scenario the fact that Mexican American or Chicano/a youth—that is, the children of families who have been in the U.S. for many decades, if not centuries—continue to have a relatively limited range of life opportunities. More than one-third of all Latinos are under 18 years of age. With a high school dropout rate around 40 percent and high rates of incarceration, many Latinos see little hope for the future....Although Latinos have a high rate of participation in the labor force...Latinos and Latinas are working extremely hard but are trapped in minimum-wage jobs. Many hold multiple jobs at low wages.

The characters of the corrido are the main narrator, a Latin American migrant and father of soldiers who fought in a war for the U.S. armed forces, the narrator's children, and an INS officer. Implicitly, the narrator mentions that U.S. mainstream society discriminates against people of Latin American descent. The places that are mentioned are the border between Mexico and the United States, the immigration post, battlefields, the United States in general, and the workplace. The values that are present in this corrido are anger, frustration, righteousness, solidarity, and courage.

Historically, the casualty rates for soldiers of Latin American descent have been high due to their placement in the most dangerous branches of the military, such as infantry and armor. The narrator calls them *carne de cañón*: "human ammunition." U.S. mainstream society has no trouble giving these jobs to people of color but has not yet found a place for soldiers and sailors of color in the national and cultural memory.

The narrator states that Spanish surnames in the workplace are perceived as a burden, but white Americans do not realize that these Spanish surnames are the ones that fill the war casualty lists.[4] This corrido, "The Hernándezes' Children," attempts to provide a voice and a space for the contributions that people of Latin American descent have made to the United States, in particular to the U.S. armed forces.

There is a symbolic inversion of roles at the end of the corrido when the INS inspector acknowledges his misperception of Latin Americans, states his admiration for the narrator, and says that he can

Mexican American
norteños who are
serving in the U.S.
armed forces (2001).
Photos by Selfa Chew.

cross the border freely. In this stanza, the resolution of the story is amicable and peaceful once the INS officer becomes aware of the situation.
Both parties open their hearts and understand each other when they
have the opportunity to express their experiences and when they speak
to each other as equals. The narrator therefore ends on an optimistic
tone. However, such an event is unlikely in real life due to the power
asymmetries between the two individuals. It is very challenging to convey the complexity of people's reception of corridos because, as I said
before, it depends not only the lyrics, the music, the performance, the
context of the performance, and the everyday life of the audience but on
the careful combination of such elements. Virginia Archuleta, a resident
of New Mexico who dances música norteña and whose family lived in
Colorado well before the Mexican-American War, expressed celebration
and *orgullo* (pride in Mexican cultural expressions), like many of the
people I spoke with. Virginia considered the corridos about immigration

a very healthy, safe, and artistic way of analyzing the migrants' situation. As she put it,

> That is how they are feeling, that is exactly what is in their heart. Do the people know what is in there [corridos about immigration]? Illegal migrants are being treated so unfairly. To me, this world is for everybody. If they feel that if they sing about it they think that it is a release, everybody feels better. They put their emotions into the lyrics. That brings a kind of sadness. I have seen how Mexicans are treated when they are over here. We are all the same. I think everybody's opinions matter. They [singers of corridos] express people's experiences that way because they cannot express them anywhere else. They really express it there [in the corridos]. They sing about somebody coming here and they did this to them; then the corrido is an outlet. I am glad they can sing about it. They have a lot of emotions. I think the music is a release because somebody is hearing it. So, it is a release and they want to talk about this. That is what makes it so pretty because the music is wonderful and then the lyrics. That is the talent I am talking about. We have beautiful talent. We [Mexicans] cover our talent. We are too shy.... In the Mexican community there are artists; there are musicians, actors, and attorneys. The people who sing corridos are great; they have talent coming out of their ears. They are beautiful. They have talent. So much spirit is going on in the corridos. They are great, beautiful, beautiful men, handsome.

Armando Chavira, who was visiting his family in Chihuahua in December 2001, has a very close connection with corridos about immigration:

> Corridos about immigration remind me of my father. He used to talk to us about his experiences when he crossed the River as a wetback. The first time he

crossed, he was very young. He told us that they got lost and since he was the youngest one, he was sent to look for water. He was sent with a container full of water and was in the desert for three days, lost. The irony was that when he was about to die, he arrived where he was suppose to arrive. That makes me think that my situation is much better than my father's. I was born in the United States, thanks to my dad. Had it not been for him, I would not have anything here. Sometimes people think that the corridos exaggerate. I identify with those corridos. I know many people who were caught crossing the River and tried to cross even risking their lives. Sometimes, we think we have many problems and that they cannot be solved, but when I see those people, I feel I am very lucky and I have to learn from them. Corridos remind me of the coyotes who charge people to cross the border and sometimes they are abandoned by the coyotes themselves. When I listen to those corridos, I feel like having a conversation with my father. I remember the stories he told me when I was a kid.

Chapter Three

Voy a contarles la historia:
MIGRANTS' PERCEPTIONS OF CORRIDOS

South Americans and Caribbeans are experiencing the same problems
we Mexicans have in the United States, but they are experiencing them
in other parts of the world...so our songs are also meaningful to them.
Some walls have fallen and others walls have been erected.
— Jorge Hernández, leader of Los Tigres del Norte, 2001

I have spent many Christmas holidays between El Paso–Ciudad Juárez
and towns near Chihuahua City. The Christmas holiday is perhaps the
only time when Mexican migrants living in many different parts of
the United States cross the border to be with their families. Migrants and
their families in Mexico go through extensive preparations for this special
occasion. Most people plan their most important events, such as weddings,
christenings, and community celebrations, for that time of year when the
people who matter most are nearby. This intense interchange of love, care,
ambiguities, and conflicts between people from el México de afuera and
their relatives back home has seemed so rich to me that I have always
wanted to understand it from their point of view. I spent Christmas of
2000 at my extended family's home and this time took notes about the stories that they, their friends, and their neighbors had told me about the way
they organize *coleaderos* and dances and the way they make sense of their
everyday life in their towns and as migrants. I did it with the support and

enthusiasm that my extended family offered at every step of the process. They knew the calendar of events and the key people I could talk with. They were available for any questions I had, from the meaning of a regional word to the description of a certain ritual. I often feel clumsy, anxious, and unfit to navigate the life of rural Chihuahua as a woman raised in urban settings. I also tend to disorient members of this community by not fulfilling my role as a ranchera—being a terrible cook, declining to dress up like the beautiful women from the ranches, not having children, devoting a lot of time to my studies, and often carrying out my work in male spaces. Often I was an intruder, although not necessarily a privileged intruder, particularly in male spaces.

I also carried out my fieldwork in Dumas, Texas. Many people in the town already knew me from my previous visits and as part of my extended family, although my previous interactions with them had not been in the format I chose for my research, with my tape recorder and my notebook, asking questions they had never been asked before. Most of the people I talked to were quite happy to help me, and many felt flattered to be asked their opinion about the music they liked, their perceptions of corridos,[1] dances, and other aspects of their everyday life. I felt much at ease in the Ciudad Juárez–El Paso area because I had known many people there since my childhood, and some of those friends helped me carry out my ethnographic work and interviews. In Albuquerque, it was *mis amigos* Nuevo Mexicanos who helped me, mainly coworkers. Given my proximity to the migrants' lives, it is not my intention to simply "record the voices" of participants and, as Sandra Harding states, to reduce myself to a "kind of (inevitably inaccurate) transcription machine." I took pains to avoid a "colonial destiny" for my research but also to offer a theoretically informed interpretation of the data (Harding 2004, 72). In this chapter I analyze the meaning of corridos about migration as perceived by migrants, singers, corridistas, and dancers.

Voz de nuestra gente: People's Definition of Corridos

Every person I interviewed demonstrated a thoughtful, well-conceived understanding of the main characteristics of the corrido. In fact, their definitions and understanding of the genre were more rounded and sophisticated than many I have read. Most study participants mentioned the epic dimension and the values embodied in the corrido as important characteristics. As one participant remarked, "I think we can understand so many things about life through the corridos. To me the corrido enters into the heart. It is not only about the words that are in the corridos, it is everything: the music, the way the story is told. From what I understand, it is a story. They are stories that were true at some point in time. The corridos make you think about what happened in the past."

Everybody I talked to could distinguish between a corrido and a canción and knew by heart at least a couple of corridos. Armando Chávez, from Ciudad Juárez, defined the corrido as follows: "I think the first thing is that corridos should sing real events, secondly, with real characters, and thirdly, those events should be known by the people. All they do is to put music into the narration. For example, the old corridos were sung only with a guitar and perhaps only one singer. Later, the instruments changed; there are more musical instruments and more singers, but the essence of the corrido has not changed. It is the same: we have a character, an event, a place. I think the main characteristics of the corrido have not changed."

People often talked about how the personal stories of the corridos become collective stories because of the level of identification with the main protagonists. This strong identification seems to create social consciousness. Manuel Ochoa in Albuquerque told me, "I am not saying that corridos have to be about a Villa or a Zapata, because people like them are very, very few, but about somebody who lived according to his/her own standards, who is genuine, strong, proud of his people, of what he is. The character of the corrido has to be one of us."

Corridos enjoy a very high credibility. I did not encounter a single person who doubted the veracity of the main argument of any corrido, old or current. People's perceptions of the credibility and role of the corrido reflect a deep sense of trust and faith in the ability of the genre to respond to people's interests.[2] As David, who lives in northern Texas and was visiting his family in La Veracruz, Chihuahua, told me, "Corridos are the best source to know what is really going on in the country, unlike the news that come out from the government or the media. The corrido say nothing but the truth. If you want to know what really happened in any situation, listen carefully to the corrido about it."

Corridos are perceived as cultural artifacts that transcend time and space because the main content of the corrido applies to many generations from different regions. Homar Prieto, who is a devoted fan of horse races and coleaderos, described this dimension of the corrido eloquently:

The fact that they are from Michoacán or
Chihuahua does not really matter. People identify
with the stories; the place and the person are not
that important. There are corridos that you really
do not know where the main character of the corrido is from. He can be from Michoacán, la Sierra,
or Sonora State. Quite often you do not know where
from, but it is the story that is liked. For instance,
"El Corrido de Los Pérez" is a very old one; it starts
"en mil novecientos once" [in 1911] and it is very popular among youngsters. What does it tell you? That
the stories are good.

In February 2001, I met Evelyn from Española, New Mexico, in
Santa Fe at a concert of Los Tigres del Norte. Evelyn introduced me to
her son, of whom she was very proud. She also told me that her son had
every single disc of Los Tigres del Norte and had followed them since
he was a child. Evelyn was born in New Mexico, but her family and fam-
ily-in-law were from Chihuahua State. Evelyn's son compared a corrido
with a good book:

The corrido makes you think about what is happening in life. Every time you listen to a corrido, you
will get a different meaning. They are very profound. It is like a very good book, a classic book.
You get different things out of it. They teach you
about life. When I listen to a corrido, the first time
I do not understand it completely. I have noticed
that corridos have a different meaning now that I
have my kids than before, although they are the
same stories. Corridos put me into a state of tranquility and serenity. They make me feel happy, they
remind me of Mexico.

Iliana Hernández, a connoisseur of corridos from Parral, Chihuahua,
told me while she was living temporarily in Las Cruces, New Mexico, that
what she likes about them is

the ability of the authors to write about an event in few words, the life of people or the feelings of a person. For example, the corridos about horses, they are written so well that one can imagine horses one never met, how they ran, their feelings, their personality, their relationship with their owners, and their loyalty to them. It is very creative. I play corridos at home, those about the revolution and other types, so that my children will get familiarized with them.

Yolanda Olivas, a friend and colleague who knew about my project, read in the *Albuquerque Journal* that Al Hurricane, the godfather and main pioneer of New Mexican music, was going to perform during the opening of the National Hispanic Cultural Center in the Barelas neighborhood in Albuquerque. Yolanda and I went together and were excited to see Prince Philip of Spain deliver a speech at the opening of the cultural center. After the speech, people gathered near the stage to see Al Hurricane. The New Mexicans in attendance knew every song he performed and showed near adoration for him. It is no wonder that he was chosen to perform at such an important event for the Chicanos of New Mexico. After his performance, I talked to him and told him that I was interested in learning about New Mexican music. Immediately he gave me his phone number so that we could meet. This conversation turned out to be most memorable since he was very generous in showing me all his materials and, as an artist, he could not help singing and playing the piano to make his points. Corridos are part of Al Hurricane's repertoire, and he knows thousands of corridos by heart. He told me,

The corridos are popular because they are very traditional; they are part of our culture. They always have a story that makes you feel to the extreme. Some of them make you cry. I cannot sing what I wrote about my child who passed away. It is like a spade on your heart, like you feel what the people [characters] from the corridos feel.

Voz del pregonero: Writing Corridos

A day before Christmas, I was invited to attend a dance that the municipal government of Satevó organized for its workers. A local conjunto norteño, Los Campeones del Valle, from a nearby town called Zaragoza, Chihuahua, played that night. The dance took place in what used to be the town hall, which, on this occasion, once again housed a community gathering. While the musicians were getting ready backstage, I asked the main leader, Leandro Rodríguez, to allow me to talk to him about his work. Don Leandro was very equable and soft-spoken. He was very inclusive with the rest of the conjunto, which consisted of his sons and nephews. After the dance, I kept thinking about this conversation. Don Leandro's way of presenting himself, his language, his mannerisms, his way of dressing, and the way he interacted with his conjunto all seemed part of an organic synchrony between singers, composers, and dancers. Don Leandro's lifestyle was not very different from the corridos he sang about rural life. He told me,

> I get inspiration from many sources. One does not really know. Composing music is something really difficult to puzzle out. Why is that? Because one does not know the time when the idea of writing, of composing is going to come. Sometimes, in the middle of the night, one wakes up and the music and words are there, everything. Sometimes one arrives from working in the field and there you have it. I can get inspiration from anything, from a friend, from myself, from our parents, our brothers, from a party, from many things.

After the conversation, Los Campeones del Valle got ready to play música norteña and the norteño dance started. Don Leandro respected the political hierarchies and dedicated the first corrido to the mayor. Later Don Leandro dedicated his corrido "Recordando al general," the one for which he got a third place in a corrido contest, to me: *Este corrido va dedicado a la Dra. Martha Chew* (this corrido is dedicated to Dr. Martha Chew). I was flattered to receive such an honor.

Don Leandro, like the corridistas and musicians, expressed a deep sense of connection with the community he wrote the corridos about and for. Many writers of corridos have a close relationship with the characters or with people close to the characters. This connection explains why they can write in great detail about the major events surrounding the characters of the corridos.

Roberto Martínez, a musician, singer, and corridista of the musical group Los Reyes de Albuquerque, illustrates the corridista's close relationship with major events that have affected Hispanics from northern New Mexico (such as the Vietnam War, the Gulf War, and the land grants movement, called "Alianza federal de las mercedes" [Federal Alliance of Land Grants]—a movement that tried to regain the land lost to white Americans in New Mexico. This movement was based on the 1848 Treaty of Guadalupe Hidalgo. According to the aliancistas, European Americans had violated the stipulations of the treaty.) and the way these events are embodied in corridos written by him. Roberto Martínez was born in Chacón, in northern New Mexico, and in 2003 the American Folklife Center awarded him and his eldest son the National Heritage Award.

I heard about Roberto Martínez while living in Albuquerque. I asked Miguel Gandert, a great Nuevo Mexicano photographer and professor, about Roberto since they are related and come from the same town. Miguel told me, "Just look at the address on the CD and call him." That was how I learned that Roberto Martínez established his own record label, Minority Owned Record Enterprises, in the late 1960s, during the civil rights movement. His home address and phone number were on the CD label. I spent two delightful and long afternoons in Roberto's home learning about corridos in New Mexico. When I arrived at his house, he was waiting for me and immediately made me feel at home. Don Roberto is very close to his family. We spent the first hours talking about his wife and five children, and his wife was on hand to help with several of the questions. It is clear that his artistic life is very closely intertwined with his family life. Martínez has a fatherly personality, with a very mild character and a soft, soothing voice. I was touched by his gentleness, politeness, and strength.

Roberto Martínez told me that he started singing corridos when he was a child:

> My father was a very strong man. I used to imitate
> him. When we used to go out to gather firewood, we
> used to leave home at four in the morning. It was

dark still. My father used to stand up while he was directing the cart pulled by a horse. He used to sing the corrido "Paso del Norte." Don Roberto sang me that corrido "Le pregunté a mister Hill que si vamos a Louisiana, Mister Hill con su risita me respondió: no señor. . . ." Look, I will be seventy-six years old, and when I was much younger, there were already corridos about drugs and people who were sent to jail because of that. I loved to hug my father's legs and imitate him while he was singing. Corridos are a way of telling a situation in a very well established manner. In New Mexico, we had *Inditas*. I remember the corrido "Indita de Juan de Dios." This is about a man who was hunting a *cíbolo* [buffalo] with a lance, and then the son of Juan de Dios accidentally knocked the lance in his body and died slowly while he was riding the horse: "Caballo alazán tostado, que tu me diste, mi vida afligido, con tu sangre me teñiste. Al lado del Río Grande, me ví comiendo sandía rodeado de mis hermano, que me hacían compañía, ahora se queda mi cuerpo sembrado como semilla."

Writing corridos is something very natural for me. I do not consider myself a composer because a composer takes a topic and writes about it. I have many friends who are composers; they can get paid to compose. In my case, I have to be inspired. I know there are corridistas who would make a corrido of any topic if you pay them and give them the plot. Compositions for me are something that comes out of my heart. Like the corrido "La prisión de Santa Fé [Santa Fe Prison]." They [corridos] come up quick, rapidly. I wrote that one, too, and my inspiration came suddenly.

When I write something, I feel a close relationship with people. Regarding the corrido "La prisión de Santa Fé," I felt compassion for the prisoners.[3] Yes, they did not do the right thing; that is why they were in prison, but what about their mothers, their wives, their relatives? They are somebody else's children, fathers, husbands. Prisoners are human beings, and they suffer. People suffer just like anybody else. Have you listened to "El corrido 720"? It is about a battalion of the National Guard who were sent to fight in the Gulf War. All of them were from Las Vegas, New Mexico. They were relatives among themselves. We have a *concuño* [the brother-in-law of his wife] and his son. We went to El Paso to say goodbye to them, because they were leaving for Kuwait. I woke up at 2 a.m. and I started to remember the number of the battalion, "720," so I started to write the corrido in the hotel before they left. I showed it to the First Sergeant and he liked it and so we recorded it quickly, and when they left for Kuwait, they took with them their corrido. It was about people I felt very *hermanado* to [close to and in harmony as one feels with a brother]. It was not about something I felt distant, cold.

When I wrote "El corrido de Daniel Hernández," about a soldier from Los Lunas, New Mexico, who died in the Vietnam War, I went to see the parents of Daniel Hernández and showed them the corrido. His father did not mind that we recorded the corrido, but his mother did not want it at first. I believe that she was suffering a lot from his death. I came back really discouraged from recording the corrido. I went back to them, talked to them again, and told them that I was not going to record "El corrido de Daniel Hernández" for the sake of making profits but to honor him, so we recorded it and we bought an organ with the royalties of the corrido: the organ is in the church of Los Lunas; it is in his honor. It was worthwhile to convince the parents because the ceremony in the church was something really beautiful.

When I wrote "El corrido de Río Arriba," that corrido is about Tijerina and his mates.[3] The way I

wrote this corrido was a little bit strange My family
and I were visiting our family, we were living in
Denver at the time, and we heard in the news that
Tijerina tried to free eight people in the county jail
who were incarcerated for unlawful assembly. The
National Guard was mobilized, and, as always happens in families, different members of one family
have different positions regarding an issue. Some people condemned Tijerina, and some were sympathetic
toward him. On our way back, I saw the newspaper
and I saw pictures of the National Guard placing
women and children in corrals. It was very touching.
The reaction of the government was very strong. In
other words, the reaction was as if they were terror-
ists and instead of putting all their efforts on the
people who assaulted the court, they included all the
people from the area, entire families with children,
young, *ancianitos* [old people], and they were all
placed in corrals. They were patrolled with tanks. I
did not personally know them, but I wrote what I
saw and what I felt. The mentality of the people in
power... in my opinion what they did is expected
from a dictatorship not from a democracy.

I asked Roberto Martínez if he was personally affected by the land
grants, and he replied to me after an intensely thoughtful moment:

My family has been in New Mexico since 1692. They
came from Zacatecas, Mexico. Originally from Spain,
I think from Extremadura, but of course through
Mexico. I always say that we [Hispanics from northern New Mexico] were victims of those who took
our lands. When I was a child, there were not fences;
we could walk more freely. I have beautiful memories
of my childhood in those places. Unfortunately, the
homestead started there and fences started to be
built. I have a very strong feeling about the land

grants because that changed our lives totally. My feelings are like, how can I tell you? I feel like they robbed us, they robbed a lot from the people. So, we had those problems. They have defeated us, very much, *pero no sin lucha* [but not without struggle].

I was fascinated by Martínez's clear understanding and sensibility of the major events that have affected Nuevo Mexicanos. I asked him if he knew Tijerina personally:

I did not know Tijerina at the time I wrote the corrido. Years later, I met Tijerina in Old Town Albuquerque. He was going to have a presentation of something. I went with my wife, Ramoncita, and I saw him. He is a big man, very impressive. I was a little bit intimidated and I said to myself, "What is he going to think?" you know. I was a little bit nervous but I went and said "hi" to him. I said, "I am Roberto Martínez," and he said, "Oh, yes, you are the one who wrote the corrido," and he told me: "Well, let me tell you that when I was taken by the police, I was placed in a police car to Bernalillo, they took me to the prison, and when I was in the basement of the prison, I was not sure if I was going to get killed or what was going to happen to me. They took me out and placed me in an elevator; I felt very down, demoralized, and when we arrived to one floor, the doors were opened and they were playing your corrido. The prisoners were shouting, "Tijerina, Tijerina," and I answered, "Yes, yes." I felt so good. What Tijerina said to me was something very special to me. Tijerina gave me a hug, and we are friends ever since. What happened was a beautiful thing. Another one that I remember is the one about the *Challenger* when it exploded. I wrote one to my friends, *compañeros* [workmates] to Jorge Benavides, who was my *guitarrista*. I wrote it when

he died. To my wife, Ramoncita, to my sister, and
others, not many, actually.

I left Martínez's house with my hands full of the tapes and CDs he
gave me and with a deep admiration for this gentle and sharp man. Many
thoughts came to my mind after this visit. We had our conversation in
Spanish, and his Spanish was very similar to the Spanish of many of my
mother's friends in Chihuahua, who are from ranches near Ciudad Juárez.
Dr. Enrique Lamadrid has often told me, "Chihuahua is the other half of
New Mexico," a concept I never understood well until I met Don Roberto
Martínez. I invited Martínez to my dissertation defense, and I felt quite val-
idated when I saw him arrive. Martínez also participated in the defense,
and at the conclusion he congratulated me and hugged me. I feel that he
is a wise, genuine man with a disarming gentility. He is living proof that
the corrido is a loyal partner of popular struggles, the recorder, or *escrib-
ano*, of every social movement.

As discussed earlier, Los Tigres de Norte, also called Los Idolos del
Pueblo (The People's Idols), is the most commercially successful conjunto
norteño. Los Tigres del Norte have made thirty-two records, sold thirty
million discs, performed in fourteen movies, and been nominated seven
times for Grammy Awards. In 1988 they won a Grammy for their album
Gracias América (Thanks, America). Los Tigres del Norte have been working for thirty-two years in the United States, Mexico, and Central America
and are very well known among Mexicans, Central Americans, and now
Spaniards. Their fans are composed primarily of two groups: the first generation of fans (people who are now in their mid forties and late fifties)
and their children (who are generally between eighteen and twenty-five
years old). The group lives in San Jose and Morgan Hill, California. They
tour forty-four weeks and take a one-month break each year.

Los Tigres del Norte migrated to the United States in the early 1970s
as musicians, and their market is the transnational community. Many factors have contributed to the success of the group, notably their charisma
and the consolidation of media that has provided the infrastructure to
record, announce, distribute, and present concerts in the United States,
Mexico, and Central America. Jorge Hernández, the group's leader, tries to
maintain a low-key image despite the group's success, and he has been
very sensitive to the needs of the marginal communities that rarely see

themselves represented in a positive light. I have always been interested in the way this legendary group selects corridos.

When I spoke with Jorge in Santa Fe, he said,

> I believe we are establishing a very direct communication with them, because we are telling their lives in our corridos. We are singing their life experiences. In so many ways, we are singing what migrants want to say aloud. We are communicating with them a great sense of love, of union, of peace, of tranquility. I believe that is what makes this communication possible. What makes them feel the corridos.

I asked him how *they* work on the corridos they are going to sing.

> We have different ideas. We give the ideas to the composers. We ask them to write what we want to say; it might be about migration, drug smuggling, politics, *en fin* [well, then]; everything we want to say and portray, we tell corridistas. Depending on the different kind of problematic that is being presented throughout time.... We tell everything so that they write a corrido and tell what we want to say, so that they can express it in less than three minutes.

Jorge and his brothers work on the topics they think are important and then ask certain corridistas to write the corridos. Thereafter, corridistas and Los Tigres work together:

> Yes, that's it exactly. I always look for positive messages, something with good messages, with meaning...because they [corridos] talk about the problems of the people, of their everyday lives. It was what happened. We try to tell the people what we can through the radio and songs. We sing true stories.

The corridistas who have worked most closely with Los Tigres are Enrique Franco, Teodoro Bello, Paulino Vargas, and Jesse Armenta. Enrique Franco composed most of the corridos about migration, although he and Los Tigres have not worked together since 1997. The end of this partnership was, in a way, the end of a very commercially successful era for corridos about migration and Los Tigres del Norte.

A los mojados les dedico mi canción: Changes in the Corridos

Quite a few people I talked to mentioned the changes that corridos have gone through over time. Because corridos have a collective political role as a means of expressing social conflict, they tend to reflect the current sociocultural and political environments. Jorge Hernández explained to me in an interview in 2001 that corridos are nearly always relevant to the lives of the common people. Conditions are always changing, so the topics of the corridos change as well:

> In every year, every generation, there are new words that need to be modified. The language that people talk now is very different from the one people used to talk before. This is what makes us change a little bit the themes of the corridos. However, the meaning is the same. We can change two or three words, but the meaning remains the same. We want to say the same things we said before with other words. We sing stories about different characters. If you have a close look at our catalogs, you will find that the corridos, all the corridos, are true stories.

Most Spanish-speaking people in the border region are well aware of these changes in the corridos. Some feel that the conjunto norteño is mixing with other musical genres, creating a hybrid version of the corrido. In general, the people I spoke with demonstrated great clarity and understanding regarding the commercial limitations that influence the production of corridos.

In my focus groups, middle-class people, particularly students on the Mexican side of the border, tended to regard contemporary corridos as inauthentic—as songs not worth listening to. These same respondents generally took a purist stance toward corridos despite the fact that they seldom listened to conjunto norteño music. As a group, they condemned the changes in corridos and characterized currently popular corridos as being too "ordinary," "vulgar," and "rusty." They often mentioned corridos about the Mexican Revolution in favorable terms, lamenting the decline of the genre in recent years.[5]

Niegan que son mexicanos aunque tengan mi color: Corridos in the Present and Future Generations of Mexicans in the United States

Most people I spoke with talked about the difficulty faced by young Mexican emigrants who try to maintain their cultural heritage in institutional settings that do not value cultural differences. According to some migrants and Mexican Americans, young Mexicans like to listen to corridos at home but deny their cultural preferences in other places, particularly those in which their "Mexicanness" has been problematized by mainstream U.S. institutions such as schools, workplaces, and other public spaces. This tendency is especially notable in contexts where there is strong immigrant bashing targeted at Latin Americans in general or Mexican Americans in particular.

Young Mexicans and Mexican Americans vary in their reactions toward such hostility. Octavio Fernández, from northern New Mexico, explained eloquently the complexities involved in denying one's culture. In his opinion, rejecting one's culture is a matter of social survival because the school system is dismissive of nonwhite students who maintain ties to their home culture. Many people mentioned the schools as sites of cultural struggle and negotiation. For Mexican American children, being a "non-ethnic" American is not an option, as it is for most European immigrants and their descendants. The pressure to assimilate, the conditional "acceptance" by mainstream society, the anti-immigrant climate of the United States, and the crystallization of anti-immigrant laws force many Mexican American children to downplay or hide their cultural heritage as a way of surviving. Migrant families and Mexican communities in the United States play an important role in providing children with a strong sense of origin. According to them, close proximity to kinship networks can provide a cultural infrastructure that sustains shared memories of Mexican culture.

Chapter Three

Octavio Fernández's narration captures part of the cultural struggle
that young Mexican descendents face in the United States:

> Are you asking if children in the U.S. like to listen to
> corridos?...I will tell you what happened to my sis-
> ter to answer your question. When I had my truck, I
> started to drive and my mother sent me to pick up my
> sister at school. I knew my sister liked corridos, par-
> ticularly those sung by conjuntos norteños. We always
> listened to them at home and she always enjoyed
> them. When I arrived at her school, I was listening to
> corridos being played on the radio. As soon as she
> was in the truck, she turned off the radio and told
> me, "Don't you see that my friends are here?" I got
> mad and I switched on the radio and I drove the
> truck around the school three times so that her
> friends heard me enjoying corridos. My sister was
> really mad at me.
>
> I think when I was young, I wanted everybody
> to like my music, that everybody who was Mexican
> would listen to music in Spanish. Again, I will answer
> your question by telling you what happened with my
> sister. The following day when my sister went to
> school, everybody made fun of her. Everybody had
> listened to our music the day before. I believe they
> were listening to Los Tigres del Norte. It was a very
> ugly experience for my sister. Her classmates called
> her awful names. It was terrible for her, but at that
> time, I did not think so much about her. I did what I
> did because I was mad at her for pretending to be
> somebody else. The reality is that not many people
> feel the way I feel about Mexico and my culture and
> I should not impose that on them. I do not think
> they will only like this music. I think that the only
> way to change things is that they start liking it since
> they are really young and that they feel proud of
> themselves. Corridos are as good as the textbook;

they have lessons, you know? Lessons of different experiences. Every corrido is different. It is about something that happened and explains that something similar can happen to you and that you have to think about the consequences of your actions. But people who do not know what our music is about, they immediately judge and reject corridos.

Gloria Anzaldúa, the Chicana feminist writer whose work has been very influential, described in *Borlderlands/La Frontera: The New Mestiza* (1987) how cultural terrorism provokes self-hate among Tejanos:

I grew up feeling ambivalent about our music. Country Western and rock-and-roll had more status. In the 50s and 60s, for the slightly educated and *agringado* [assimilated] Chicanos, there existed a sense of shame at being caught listening to our music. Yet I couldn't help stop my feet from thumping to the music, could not stop humming the words, nor hide from myself the exhilaration I felt when I heard it (61).

Interestingly enough, migrant children whose families moved frequently tended to have a stronger Mexican cultural heritage than those who moved less often. It seemed that if a family got settled in one place, even if the family spoke Spanish at home and visited their relatives in Mexico frequently, the children tended to be more influenced by the cultural context outside their homes. On the other hand, the children of migrant workers who moved frequently tended to rely on their immediate families for the construction and development of their cultural identities. Armando, who was born in Texas but visits Chihuahua for the holidays, was raised in a family of migrant workers. His experience illustrates the closer attachment to música norteña for migrant children. I asked Armando if children in the United States like to listen to corridos.

Over there [in the United States], children have another language. They listen to music in English.

The ones from over here listen more to our type of
music. I think what happens is that you listen to the
music that you are used to listening to in your home.
If you are young, your parents instill in you this
Mexican music, and you will like that music. It
really depends on the kind of music that is listened
to at home. Children over there have many pressures
at school. My case is different: I love corridos and
people find it very strange that although I was born
there, I like so much Mexican music. I think it was
due to my father. I always liked the way my father
and my uncles are. I always wanted to be like them,
dress like them. Since I was a child, I used my cowboy hat and my boots. I got used to listening to corridos and canciones norteñas. It is difficult to
maintain the liking for corridos because you see
other ways of living, other tastes. What happened
was that I never had a chance to make many friends
because my family kept moving from one place to
the other, depending on when my father had work.
Most of his work was seasonal. We lived in Arizona,
California, Texas; you know, wherever there was a
job for my dad.

Virginia Archuleta is a living example of resilience. Like many people
I met in Albuquerque, she is one of those Mexicans born in Colorado and
whose family was living there before the U.S.-Mexico war. Her personal
history weaves a route between Colorado and Chihuahua. She was married
for a long time to a Chihuahuense with whom she shared the love of
música norteña that her father installed in her. I asked Virginia if she
thought her preference for corridos might subside over time, and she res-
olutely told me,

No, it will go on forever; our lives and souls never
change. I have to instill in my daughters their values, and my daughter has to instill them in her kids.
I do not think it will ever vanish. I say this because

nowadays people are getting to be more assertive in
what they are. Before, if you were in school, you
had to hide your tortilla, because you were kind of
ashamed of tortillas; you see how Mexican food is
all over. If Mexican food is popular, why not the
language...the music? I think it is going to be on
and on. It is never going to vanish. We have the
same spirit, drive. I do not think it is going to vanish anytime soon, no. No, it is not going to go away.
If it is going to go away, then everything else is
going to go away. Absolutely no!

Jorge Hernández feels that music has to talk to people—to express the
reality of their current situation—in order to be relevant among the
younger generation:

It is very difficult, the task of creating new stories. I
think that as long as we continue singing new stories,
stories that are relevant to the youth, to the type of
youth we are singing for, the corrido will be main-
tained among us, particularly among the youth. It is
very difficult that only one group establishes communication with them. Nowadays they are communicating with so many different genres.

According to Jorge Hernández, today's adolescents are exposed to
musical genres that have no roots in Mexican culture. This is especially true
within the United States. In his opinion, however, the favorite songs of
Mexican American youth are drawn from a wide repertoire that includes
both corridos and música norteña. This situation is not necessarily contradictory, given people's multiple subjectivities and exposure to different
genres. Hernández told me,

We have a little bit of everything. People from the
United States, from Latin America, Mexicans, Mexican
Americans. The new generation, the one you are see-
ing now, the ones that already live here, who go to

school here, who can communicate in English and Spanish, they are communicating with us too, they are also part of our audience.

XEBU, La Norteñita radio station, plays corridos and conjunto norteño all the time. Like most Mexican stations, the DJs frequently play specific pieces requested by their audience. Manuel Pineda described the reception of conjunto norteño music at XEBU:

> Young people love this music; the proof of that is the type of phone calls we receive. Even small children from the city [Chihuahua City] and obviously from the ranches call us to make requests. This Christmas season and even in the normal season we receive phone calls not so much from the small children population but from youngsters, people who are between...I would say...twelve and eighteen years. That is what we consider a juvenile audience. The music that the grandfathers listen to is more or less the same as the one that the grandchildren listen to. There are young people who ask us to play the very first corridos that Los Tigres del Norte, "Ramón Ayala," used to play a long time ago. Young people are raised with that music. And it is precisely because the family listens a lot to radio stations and La Norteñita that they continue this tradition.

El otro Mexico que aquí hemos construido en este suelo que ha sido territorio nacional: Re-creating Home Away from Home

Immigrants construct their ethnic identities partly through memories of their lived experiences in their countries of origin. They also carry along the cultures and values that are crystallized in their everyday lives. Informal but strong social networks serve as a cushion against the isolation and rejection they experience in the host country. They visit Mexico, call their relatives by phone, and meet with other Mexicans in the United States who have gone through similar experiences. These activities seem to be a mechanism for survival and solidarity as much as a response to racial discrimination and exclusion in mainstream society.

Rosa mentioned some of the ways in which migrants keep informed about their homeland and the ways in which they try to help their relatives or acquaintances in their towns:

> We always know what is happening in town [in Mexico]. I call every week or every two weeks and they tell me the news of the town. Many of my workmates are from the same town and they call, too. So in our workplace we talk about the news of the town. So every day, when one of us does not call, the other does. What happens here [in Mexico] is known over there [in Texas] in a very short period of time. That is how we keep updated of the news. I call home; my family is always in my mind and more if you know that in one way or another you want to help them. They are always in my mind. People let me know when they are coming to Mexico [from the United States] and I send clothes to my family or the things I know they need. I am always storing things that I know are going to be useful for my people and when it is time to come or I know somebody is coming to Mexico, I send them. I know people make very good use of the things we buy and keep for them. I wish I could bring everything they need. It is hard sometimes, but I always bring what I can.

Hasta lloró de alegría cuando le dije me "quedo": Family Separation

A common hardship some migrants mentioned to me is the disruption of their family life. It is common for migrants to leave behind their partners when they migrate to the United States and to visit their families during their work breaks.

Benito Mendoza and his wife, Cipriana, live at La Garita ranch in Satevó County. Benito is in his mid seventies and has worked more than forty years in the United States. He has retired and now lives in Mexico. During those forty years, Benito visited his family in cycles of two or three months and often risked his life crossing the border to visit his family. Doña Cipriana told me,

> It is very hard to migrate. I was on my own for over thirty years. My husband visited me every two or three months and he was working in the United States. It is very hard to bring up your family on your own. I did it without my partner to help me raise my eight children. The two parties suffer a lot, but we did not have an option. The thing is that both of us suffered the separation...but we could not be together.

Cipriana and Benito have been together again since 1996, when Benito had a stroke and could not work anymore. The first time Benito went to work in the United States was in 1954:

> I went with the bracero program from 1954 until 1962. Later on, I went as a *mojado* [undocumented]. In the 1970s, I managed to get my permission and later I became a U.S. citizen. The first time, I went to Michigan to the beet fields and then to the cucumbers. Later, I worked in Deming in the fields with alfalfa, cotton, and wheat. I learned about the bracero program through friends. There were groups. What they did was to contract twenty, twenty-five, or thirty men from every county. There was a raffle and they contracted us based on the results of the raffle. I used to earn fifty cents an hour. I always managed to save money. If I earned thirty dollars a week, I used five for my food and I saved the rest for my family. I used to send my family money with other people who I knew came to town and I used to tell my friends when I was coming so that they could give me money to give to their family.

I asked Benito and Cripriana how the bracero program allowed them to maintain their relationship. Benito said that he really never liked to work too far from the border so that he could visit his family often.

> We went by contracts of ninety days and after the end
> of the period we could renew the contract. So I used
> to come to visit my family in between the contracts.

Benito always missed his family, and he crossed the border every two or three months, even as an undocumented migrant:

> I could not stand it longer. I missed them very
> much....I used to stay fifteen days, no more. My
> boss used to tell me, "If you come back in fifteen
> days, I will keep your work [for you]." If we did
> not comply, we would lose the job and had to look
> for another one. But I never had to do that. One
> has to work, hard, hard, hard, to meet the needs of
> the family. And it was like that for forty years. I
> know people who can last longer in the United
> States... or they get married to another woman and
> forget about their family in Mexico. I know it hap-
> pens because I saw many people who did it.... Now
> I am *encantado de la vida* [enchanted with life]. Now
> that it is Christmas, my sons came to visit me. We
> have serenity. The good thing is that they live in
> Texas not too far from here. I am grateful to God
> for what I have received.

The corrido is perceived by most study participants as reflecting and critiquing the political, social, and economic conditions of the common people. All of them demonstrated a high degree of understanding of the main components of the corrido: its role, aesthetics, and history. Corridos enjoy a high degree of credibility among people. None of the participants doubted the veracity of the corridos. People often referred to the corrido as an instrument that not only analyzes important events of the commu-nity but also incorporates the feelings of the characters and the people involved in such events. In this sense, the epic element of the corrido is complemented by its lyric element. The corrido is also perceived as an expression that is always present in moments of transformation and crisis, both at the individual and collective levels.

All the participants learned some corridos at a very early age. While some students at the Universidad Autónoma de Ciudad Juárez tended to prefer ballads, Spanish-language rock, and other genres, all had danced corridos at family and community gatherings. All regarded the corrido as an instrument for the preservation of the community's memory and values.

People who listened to and performed contemporary corridos did not see the transformation of the corridos as a problem, however. Their position reflects an attempt to understand recent changes rather than condemn them. Among the changes that people perceived were the topics and the length of the corridos. According to musicians and people who listen often to corridos, these changes are directly related to the changes in society, since corridos narrate the events that happen in society. One of the topics that has been popular in recent corridos is drug smuggling. The reactions toward *narcocorridos* were contradictory and ambiguous. Some people tended to see the main characters of the narcocorridos as social bandits—as transgressors of the existing class system. Other people thought that narcocorridos glorified delinquency, and some even felt that the production and distribution of narcocorridos should be prohibited. Such comments were derived particularly from radio stations and from middle-class participants, who tended to see drug smuggling as a problem limited to criminals. In general, the participants who were against narcocorridos were more vocal and assertive about their beliefs than those who perceived drug smuggling simply as another aspect of the reality of the border region. Perhaps the latter groups of individuals were less assertive because they implicitly acknowledged the negative elements of drug smuggling.

Migrants I interviewed in Mexico talked in less detail about their migrant experience than those I interviewed in the United States. I sometimes interviewed people in Mexico in the presence of their relatives, and some of them preferred not to talk about the hardships they had experienced in the United States. (These migrants are a source of pride and moral support, as well as economic support, for their families.) I often felt that being silent or talking about the subject only superficially was a means of preserving their dignity with a stranger. This attitude reminded me that migrants, like everybody else, must continuously negotiate multiple social contradictions such as the coexistence of marginalization, survival, and love of their families.

All the migrants I talked to are low-wage workers who clean yards, serve food, sew clothes, harvest, plant, drive, manufacture fiberglass, take care of other people's children, construct houses, milk cows, and in general provide all the services that make life more comfortable for those who reject and marginalize them. During the conversations and the focus group interviews, they expressed multiple subjectivities that make their migrant experience transcend their identities as workers: these migrant workers are also mothers, fathers, sons and daughters, neighbors, religious people, and community members in their homeland, marginalized and at the same time empowered in Mexico and in the United States. They are members of complex social networks that help them gain at least partial autonomy from the dominant culture. These social networks or communities generate distinctive experiences and values that accept, reinforce, and transmit the elements of their migrant experiences as well as the culture they prefer to keep, create, or incorporate into their everyday lives.

One cold winter I was having a cup of coffee and enjoying the view of the sun coming into the kitchen of my extended family's house. There were many activities going on in the adobe house of Satevó, particularly in the main patio and the *solar*. It was the day after the annual *matanza* (pig slaughtering) the family has.[6] Men were in the solar that was behind the house, reclined on the wall, in a typical vaquero posture and custom, chatting among themselves. I was watching *mi compadre* doing her laundry and cleaning the patio after the big family reunion that was the matanza. David, *mi compadre*, came to kitchen to have a piece of *chicharrón* (crackling of pork). He asked what I was doing while he warmed some tortillas to have with the fresh chicharrón from the day before. He prepared himself a coffee, sat next to me, and was curiously looking at the transcriber and the laptop. I was transcribing some tapes and I could not help but ask him some questions about corridos. Mi compadre David is a very hardworking and very gentle person. He is from Satevó municipality and has been working for a slaughterhouse in northern Texas for over ten years. David visits his family in Chihuahua at least once a year, particularly during Christmas. He does not speak much, but his smile and actions make people feel very welcome. David knew what I was doing for my research, but he still felt quite uneasy about what he perceived as a formal conversation with him. David's wife encouraged him to help me, telling him how easy it was to talk about something he knew. His wife's explanations did not help much to make him feel at ease. It was Marimar and Brianita's, my goddaughters', playful interaction with us that made David start to talk. One of David's daughters started to play with the tape recorder and pretended to be interviewing us. The girls kept hearing in a very solemn way the whole conversation with the headphone on their heads, and their mother was on the patio, also paying attention to what was going on in the kitchen while doing her chores. The situation turned serene and delightful. During our conversation, David mentioned something that touched me very much:

> Many corridos about immigration talk about the deaths of people in the river [Rio Grande/Bravo]. Let's not go too far: not long ago, here in town [Satevó, Chihuahua], a friend of mine was found drowned in the river [Bravo]. He was a very good friend of mine. He was with his brother. He was a little younger than me. The current [of the river] pushed him and he drowned. His body was recovered, but he was already...[dead].

This issue was so delicate and powerful to him that he did not even want to pronounce the word *dead*. David's dignified silence was quite telling of how close to his heart the narratives described in the corridos were. I had never spoken to him before about such serious matters. I knew that he had a quite large collection of such corridos, but this conversation was very special to me. David prefers listening to the narratives of the corridos about migration, a phenomenon he knows so well, to talking about such painful situations. I could not help but feel like an intrusive person when I saw his pain. I also kept silent for a while. David told me that listening to corridos brings him a lot of peace—they seem to have a cathartic role in his life.

Chapter Four

De parranda con el diablo:
PERFORMANCE AND THE AESTHETICS OF CONJUNTO NORTEÑO DANCE MUSIC

It is not what you play, but what you play for...not about music or lyrics
but about feelings. You have to make people feel it.... In the case of
música norteña, the blend of music and culture cannot be separated.
Leandro Rodríguez, musician and fisherman from the conjunto norteño
— Los Campeones del Valle, Zaragoza, Chihuahua, 2000

On February 4, 2001, I attended a dance at the Genoveva Community Center in Santa Fe where Los Cadetes de Durango, Los Yoniks, and Los Tigres del Norte were playing. The ticket cost thirty dollars and the event started at seven. I arrived an hour and a half earlier to contact Los Tigres del Norte's manager, Alfonso de Alba, and asked him to allow me to interview the group. Cars were already parked in the lot of the center, and young people were standing in a line at the entrance. Most of the young men were very well dressed, wearing cowboy hats, some in silk shirts and cowboy boots, and the women were wearing elegant evening dresses and high-heeled shoes. There were also groups of middle-aged men and women and some couples with their teenage children. Outside the main entrance of Genoveva Community Center was a sense of camaraderie and a willingness to relax and establish a rapport with the other people who were waiting for the doors to open.

People were asking each other where they were from, and smiles were exchanged all over. A man in his mid sixties started talking to me, smiling and acknowledging me as a countrywoman. He was very excited about having the "unique opportunity to see Los Tigres del Norte." He asked me which part of Mexico I was from, saying that he was from Chihuahua State and that he had just come back from Chihuahua, where he usually spends his Christmas holidays. He told me, "I live in Chihuahua; that is my home, but I come to work every two months." That was not an unusual answer, since many Mexicans spend years or even decades working in the United States, going back and forth every two or three months. Evelyn, a northern New Mexican in her fifties, and her fifteen-year-old son asked me where I was from. She asked me if I was on my own and, when I replied that I was, immediately told me to stay with her family. She instructed her son to stand next to me. The situation reminded me of the Mexican custom in which senior people, particularly women, are protective of women who are alone and who look relatively young. Evelyn's family did not separate from me until the event finished. Evelyn kept asking why I was alone. I told her that I was trying to learn about the music that is most liked by Mexican immigrants. She became interested in the topic and started telling me that she and her family never miss an opportunity to see Los Tigres del Norte when the group performed in New Mexico. Evelyn said that her sons had all the Los Tigres del Norte CDs and that she was very happy to be attending the event.

Before the dance started, I talked to a security guard at the entrance of the community center and asked him to give my business card and an accompanying letter to the manager of Los Tigres del Norte. I had written to express my interest in an interview. The security guard came back and told me that they'd be happy to meet with me but that the interview would have to be held after the event.

We entered the community center a little before seven. The dance took place in the basketball court of the center. On the side of the field were about twenty tables with six chairs at each table. There were temporary stairs on the side of the court. The crowd of about fifteen hundred people was minuscule by Los Tigres del Norte standards. The group routinely plays before audiences of ten thousand people or more on both sides of the border. The first two groups were presented on one end of the basketball court. During their presentation, couples were dancing and people on the sides were chatting and getting to know each other. Each group played for an hour. The first group, Los Cadetes de Durango, played música norteña music. Los Yoniks, a well-known and established group from Acapulco, played romantic songs. For Los Yoniks, it was the first time they had performed in New Mexico. While Los Yoniks and Los Cadetes de Durango were playing on one side of the court, the stage for Los Tigres del Norte was being prepared on the other side. The stage had some rocks and tigers made of fiberglass. As the choreographers were preparing the final touches, people started to get closer to the stage of Los Tigres del Norte. About 8:30 p.m., most dancers did not continue dancing. Instead, they chose to get closer to the stage of Los Tigres del Norte so that they could get a good spot to see them performing. At nine, a five-minute prerecorded collection of the most well-known songs of Los Tigres del Norte was played. That was the call that meant they were about to start performing. Los Tigres del Norte started their performance with the song "El mojado acaudalado" (The Rich Wetback), followed by "De paisano a paisano" (From Countryman to Countryman). Thereafter, they played by request. Jorge Hernández, the main singer of Los Tigres del Norte, stopped to take requests that the audience scrawled on scrap paper and gave the pieces of paper to one of the band's helpers. From then on, all the songs they played were those the audience had requested.

On the far end of the stage, images with the photographs of each member of the band were displayed. The images were changed constantly and showed the band member who was singing at the time. Between songs, Los Tigres del Norte praised people from Chihuahua, Mexico. They were certain that most of their audience in New Mexico was from Chihuahua or had strong links with that northern Mexican state. The band read some greetings that members of the audience were sending to their loved ones or family members. One of the greetings and dedications they read aloud was, "Saludos a Esteban, Patricia, Noemí y Laura de Verónica" (Greetings to Esteban, Patricia, Noemí, and Laura from Verónica). It was a great pleasure to see people sending pieces of paper to Los Tigres del Norte and hear them pronouncing their names and hometowns. In the middle of the performance, confetti, balloons, and balls with the Los Tigres del Norte logo slowly descended into the audience while the lights were focused on the crowd. It was a slow-paced moment in which the audience and Los Tigres del

Norte had a strong sense of communion. All of us were participants in this cathartic event.

Los Tigres del Norte played for over three hours, until most of the people in the audience were exhausted. After the event, there was a photograph session with the fans. The fans lined up backstage and the members of Los Tigres del Norte were asking them questions about their places of origin and praising them. The band was attentive, gentle, modest, and cordial. Octavio Hernández, Evelyn's son, came back from the photography session:

> It was so beautiful. They are really modest. They treated me as if they had known me for a very long time. I do not know, like a brother, *muy bonito, bien bonito*. They talk to you and ask things about you. The first time I saw them, I was sixteen and I loved them so much, I wanted to be part of them. The first time I saw them, they were more simple but with a very good style. I have seen how they have changed. It has always been something very beautiful to see them. They are now more modernized. Did you notice that people stopped dancing and then went to the stage just to listen to them? Let me explain it to you. I knew this was going to happen because the first time I saw them, I did not expect that to happen. When the two bands played, everybody stood up to dance. When Los Tigres appeared, everybody stood in front of the stage just to see them. That is because they are great, very famous. They enter into the heart of the people. When I saw them when I was a kid, I always wanted to be like them; I wanted to play and watch how they played. I stayed in front of them to see their faces to have the illusion that I am there with them, to feel that I am in what they are saying.

After the performance but before the photograph session, I talked to Jorge Hernández, the spokesman of the group and main singer. All the members of Los Tigres del Norte radiated tranquility and self-control.

Their voices were soft and amicable. In fact, they seemed to personify many of the family values that are idealized in Mexican culture: the Hernández brothers seemed to enjoy each other's company, respected each other, worked in harmony, and looked very serene and peaceful. They walked out slowly toward their fans who wanted to have a picture with them. I was treated by the band with extreme gentleness, not with a patronizing attitude but with respect from the moment I asked for the interview, when I went up to the stage, while I was interviewing Jorge Hernández, and after the interview. Even though the band had a very tight schedule, they managed to maintain an attitude of serenity.

The eldest of eleven siblings, Jorge was fourteen years old in 1968 when the group was hired to play for the Mexican Independence Day parade in Parque de las Flores in San José, California, a park where the Mexican community used to get together on Sundays. Los Tigres del Norte were so young when they crossed the Mexico-U.S. border that they had to convince a middle-aged Mexican couple to pretend to be their parents. At that time, the band had no name. When they crossed the border to play in San José, the immigration officer who issued their visas kept calling them "little tigers" in an affectionate way. Jorge Hernández said that he thought, *Call us what you want, but let us cross.* The name they chose for the band was Los Tigres del Norte because they are from the northern part of Mexico, they were playing northern Mexican music, and they were heading north.

The first successful song of Los Tigres del Norte, "Contrabando y traición" (Contraband and Betrayal), was the first one they recorded in 1972. Their first song was the most successful of all. According to Jorge Hernández, the main distinctive feature of the corrido is its expressiveness. The topics of the corridos change because they reflect the circumstances of the community, which are always changing. Regardless of whether the main protagonist of the corrido is good or bad, the corrido always expresses, in a very strong and dramatic way, the main features of the protagonist. Jorge told me that the corridos have two or three layers of meaning, and the public will decide which one is most relevant to them. The meaning will depend on the community they are singing for.

Conjunto norteño musicians are a fundamental part of the social fabric of northern Mexican communities and of Mexicans from that region who migrate to the United States. Most musicians belong to the community they play for or at least share the core characteristics of their

Saxophonist of the
conjunto norteño Bego
playing norteña music in
El Sinaloense dance club
in Ciudad Juárez (2004).
Photo by Selfa Chew.

audiences, such as having a working-class background and being from
the same geographic region. Even though Los Tigres del Norte are now
wealthy artists, their origins were humble. As Jorge explained to me,

> Once we were here [in the U.S.], we helped [the fam-
> ily back home], and we didn't want to go back but
> rather to keep working here, sending them money so
> that they could make a living. That was one of the
> reasons we were insistent on playing music, because
> we wanted my father to be okay financially and to
> have enough to sustain himself every day. That was

a goal, not an artistic goal. We wanted to work to sustain our family.

Don Leandro Rodríguez, the leader of the conjunto norteño Los Campeones del Valle, from Zaragoza, Chihuahua, told me how he got into playing music:

> My father was a very busy person who worked hard in the fields. He was a musician too and taught me a little bit. My father gave me the first *empujón* [push], but a lot of what I know is because I learned it by myself. I was close to people who knew how to play [musical instruments of conjunto norteño music]. That was the way I learned, little by little. I am saying little, because that is what I know, little. I normally play within the region, but we traveled only in a small region. We almost only play in the Zaragoza Valley, Parral City, San José del Sitio. This is the first time we played in Satevó. We are advancing little by little.

Don Leandro is a very modest, extremely polite, and dignified person. When I asked him if he had other jobs apart from being a musician, he told me: "Yes, and I appreciate your question. We are fishermen and we are very proud of being so. We are fishermen in the Zaragoza Valle. We live on the shore of the Toronto Lake. Some people call it La presa de la Boquilla [Boquilla dam]; other people call it Rancho del Toro. We live there a *sus órdenes* [at your service]. So, we work as musicians and as fishermen."

My friend Yolanda Olivas took me to Tumbleweed, the most popular dance hall among Nuevo Mexicanos and people from Chihuahua who live in Albuquerque. I went there on several Fridays and Saturdays to carry out my fieldwork. The popularity of the dance hall among New Mexicans is still very strong. Friday is the day for strictly New Mexican music and Saturday for Mexican music (mainly conjunto norteño, but also *música banda*). Al Hurricane and his family were the first owners of the Tumbleweed restaurant and dance club. They, Roberto Martínez, and the first owners of Cristy Records are credited with the first serious effort to record music in Spanish for Mexican and New Mexican audiences. This was a major struggle for these artists, whose talents had been consistently undervalued. Paradoxically, multinational companies took over and pushed these musicians out of business as soon as the market had grown sufficiently. As Al Hurricane explained to me,

> When we started, there were no record studios in New Mexico for music in Spanish. People would ask us, "Why don't you perform in this nightclub?" We had to go to Las Cruces and California to record our music. My family and me started to have our own record label called "Hurricane," and then we thought it was better to buy the nightclub because if we played in other people's nightclubs, we had to pay a lot of taxes. This club is called now Tumbleweed, but it used to be called Farwest. We sold our products to different stores, and the managers noticed that our music and the music in Spanish was demanded and liked it. So, the story is quite long. All I can tell you now is that now the nightclub does not belong to us and that music in Spanish is sold in Wal-Mart and Kmart. It took a long time to acknowledge our music, and once they saw the market, we were pushed aside.

The first time I went to the Tumbleweed, I introduced myself to Mr. Manuel Granillo, the leader of Grupo Diamante, one of the conjuntos that plays often on Saturday, when Chihuahuenses are there to dance. Mr. Granillo was very helpful and very polite to me when I explained why I was interested in learning about him and his conjunto. My visits to the Tumbleweed were often tense and uneasy because I do not often dance música norteña in dance halls or other public places. I was in a liminal position, sometimes being a full participant in the dances because my profile matches that of the frequent dancers, at other times trying to detach myself and take notes as events of interest were happening. When I was invited to dance, I sometimes accepted, but most of the time I remained with my friends, watching what was happening and enjoying the música norteña.

The entry cost was quite high for a graduate student (twenty dollars), and I could not afford to go as often as I would have liked.

I told Mr. Granillo that I often felt awkward doing research in a dance hall. I did not always feel safe, since some of the frequent dancers assumed I was there to dance or to find a boyfriend. Mr. Granillo told me in a decisive and protective manner, "There is nothing wrong in doing this kind of work that you are doing here. On the contrary, it is very nice work. We can see you from our stage, and if you want, you can just sit next to us." I felt quite relieved, and we had several conversations after that. The most vivid one occurred on the porch of Mr. Granillo's family home. Mr. Granillo was very generous and gave me several tapes of their music. He said to me, "Occasionally I play in Chihuahua, but most of the time I play in Albuquerque. I have been working in roof construction for over ten years. My son has always been with me, and I did not want to leave him alone while I was touring; you know how hard things are for young people now." Mr. Granillo told me that although he had many opportunities to tour, he decided against it because he felt his family life was more important and wanted to be close to his wife, daughter, and son.

Conjunto norteño musicians learn to play music almost as their mother tongue by listening to it, practicing it, and performing it through very informal means. None of the musicians I interviewed had gone to a formal school of music. The members of Los Tigres del Norte did take formal voice lessons, but only after they were already established musicians in their hometown.

Los Misioneros de Chihuahua is a conjunto norteño that often plays when there are *chicharrones de marrano* or matanza in my extended family house in Satevó. Whenever relatives who live far away come to town, they have a *marrano* (pig) or a matanza. At one of those matanzas, I talked in great detail with Los Misioneros de Chihuahua about their work. We were talking over a *cerveza* and a *taco de chicharrón* on the patio. Some of my female cousins and sisters-in-law listened attentively to our conversation, while the rest of the family carried out their duties for the matanza. (They still listened in whenever possible.) Most of the musicians in Los Misioneros de Chihuahua are from ranches near Chihuahua City: Nonoava, San Juanito, and Delicias, for example. They told me that they learned to play music just by listening, without any formal training.

Guitarist of the conjunto norteño Bego (2004). Photo by Selfa Chew.

Roberto Martínez of Los Reyes de Albuquerque learned to play in a similar way:

> I got used to [playing] in my house. We did not listen to other music [than ranchero music]. Since I was very small, I used to sing with my dad. When I was nine or ten years old, my uncle made a guitar for me. A very simple one made of a gas recipient and some wires. I loved it and used to play it and sing and sing.

Jorge Hernández of Los Tigres del Norte learned to play and sing by listening to his relatives:

> I've always liked to sing corridos, since I was a kid. People looked for us on the ranch to sing them stories. Since I would listen to other singers doing corridos like "Gabino Barreda," "Custodio," "Lucio

Vázquez," "El Corrido de Siete Leguas," and "Rosita Alvírez," I learned and sang them. I knew I could get attention with the stories, and I could earn a peso for my family. We started playing on our ranch; there we played and sang. We did not have many opportunities, and all the music we played was to sustain our family. Our daily earnings were to meet basic needs. . . . I was fourteen years old. We were about to come to San José. The conjunto that influenced me, among many, I mean the influence I remember the most, is "Los alegres de Terán" [The Happy Men from Terán].

I had the support of my mother. Although my father liked very much the idea that we dedicated ourselves to play music, he always demanded that we study. We were so young that we could not play in public places. We had to play in restaurants and in parties. From time to time, the police caught us because we were in places we should not be in. The music comes from my maternal grandfather. He was a musician who used to sing at home with friends. Almost all his family played the accordion and were musicians whom people sought out when they wanted to have a good time. They were musicians from another ranch, the Limón ranch.

Almost all conjunto norteño musicians told me that the internal organization of the conjunto is crucial to its success. The leaders of the conjuntos norteños are the ones who keep the conjunto norteño disciplined. As Mr. Granillo told me,

There should be discipline. I tell musicians not to drink and that they should behave as in any other kind of job. This job should not be any different. The saxophonist is my right hand. He is very responsible, and if one of the other musicians is playing good, he can bring the group together.

Manuel Márquez is a very talented conjunto singer and very much part
of the transnational community. He was born in Satevó but during his adult
life has lived between Chihuahua State and Dumas, Texas. He created the conjunto Los Ciclones de Manny Márquez (The Cyclones of Manny Márquez),
which plays on both sides of the border. Manuel is a truly transnational musician who knows the way performance works in Mexico and the United States.

I met Manuel, or Manny, in a Wal-Mart store in Dumas, Texas,
while I was with my extended family. Manny greeted them with great
love, since he is from the same town in Chihuahua. He invited us to
attend a *quinceañera* that was organized for one of his nieces. We did
attend the quinceañera, which took place several months afterward. The
whole community of Chihuahuenses in Dumas was getting ready for
this big event. Everybody cooperated in different ways, preparing the
food, organizing the dance hall, and helping with the expenses. An
interesting aspect of the music at the quinceañera was that the songs
requested by the people in attendance were the same ones I had heard
earlier at a similar event in Satevó. Even the order of the songs was very
similar. Over two hundred people attended the event. Manny sang a
couple of norteña songs at that quinceañera. Like Mr. Granillo, Manny
stressed the importance of discipline:

> It is very hard to be a musician because you have to
> be close to the fire without getting burnt. That
> means that there are all kinds of temptations in the
> dance halls, alcohol, sometimes drugs and young
> girls who become fans and are following you, but
> musicians have to behave professionally.

Conjunto norteño musicians gain greatest satisfaction when they can
convey positive, happy feelings to the people they are playing for. They feel
that the contracts they receive are representative of their talent, since almost
all their jobs are arranged in response to referrals from previous clients. Manuel
Granillo reported that the task of making people happy can be difficult when
the audience members are gathered in response to a sad or unfortunate event:

> When we used to work four days a week, we earned
> good money. That was how I managed to get my

Drum player of the conjunto norteño Bego playing norteña music in El Sinaloense dance club in Ciudad Juárez (2004). Photo by Selfa Chew.

little house. The money we earn in the construction industry for a week is less than what we earn in one day playing music. What is nice is to be acknowledged by people. We have played in Chihuahua with people who have money and pay for all our expenses from Albuquerque. It is a very hard job in the sense that it does not matter what are your feelings, you still have to play. Five years ago my brother died. We went to Chihuahua to his funeral service, and as soon as I came back, I had to play. Even my soul was hurting, and I still had to play because that was my job.

Sometimes it is sad, but most of the time it is a happy job. I work in what I like to do; what I sing, I do it with all my *ganas, no a fuerzas* [with all my might, not forced]. Since I am a norteño, I enjoy playing the music of *mi tierra* [my homeland]. We have

been asked by rich people to go and play our music
to Chihuahua State. It is so rewarding and nice to
feel acknowledged. I go very often to Chihuahua
because my father lives there and I do not like leaving him alone. Música norteña is in our veins. Even
small children want to know how to play it. My two
grandsons want to know.

Leandro Rodríguez, leader of Los Campeones del Valle from
Zaragoza, Chihuahua, said that what he likes most about being a musician
is that people enjoy themselves and value his music:

As a musician, one has to play really well regardless
of whether there are three people dancing or many
people....One has to be a musician at heart. Of
course, many people gather together at the weddings,
and the more people there are, the more enthusiasm
we have and of course one puts in more effort. I
think that being a musician implies that it should not
matter the number of people that are dancing; one
has to play very well because this work is very difficult and competitive. I tell that to my sons and
nephews and they should not be discouraged; they
should look forward, forward, and forward, because
that is the nature of this work.

Escuchen este corrido que alegre vengo a cantar:
Genres and Occasions to Play Conjunto Norteño Music

According to musicians, música norteña can be characterized by the musical instruments used to perform the piece: accordion, drums, saxophone,
bajo, and bass, and the rhythm of the music, which is very close to that of
the polka. The main genres that conjunto norteño play are cumbias, baladas, boleros, and corridos. In order to differentiate other types of rhythms,
people normally add the word *norteño* after the genre. For example, if the
corrido is a cumbia, they would refer to a cumbia played with conjunto
norteño instruments as a *cumbia norteña*. Manuel Granillo told me that conjuntos norteños play different genres:

Cumbias, baladas, boleros, everything. The difference is the instruments. All those genres become part of the música norteña if we play with accordion and saxophone. We need to study and see the lyrics and the musical notes and put them in the norteño style.

Likewise, Manny Márquez stated,

We play a little bit of everything but with our accent, the norteño accent. There are some young people who like very much cumbias, cumbias norteñas, like the ones Los Tucanes de Tijuana play. Some people like romantic rancheras sung by El Conjunto Primavera. They are a typical example of *baladas norteñas*, or romantic music, but with conjunto. We can play music that originally was for mariachi or for trio the very same, and we make it norteño style with the instruments, our voices. Yes, there are places where they use more certain instruments. For instance, in Sinaloa, the band is used more with wind instruments, with more musicians, up to fifteen. In Chihuahua the corridos are sung with five musicians and with the norteño group. It is only different styles more than anything because the corridos are the same. The difference is the type of instruments, only that.

Another unique characteristic of conjunto norteño is the singer's voice. Traditionally, conjunto norteño music is sung in a nasal, high-pitched voice. While high-pitched voices are normally associated with female singers, norteño voices are more evocative of seduction, intimacy, youth, sincerity, and intense feelings. Manny Márquez spoke in more detail about the nasal, high-pitched voices typical of this kind of music:

The norteño style requires a different way of singing than the mariachi. It is higher. The highest part of the *canción norteña* comes from the *estridillo* [chorus],

in which normally two or more singers sing together.
The estridillo takes place more or less in the middle of
the song.

Mr. Granillo added,

> The música norteña is sung with a shrill and voice
> high. The typical norteño style should be this way.
> Many people think that it is very easy to sing norteño
> music, but when they try, they cannot [sing it]....It is
> hard....It is very high, higher than mariachi music.

Hiring a conjunto norteño for a family event can be expensive. Indeed,
it is the most expensive part of any celebration. However, people appreciate music so much that they are willing to contract musicians even when
they have to pay high prices. The way people cope with such expenses is
by sharing them among the members of the community. In the case of
weddings, up to forty godparents may share the cost. For community fiestas, people are charged a fee at the entrance, and any profits go to the community. Dances have a cover charge of thirty to forty dollars in the United
States and approximately ten dollars in Mexico. Homar explained the pricing to me:

> For the weddings, the amount of money for the
> music will depend on the number of godparents.
> That is, if the godparents are very few, then the monetary resources will be little. Therefore, most people
> try to put together up to twenty, thirty, or more godparents. This is with the objective of raising more
> funds, because the godparents are the ones that are
> going to pay for the music. It depends on them the
> type of mariachi they are going to hire and above all
> the musical band that is going to play in the party.
>
> The most expensive part of the wedding is the
> music. There are conjunto norteños that charge up to
> six thousand U.S. dollars, four thousand, three thousand dollars depending on how famous the conjunto

is. They normally charge by the event. In general, they play five hours. For a quinceañera it is different. The father is the one that has to pay everything. The male dance companion of the quinceañera is only a friend, but nobody helps the father of the quinceañera to pay for the music. So, in these cases there are less possibilities of spending money. The quinceañeras use conjuntos that are less expensive. In the weddings you have economic support from others; in the quinceañeras you do not. As a father or as a mother, you are the only one who has to pay. For instance, in the ranches, everybody eats in the house of the bride. The family is invited to be there. And if there is a community dance hall, then they use it free of charge. The community provides it. If there is no community dance hall, then they use the basketball court or even the patio of the house of the bride. But nowadays this is more rare. As I said before, this is due to the fact that the musical groups are more sophisticated. Men are the ones who contract the musicians. The issue is treated as a contract among men. The father of the bride or the bridegroom, or the father of the bridegroom, looks for the musicians, talks to them, reaches an agreement, and pays them.

Voy a contarles la historia: Interaction of Musicians with Their Audiences

There is an indissoluble and organic relationship between the musicians and the community for which they play. In fact, frequent dancers repeatedly evaluated conjunto norteños based on their interaction with the community more than by their artistic qualities. It is very important for the conjunto to know the members of the community, their lifestyles, their major local events, and the songs a particular community likes most. In other words, the value of the conjunto is not in its quality per se but in the capacity of the conjunto to create affective and emotional alliances with the community it is performing for. The musicians' knowledge of the community is displayed in their *saludos* (greetings) and *dedicatorias*

(dedications). In these segments, the musicians always comment on specific people and events in the communities in which they are playing.

Homar Prieto told me in detail about this interaction between musicians and their audiences:

> To your question on what it will take to ask a con-
> junto norteño to play for a particular event, I would
> say that very often you like the [musical] groups just
> by the way of singing or the way they interact with
> people. For instance, nobody matches the Vendabales
> to entertain in a coleadero [a special event in which
> a group of men throw the bulls by twisting their
> tails]. Why is that? Because the singer of that group
> knows everybody from the Municipality of Satevó.
> He greets people by their name, with the micro-
> phone. So, people love to receive greetings in public
> events. If you go to a coleadero, he might say, "Here,
> X and Y are coming; they are from this ranch." So
> people love that. Sometimes they [the artists] say
> humorous things that only people from the ranches
> appreciate, those types of jokes, or he might use the
> same vocabulary people from the ranches use. Then
> people really identify with him. That is why they
> are in every coleadero.
>
> On the contrary, a group from Chihuahua City
> does not know anybody. The singer cannot greet
> anybody, cannot say jokes that people like because
> they do not know the traditions of the ranches. So,
> the Vendabales know everybody, they know it is
> important, and so they send greetings to everybody
> who is present. He [the singer] might also send
> greetings or regards to the girls from the ranches.
> To say something like, "This song is dedicated to
> Irasema, who is this and that and who was in the
> dance of...last night." So, he already mentioned
> before everybody your name, and of course you like
> it. You know what I mean? It is a way of being liked

by the people and attracting people and, of course, apart from the fact that they sing the songs that are popular at that moment.

So, in the coleaderos they know the songs that people like and they play them. In the coleaderos, people do not ask for the songs all the time. I mean, it depends. In the ranches... very often people do not make requests because they already know which ones they are going to sing. They already have in their program songs that they know people like. No, they already have their repertoire. However, people may ask them to play corridos or other songs. For instance, they may be asked to play "El corrido of the Mendozas" or " El corrido de los Pérez" that talks about horse races.

Musicians often stressed to me the importance of playing songs requested by the people in attendance, particularly at family reunions, such as quinceañeras, weddings, and christenings. Normally, musicians have a core of pieces to play in case people do not have specific requests, but the order and genre of the music is subject to change depending on the people who are listening or dancing. Songs by request are very much part of the culture. When people do not ask for songs, musicians feel that they are not having a dialogue with the people. On the other hand, there are times when different people ask for the same song several times at a single event, and even though the musicians might want to show their versatility by playing a wider range of pieces, they still play the same songs because that's what the people want. As Mr. Granillo explained,

When one is on the stage, one has to know what people like, what are they accepting. When we do not fully know the songs they are requesting, we still play the parts of the songs we know. People do not mind that, as long as we try to please them. I always tell the musicians, "You have to have it clear in your mind that we are not going to play what we like. Forget about it. We are going to play what people

Dancing conjunto norteño
music during the winter in
El Sinaloense dance club in
Ciudad Juárez (2004).
Photo by Selfa Chew.

like us to play." Sometimes we play the same song
many times. I do not like that, but some songs are
quite popular and we have to play them if people
request them. In those cases, I announce in the micro-
phone that we are playing the same piece because
people keep asking for it....

How do I know what the people like at that
moment? Well...for instance, if one plays a cumbia
norteña and the people get happy and dance, that is
what we play. One has to be very sensitive and to
look carefully at what is going on in the dance floor.
Sometimes all they want is *canciones corridas*; then
that is what we do. It is difficult to play beautifully,

with feeling, with *ganas*. That is the difficult part. We really have to be updated in what is going on. There are youngsters who are very good, and we are competing with them. There are very good musicians, extremely good, but they have not been able to make it because they do not have the special charisma that Los Tigres del Norte radiate. The most popular conjuntos norteños are popular not because they are the best but because they have charisma. They are very good at knowing what people want. When one is onstage one needs to know what people want. We really have to be jealous of one's prestige. I always say to my musicians, "Nobody is an obstacle here, but nobody is indispensable either." My son and me have made many sacrifices and put a lot of money into our equipment. We have very good equipment so that we can rent it. Our equipment costs forty thousand dollars. We are very responsible musicians; that is why people who contract us know that they can trust us. The very best música norteña comes from Monterrey. There almost every single group is good. There are not bad groups. Then you have people from Ojinaga, a small town, and there are excellent musicians.

Leandro Rodríguez described some of the interactions with dancers and dance audiences:

People come close to the band and ask for the song they want us to play. They ask me, "Excuse me, do you know this song?" Sometimes we answer, "No, we do not know, but we can change that one for this other one." That is the way we work, or if we know a little part of it, we play it...and they get happy if we try to play the little part we know. In some places we are very lucky because we know all the songs they ask us to play. Thank God! But in other places

it is very difficult. One has to guess the kind of
music they like. This is because people do not feel
comfortable enough to make a request. So, that
makes us feel uneasy. When people do not approach
us, I start thinking, *Well, maybe we are actually playing
things that they do not really like.* This situation is very
different from a band that is already known and
established because they already have their repertoire and so people already know that is what they
are going to listen to.

Musicians often told me that the songs people request provide interesting information about their communities. In communities where the
main economic activity is cattle ranching, people tend to ask for corridos such as "Los quinientos novillos"[2] (The Five Hundred Steers) or "El
hijo desobediente" (The Unruly Son)—corridos that reflect their lifestyle.
In communities where drug smuggling is an important part of their economy, they tend to request narcocorridos. Several musicians expressed
frustration with the corridos people want them to play. Because some
corridos are specific to a particular community and may even incorporate
lyrics about local individuals, many musicians have a difficult time keeping up with all the songs they are expected to know. As Leandro
Rodríguez explained,

In some places people even ask you to play corridos of the region, where the very people from the
region are the characters of those corridos. To
give you an example, in Valerio there are corridos
about people from the same town. In the Zaragoza
Valley, there are corridos about the valley and
about people from there, but not all of them are
known outside Zaragoza. People often ask for corridos that we do not know or that we are not
aware they existed. What happens is that people
compose their own corridos and expect us to
know them. The problem is that often we have
not even heard of them.

Música norteña: Fashionable Music Enjoying a Period of Popularity

According to musicians, radio executives, and promoters, música norteña has always been popular among people from the northern states of Mexico. In that region, people from every socioeconomic class dance conjunto norteño music. However, música norteña is regarded in many other areas as the music of the uneducated and the poor. Only very recently has conjunto norteño music enjoyed acceptability among the social elites of Mexico. Manuel Granillo described the recent increase in the popularity of this genre:

> What people like is música norteña. It does not matter where they live. If you, as a musician, do not know how to play música norteña, you are out. However, now more than ever, música norteña is enjoying a lot of popularity all over Mexico and the U.S. There is a lot of work. Look, for example, to other genres. What happened with the *quebradita*[3]...well, it died away. That has happened to other genres and rhythms. However, the música norteña goes on and on. If you want to play in any dance hall, the very first thing they will ask you is if your group has an accordion and a saxophone. As a musician you cannot find a job without those two instruments.
>
> Música norteña is being promoted, and it is being accepted more by people. Before it was only popular and liked in the states of Tamaulipas, Nuevo León, Coahuila. In the state of Chihuahua, even in the most elegant dance halls or parties, they have to play norteño music. The dance floor is more full when they play norteño music. Old, young, children. Everybody dances it. I have seen this more frequently in Chihuahua than in other places where they mix more cumbias....In Chihuahua, música norteña has always been popular. In the north, in general, all social classes dance it.

A couple dancing *cumbia norteña* in El Sinaloense dance club in Ciudad Juárez (2004). Photo by Selfa Chew.

It is possible that Mexicans living in the United States have made música norteña familiar to other Mexican emigrants who had not listened to música norteña in their communities of origin. For example, conjuntos norteños from Michoacán and Guanajuato, Mexican states with a strong tradition of emigration, have been widely disseminated throughout the United States. The seasonal and economic cycles of movement between the United States and Mexico have contributed to migrants' growing familiarity with a wide range of regional cultural expressions. In some ways, música norteña has become an important cultural element for Mexicans living in the United States and elsewhere. As Manuel Pineda, the DJ of the radio station XEBU, La Norteñita, in Chihuahua City, told me:

Música norteña has penetrated into the center of the
country. Traditionally, in the southern part of Mexico
people listen more to Colombian rhythms, tropical or
the type of Los Angeles Azules that is more of the
vallenato[5] genre. But now música norteña is penetrat-
ing the south. Obviously, this is due to the support of
the recording and promoting companies, particularly
Fonovisa, which is the company that records the most
norteño music of renown. I think it is due to the
market. They took this music over there to the U.S.
and realized that with a little bit of diffusion of Los
Tigres del Norte, Los Huracanes del Norte, Los
Tucanes de Tijuana, and others, they could sell a great
deal because people love them. They had an out-
standing popularity, and obviously they check out in
the dances. The organized dances were quite profitable. With time, those groups started to be quite
popular, particularly among migrants. Nowadays, you
have conjuntos norteños everywhere, in the south in
Mexico, D.F., in Oaxaca. Immigrants from those
regions start to dress like people in the northern parts
of Mexico. So, the industry knows what is going on.

Chulas Fronteras ¡como las extraño!: Radio Stations and Transnational Interactions

Música norteña has crossed and pushed physical and cultural boundaries,
and it can now be found wherever immigrants live. Conjunto norteño
music has achieved unprecedented success due to the insistence and per-
severance of independent recording labels (and more recently due to
transnational marketing and promotion). Cultural transnational interactions are reflected in the conjunto norteño music itself. Conjunto norteño
has gone through several innovations in promotion, performance, sound
technology, production quality, and instrumentation. With these innovations and appropriations, música norteña is also pushing the boundaries
of regional identity. In a sense, it demonstrates the capacity to defy cultural essentialism. According to the musicians who participated in this
study, the changes in conjunto norteño are less about assimilation and

more about the adaptation of the social, economic, and cultural context in which the music has been created and re-created. At the same time, certain older, traditional corridos are still popular among younger listeners. Thus, there are strong elements of both cultural maintenance and change. As Leandro Rodríguez states,

> Old people ask for old music. Actually, I would not call them old songs, because they are very much alive. Almost all contemporary groups are recording songs that were very popular thirty years ago. So, they are very popular again. That is why I would not say that they are old songs, because they are alive. Songs like "Prieta orgullosa" [Proud Brown Woman] and "Te quiero mucho" [I Love You Very Much] used to be played when I was a small child. They are very popular now. Young people think that those songs are new because they did not have the opportunity to listen to them before. I tell my sons and nephews that those songs are beautiful, and a proof of that is that they are alive. For instance, songs written by José Alfredo Jiménez and the like are songs that were played long, long ago but continue to be played all the time and liked by youngsters.

Musicians who perform on both sides of the border told me that they do not have to modify their style or repertoire for American (or Mexican) audiences. The core elements of the music are the same, perhaps due to the transnational movement of migrants or the transnational distribution and promotion of the genre. Manny Márquez stated that the only advantage of setting up a conjunto norteño in the United States is the greater availability of credit. Musicians charge approximately the same fees in both countries.

> The musicians who play there [Mexico] are the same that play here [the United States]. People look for them well in advance, and they go to play where they are demanded. They are the same musicians. There

are many advantages in playing on both sides of the border. I can play for more people; thus we can and have more contracts. In reality, it is not much different. Here [the United States] is like being in Mexico, except that here you can ask for credit and in Mexico everything has to be in cash. I can move more easily in Mexico because I already know the country.

To your question that if the dances have a rhythmic sequence, that if they start with smooth songs and then there is alternation, I can tell you that that does not happen in the ranches. In Chihuahua State, the music starts happy and ends happy. In Chihuahua City, it starts with a smooth rhythm, then fast music, and then romantic music, and the dances end in that tone. In the ranch, from start to end we have fast music. Perhaps sometimes, there may be a bolero, but only on few occasions. And that is what people like to dance. If you play something else, they do not hire you again. They like only norteño music and ranchero music.

Most conjunto norteño musicians prefer to record in the United States, if only because credit is more readily available and the purchasing power of migrants in the United States is greater than in Mexico. Quite often the new songs and trends in conjunto norteño music travel from Mexico to the United States. This illustrates the effect of economic power on the partial contribution of cultural elements. However, there is a continual process of cross-fertilization across the border in terms of fashions and styles. As Gregorio Domínguez, leader of Los Misioneros de Chihuahua, said:

We can differentiate people who come to Mexico for a visit from those who live here by the songs they request us to play and by the way they ask us to play songs. For instance, they tell us, "Play this song that is very popular in Dallas, Texas." You see, they are produced first there, and we have not even listened to them, but they demand us to know them. We need to listen to these songs first to be able to play them and to learn them. They are played first there and every-where in the U.S., and we are the last ones to listen to them. We are a little bit behind in music for those reasons. When songs have already been heard a lot over there, they arrive here. The problem is that they ask for them and we sometimes do not know such songs. In Ciudad Juárez, it is very different because musicians from there are able to listen to songs that do not arrive here [Chihuahua]. They have another repertoire. The repertoire changes a lot from there [the border] to here [central Chihuahua].

Regarding the differences between the audiences, Don Leandro Rodríguez told me,

You can immediately differentiate them. Over there [in the United States], the big bands are the most popular. They always ask us for songs sung by those bands. They tell us, "Excuse me, do you know songs sung by Los Tucanes or Conjunto Primavera?" That is, people from the U.S. ask for music played by those bands that record in the U.S.—not the local ones. We can identify the people who come from north of the border by the type of corridos they request. The songs requested are not local; they are played by international bands.

¡Que me toquen el quelite, después el niño perdido...!: Promotion of Conjunto Norteño Musicians

Conjuntos norteños use two major promotional methods. One of them is quite informal: whenever they do a performance, people ask for their business cards or telephone numbers to contact them. The local bands are well known, and clients commonly find musicians through friends, acquaintances, contact addresses, or telephone numbers. Most groups prefer to have a promoter. The promoter is in charge of finding clients for musicians, and he or she gets a commission in return. As Homar explains:

Well, perhaps because I heard them playing in a dance, or in a party, or in a cantina. If I like them, I ask for their basic information. Friends recommend you groups. They would tell you, "This group plays nice; this group is more or less good." Or, thereafter, for instance, in the horse races, there is a group that plays there and you like the way musicians of the conjunto norteño play and ask them for their business cards and thereafter, you hire them. That is at the family, small-party level. At a higher level, they are commercial bands. There are organizations that promote them. For instance, these companies have fifteen or twenty bands and promote them through the radio: "The musical group X can be hired and contacted at this phone number." They have an office where you can hire them. That is the office of the organization that contracts them. In case the group cannot make it for the date you want, the same organization recommends another one. They might tell you, "This group is not available for that date"; to give an example, "The group Los Vendabales is not available, but Alma Norteña is available, and they charge this much." That is the way it works. Normally, the nice groups, the beautiful ones that have already recorded music, are hired for weddings. For a quinceañera it is different. The quinceañeras use conjuntos norteños that are less expensive.

Don Leandro Rodríguez told me that he promotes his conjunto through personal connections:

Well, I do a little bit of everything. For example, for this occasion, I established communication with the mayor of the municipality. And also we talk with people, particularly musicians. We tell them, "I would like you to connect me with this or that person or with your representative." It works like that.

> Little by little, we are progressing. The idea is get-
> ting to know more musicians and the people who
> work in this environment as well as in the radio. We
> have to keep looking.

Promoters are the people who organize the dances and bring famous groups to the city. They are in charge of finding accommodations for the musical groups, arranging local transportation, booking a place for the performance, announcing the dances and concerts through radio and television, and selling the tickets. Promoters talk to the representatives of the famous bands, planning the dances in accordance with arrangements they have with the representatives of the bands. One of the main concerns of the representatives of the band is that they sing within a "route." That is, they try to follow a geographical route that minimizes expenses and does not burden the musicians. Famous bands ask for a minimum guarantee in case not enough people come to the dances. These guarantees can range up to ten thousand dollars.

At dances, famous bands are often alternated with two or three less famous bands. For bands that are still in the early stages of their careers, it is very important to alternate with famous conjuntos in order to get exposure and to have an outlet for their work. These bands earn very little and sometimes even pay the promoters in order to alternate with famous groups. Promoters also serve as representatives of local bands. Some of their duties are to deal with contracts and promotional efforts. Most local bands need a representative to have more connections and therefore more possibilities of finding work. Interestingly enough, there are not many promoters in each city. In fact, most cities have only a single promoter, perhaps because the way they organize dances and make contacts with local bands is based heavily on long-term friendships. New promoters in the same city would have to develop the trust and friendship of the people they work with—not an easy thing to do. Manny Márquez described the role of the promoter in more detail:

> The amount of money promoters charge depends on
> the show they bring, the choreography, and how well
> known the bands are. If the bands are not very well
> known, a high percentage of the profits goes to the

promoter.... The representative of the bands is the
one that promotes the dances. Very often they are the
ones that have their dancing hall; he makes the radio
spots for the dances, the preparations, and the contracts. They talk to the representatives of the bands,
for instance. It is a very risky business because sometimes there are dances with great publicity and people do not go to these dances. Sometimes, the groups
ask for a guarantee and the promoter makes enough
profits just to pay for the guarantee.... Every region
has its own promoter in the U.S. Every year there is
a meeting in Las Vegas, Nevada, where representatives of musical groups, CEOs of major radio stations, and promoters meet.

También las mujeres pueden: Mujeres Who Sing Música Norteña

The presence of female singers is quite relevant to any discussion of
Mexican music, particularly in *música ranchera* and mariachi. In the 1940s
and 1950s, women tended to be included in duets in *carpas*[4] or theaters.
Conjunto norteño musicians have historically played in cantinas and night-
clubs, particularly during the 1960s and 1970s. In those decades the conjunto norteño musicians were more *taloneros* (musicians who pound the
pavement day and night); that is, they were on their feet from cantina to
cantina or restaurant to restaurant, singing. Women could not be taloneras
since this is a very unsafe way of singing for them. Duets were normally
sung by sisters, with all the family traveling with them on their tours.
Their artistic performances were often part of the family tradition. Women
used to sing more "classic" corridos, rancheras, and boleros.

Most conjunto norteños consist entirely of men, although recently
some women have joined them. Women are seriously underrepresented in
almost every aspect of conjunto norteño and música norteña musical
activities. Most female radio executives were quite aware of the unequal
treatment between men and women. In a new trend, female norteña
singers have become more visible, particularly in TV. The performance of
these new singers relies heavily on their bodies, choreography, and clothing that overemphasize their sex markers. It is not a coincidence that the
limited space given to women in this genre is almost limited to many

young models, actresses, and former singers of different genre (such as Pilar Montenegro and Thalía). Older female singers and musicians and artists who do not portray themselves as sex objects are rarely featured.

Female executive directors told me that the radio stations have an important role in shaping the taste of the audience, and those DJs seldom support female conjunto norteño singers. When they do, they tend to support artists who have very good connections with the main companies that produce and distribute CDs—not necessarily the best musicians. Most of the people I talked to could name very few female norteña singers. This situation reflects that women in music, as in most parts of the world, still do not have equal opportunities for paying jobs, careers, and public recognition. The female norteña singers most often mentioned were Prisicila y sus balas de Plata, Dinora, Lupe Castro, Mercedes Castro, Jenni Rivera, (the group "Sparks"), Rosenda Bernal, and Alicia Villarreal y Su Grupo Límite. Most of today's female conjunto norteño singers concentrate mainly on *baladas norteñas, cumbias norteñas,* and *canciones románticas* in *norteño* style.

Con este ritmo, se mueven todos, nadie se puede quedar sentado: Dances with Conjuntos Norteños

Dance is a cultural production influenced by the social, economic, and historical context in which it is produced. Consequently, dance provides a rich opportunity for studying the relationships among the social classes that participate in the dance, the relationships between men and women, and the relationships between humans and nature. We can also learn much about the worldview of the group that performs the dance. According to Dallal (2000, 32), "Dance is communion.... It is older than discursive language. The movements of the body as a vehicle of transmission and communication are older than the words and signs.... Dance always offers possibilities of re-creation and re-invention with immediate capabilities of reproduction."

Dances are ephemeral in some ways, yet perpetual in others. Except in the case of particular rituals or formalized dances, there is no way to rely on written materials to reconstruct a particular performance. On the other hand, dance can leave an indelible impression on the memories of the spectators and performers.

Dance spaces are powerful sites of solidarity (intergenerational, gender, regional, and class), mediation, collectivity, mutuality, restoration, self-empowerment, re-creation, adaptation, and self-centering. In dance spaces, cultural performers are also social performers who act under specific learned rules and adapt those rules to the performer's individual experience. Dance, like other manifestations of culture, is inseparable from the social group that produces it.

To arrive at a complete picture of the dance of música norteña with conjunto norteño, it is important to consider the organizational structure within which the dancers perform, the economic and political circumstances of the actors involved, the protocols of the dance, the meaning of the dancers' clothing, and the social relations between the dancers, the musicians, and the community. The next few sections outline some of the circumstances in which dancers typically perform música norteña.

Virgen Morena ampárame: Religious Events

Religious festivals are celebrated in accordance with the Christian liturgical calendar, the main one being the Semana Santa (Easter). Every town and ranch has its own religious festival. These festivals are often carried out to commemorate patron saints. During the festivities of the patron saint, the community organizes a dance for the town along with a coleadero (a special event in which a group of men throw cows or bulls to the ground by twisting their tails). Every family with a child in school contributes by lending one head of cattle for the coleadero. The money raised at these events is donated to the local school and the church. David Mendoza, who lives in Dumas, Texas, but visits La Garita ranch in the Satevó municipality every Christmas, explained the situation in Satevó:

> [We have] dances often. On December 3 for sure we
> have *fiesta* that is, the day of San Francisco Javier.
> The name of the town is San Francisco Javier Satevó.
> If it is not a family gathering, the dances are impor-
> tant to raise money. The event may be the fund-rais-
> ing activities of the church or the school of the
> town. Every town or ranch has an important date
> related to the saint of the ranch or town. For
> instance, in Satevó, the third of December is the
> most important date for the town because it is the
> date of San Francisco Javier de Satevó. So the money

from that dance goes to the church. In the ranch San
José de Hernández, they celebrate on December 25
of every year. And the money goes to the chapel of
the ranch and to the school. Every year we have a
fiesta. In San Juan Bautista...the fiesta is in July, the
day of San Juan. They also have their coleadero, and
the money goes to the church and to the community. Every coleadero has to have a conjunto, but people do not dance in the coleaderos. The conjunto
sings to make people happy, to motivate them. They
play mostly corridos, boleros, and cumbias. The
coleaderos are really family events. So, most family
members can go to them. But only men "colean"
[twist the tail of the bulls]. Everybody goes, children, the wives, almost all the inhabitants of the
ranch or town go to those festivities.

Most Mexican towns celebrate November 20, the day of the Mexican
Revolution. The holiday itself commemorates the day in 1910 when
Francisco I. Madero denounced President Porfirio Díaz, a dictator who was
in power for over thirty years, and declared himself president of Mexico.
In the towns near Chihuahua City, the day of the Mexican Revolution is
a special civic festival. Primary school children and the local governments
participate in a patriotic parade, and the celebration finishes with a dance
for the town where a conjunto norteño plays.

Cuando pedí tu mano: Weddings and Música Norteña

Weddings are another cultural event where música norteña music is played
and danced. Most people in the community participate directly or indirectly in weddings. Normally, many godparents participate. Most family members of the couple contribute to the payment of the musicians and to
other wedding-related expenses. The dance usually takes place in a facili-
ty that belongs to the community or the municipality, and it is a common
understanding that these facilities are free of charge for weddings and
other community festivities. Ranches without a municipal hall might use a
basketball court or some other place, depending on the facilities available
at each location.

A vaquero showing his horsemanship skills by taking the cow by the tail in a coleadero. Norteño music and corridos are played through the coleadero (1999). Courtesy of Homar Prieto Barrera.

In ranches that are more isolated, the dance takes place in the bride's house. Usually the wedding ceremony, civil and/or religious, takes place at midday. Thereafter, people participate in the wedding banquet. In principle, everybody is welcome to have dinner in the bride's home. However, in reality, the provision of food is more of an event for guests who are closest to the family. Dinner invitations are not sent to guests, since most people know who is close to the new couple and who is not. If there is enough money, the couple hires musicians to play during the banquet for two or three hours.

Women are in charge of taking care of the guests, preparing the food, decorating the house, and preparing the wedding souvenirs. The main, traditional dish at weddings is *chile colorado*, made of pork and red chile. Men are in charge of slaughtering the pig and in some cases the cattle, arranging the seats and tables, receiving the musicians, and overlooking the general behavior of the people. The dance in celebration of the wedding is open to everybody and usually lasts for about five hours. Rosa Mendoza explained how these dances are organized:

[It] depends on the type of event that we are talking about. Let's start with a wedding. A wedding dance organization starts by looking at the number of godfathers available. Regarding the conjunto, the men are the ones who talk to the musicians and make arrangements with them. It is an agreement among men. Whoever is closer to the godparents from the bride's family or the bridegroom's family invites people to be godparents of the wedding. Normally, your mother or aunt helps you to do the *bizcochos* [special cookies for weddings]. The mother of the bride has to organize almost everything.

In the ranches we have this custom that we miss very much in the U.S. Here [in Mexico] everybody can go, eat, and dance. People tend to be more selective during the banquet, people who feel close to the family of the bride or the bridegroom. It depends. . . . The wedding ceremony usually takes place in the afternoon; from there we eat, and then the dance starts at approximately 9 p.m. and lasts about five hours. Normally, the religious ceremony is at midday. It was a custom that small bands played in the afternoon while the people were eating at the bride's home. They used to play there two or three hours and then approximately five hours in the dance. Eight hours in total. Nowadays it is different because the musical groups are more sophisticated and they like to play only in the dance. So, there is usually no live music in the bride's house while people are in the banquet.

Eres mi tierra norteña, India vestida de sol: The Role of Mexican Immigrants in Northern Mexican Weddings

Most weddings and christening events take place during the Christmas season. During Christmas, most family members try to get together in Mexico. Families who live in Mexico are often honored to have their U.S. relatives as godparents or just in attendance at the ceremonies. On the other hand, Mexicans who live in the United States receive what they miss most: the sense of belonging associated with membership in their home communities. Mexican migrants contribute financially to the religious events; their contributions are often substantial. Homar Prieto explained the importance of these migrants in the organization of the festivities:

> The economic matter is very important from the moment you want to get married. Most people sell their cows or save money for a long time. A wedding starts to be planned and organized six or more months in advance. To start with, we are talking about *rancherías* [small towns or communities]. Many people are actually working in the United States. Most people program their holidays for Christmas. And if you are going to get married, it is only logical that you would want your whole family to be reunited. You want your friends to be with you that special date, and also you want them to help you. It is also much easier to reunite your family in December than in any other season of the year because everybody wants to be with their family, in their ranch. So what happens? Everybody who is important is around the area during Christmas.

¡Ay! ¡Cómo me gusta el gusto!: How People Learn to Dance to Música Norteña

Most study participants had learned to dance to música norteña in their families. Their brothers, sisters, mothers, cousins, and friends taught them how to dance. They in turn will teach new generations. The aesthetics and knowledge of dance are transmitted orally and without formal training except for the practice that takes place during formal dances. Most of the respondents from Mexico reported that they often dance with their family members and friends (those who taught them to dance) even though they might prefer to dance with other people.

Because dance is part of the family, ranch, or town communion, it is acceptable and even expected that people will dance with their families and friends. Virginia Archuleta, whose family has been in Colorado since before

Dancing conjunto norteño music in El Sinaloense dance club in Ciudad Juárez (2004). Photo by Selfa Chew.

the Mexico-U.S. war, dances música norteña. She told me that she learned it at home:

> I used to like watching my mom and dad dance; they danced pretty good. I asked my brother to dance with me so that we could practice. I like music and dancing. I grew up watching dances, and I used to say to myself, "When I am a grown-up, I am going to dance."

For Rosa Mendoza, learning how to dance this music was such an organic and natural, embodied knowledge that she does not remember when she learned to dance norteño:

I guess since a very early age. When I was very small.
I saw people dancing, my father....Later, I used to
practice....I really do not know when I started....It
was very natural.

Iliana Hernández told me that it was very important for her to pass this
embodied knowledge to her children:

I taught my son how to dance and how to direct
women properly when dancing. It is important. I
always tell my son that if he does not learn to dance
properly, then nobody will dance with him because
we women like to dance with men that know how to
dance norteña. Norteñas are part and parcel of
dances. He did not dance well at first, but he is getting better. You know some men are always out of
step when they dance. I dance just for the sake of
dancing....I love música norteña, and I do not like
being sitting when the band is playing it. I like to
dance norteña music because it is very lively. When
nobody invites me to dance, I ask my son or nephews
to dance with me.

It is the custom that most young people go to dances with their
friends of the same sex. Usually parents or other family members go to
the dances, too. In many cases, young girls are not allowed to go to dances
unless one of their parents goes with them. Many of the older generation
tend to complain about parents' lack of care in letting their daughters
attend. Young boys do not have the same problem, although the entire
community generally knows who attends the dances. The bodies of young
girls are highly monitored by their parents and the community in general, so their presence in public spaces is limited for fear that the girls will
earn a bad reputation. Women's reputations are very much based on the
extent to which they are capable of controlling their sexual desire and
abiding by community standards of sexual decency. However, it seems that
they make the best of their private (or semiprivate) spaces within the
home to forge a female youth identity within those restrictions. In their

bedrooms, girls experiment with their makeup, try new hairstyles, listen to music, read magazines for girls, size up the boys, and chat. All the same, there is often a very strict protocol for girls' attendance at dances. As Rosa Mendoza told me,

> I used to go to the dances with my girlfriends. What happened was that I lived exactly opposite to the plaza and exactly next to the dance hall of the town. My father was always keeping an eye on me. We always went with friends; you will rarely see a girl going to dance on her own. For some girls, if their dad or mom did not go, they were not allowed to go dancing. It used to be a custom that parents took their *hijas* [female children] to the dance events. When they said, "Let's go," one had to agree and leave the dance when they said so. That has changed, but still you have to ask for permission to attend a dance.

¡Suénele con fé al bailazo!: Characteristics of Good Dancers

The traditional way of dancing norteño music is a hybrid form of dancing that has been strongly influenced by the *paso doble*, the polka, and the schottishe. The paso doble was originally patterned on the movements of matadors during bullfights—particularly the small steps that follow the music. In música norteña, men are the focus of the dance more than in any other popular dance in Mexico. For this reason, men have a clear responsibility to guide their dancing partners. Iliana Hernández told me that women must have be able to follow their partners properly and that

> a good dancer feels the music and is able to transmit this feeling to you. When people are good dancers, you relax and do not concentrate too much. You just enjoy it. Men with confidence can guide you, and also they dance with the rhythm of the music.... They have to feel the music. When [a couple is] dancing together, [the man's] left hand is very important to guide the girls about how to move their feet. They have to watch out not to bump into too

many people. I think that there is more pressure for men to dance better because they take the lead. A good dancer is the one that knows how to direct the dance, that can change speed when it is necessary... that does not step on you... that knows how to do the turns gracefully. A woman has to know how to follow the steps. The música norteña is a happy kind of music, very lively... but you do not dance it too close... not like *la lambada*. In fact, la lambada did not last in Mexico or among Mexicans. People did not dance it much. I think this was so because it was too sensual; couples were too close. *La quebradita* has many steps similar to swing. That was fashionable, but it did not last that long.... I mean as the norteño dance.

Several people told me that the best dancers of música norteña in the state of Chihuahua are people from small towns and ranches. They pointed out that dances are quite important for those communities and that people therefore tend to take dancing seriously and develop stylish steps. In Chihuahua City and Ciudad Juárez, people have more options, and they tend to dance other musical genres as well. This is reflected in the way people from Ciudad Juárez, Chihuahua, dance música norteña—not quite as well as the dancers from smaller communities. However, people from small towns and ranches who migrate to the cities tend to keep the stylish ways of dancing associated with their places of origin. As Domingo, the conjunto norteño musician of Los Misioneros de Chihuahua, told me,

There are differences in the way of dancing in the different regions. Every region has its own dancing style. For instance, in Monterrey, in Torreón, each city has its own dancing style. Sometimes you invite a lady to dance and you cannot follow her properly because she has already her style. In Coyame, Ojinaga, they have another style. They dance like the people who come from the United States, for example. That is because people come and go from the

Moving to norteña
music in El Sinaloense
dance club in Ciudad
Juárez (2004). Photo by
Selfa Chew.

United States in seasons and so they learn the style of
dancing in the United States and bring it here.

Pineda, the DJ from the radio station La Norteñita, agreed with Domingo:

> Here in Chihuahua City, people are a little bit care-
> less in the way they dance música norteña. But in the
> ranches, people grow up with this music. They dance
> in a more stylish way. They are more careful in danc-
> ing it. That is the commonality among the people
> from the ranches. Yes, I can tell the difference. For
> instance, I had to work in a place called Palo Blanco,
> also in a ranch called La Joya, and in Cuauhtémoc,

and yes, you can see the differences. In general, in the ranch people are very good dancers and they take it very seriously; it is not like that in the cities. But then, there are differences between the ranches. It is hard to tell. There are also differences between generations. For instance, *los viejitos* [the old people] do not know how to dance separated from their partners...and *los jovencitos* [the youngsters] know how to dance banda music and other genres that are more mixed.

Mamá no tengo la culpa que a mí me gusten los bailes: Sexuality in the Dance

The sexuality of dance and its potential to excite dancers and often alter states of consciousness has been a topic of much discussion. The inherent sexuality of dance explains the universality of dance as well as the monitoring of dance. Dance, like sexual intercourse, generates a sense of pleasure and relief. In both activities there is courtship, foreplay, arousal, the evocation of erotic images and sentiments, excitement, release, climax, and exhaustion, and there are multiple references to domains of power. Dances for courtship are an outlet for displaying sexual attractiveness and an arena for announcing sexual availability and arranging liaisons. The spaces where dances occur are very much regulated by the roles the community assigns to each sex. In general, people from Chihuahua City and the nearby ranches told me that they felt that the relationships between boyfriends and girlfriends are regulated by the limited amount of time they are allowed to spend together and by the days on which boys can visit their girlfriends. Usually the boyfriend is allowed to visit his girlfriend only on Sundays and just for a couple of hours. The couple must be in public to demonstrate to the community that they are behaving respectfully. Under those circumstances, dances are one of the few opportunities young couples have to see each other and talk to each other in physical proximity. Very often, dances are taken as the opportunity for couples to "escape" and to start living together as husband and wife. As Homar Prieto said,

> The events where you can meet girls are really very
> few in the ranches. Dances are in reality the only

The aesthetics of norteño identity is based mainly on the way men dress as vaqueros, as in this couple, who are dancing to norteño music (2004). Photo by Selfa Chew.

occasions for that. It is really there where you can meet them or if you already know someone you like, then what are you waiting for? Well, you want to go to the dances where you know you will see her again if you want to have a small chat or socialize more with the girls... or with the person you more or less know that might be your partner. It is in the dances where people become boyfriend and girlfriend, where you meet your future wife. Here, it is common knowledge that if you and your girlfriend spend an evening together, usually after a dance event, that means you are married; that is a "law". So, many people wait to meet in the dances and "get married." That is, couples plan to wait for a dance event and "escape" from the dance, spend the night together, and live as a married couple for life. This happens often. Actually, it is a way of "getting married" when the couple does not have many economic resources; then he takes her with him. Or if you go to visit your girlfriend and you want to "get married" you place her inside the truck and do not come back until the third day. Then it is a fact that you will have to marry her. The thing is that according to the tradition, it is not well taken if your boyfriend goes and visits you every single day. He has to see you every Sunday, for a couple of hours and in front of everybody. You have to chat in a place where everybody can see you. One of the few occasions where you can chat comfortably is in the dances.

I asked Rosa Mendoza why dances are important on the ranches, and she told me that dances are almost the only way of meeting people:

> It is when you can see your boyfriend. If you do not have a boyfriend, you can see the boys. You see, the ranches are very far one from the other. So, if your boyfriend is from another ranch, the only chance to see him is at the dances. In the ranches, it is very common that the boyfriends and girlfriends meet at the river. It was common for girls to say, "The ones from San Pedro ranch are in the river." In this town we have a plaza; we did not go to the river. People on the ranches talk in the river.
>
> You are allowed to see your boyfriend every Sunday. It is not acceptable to see your boyfriend every day. In the dances you can take the opportunity to talk in a comfortable manner with him. If parents are at the dance, you cannot talk comfortably with a boyfriend, so then you pretend that you are going to the restroom. Not long ago you were not

allowed to bring your boyfriend home to visit you.
Our family used to say that that was very awkward
and embarrassing for the family. Things have changed
a little bit. . . . Frequently the couples arrange to start
living together after the dance. People knew when
[the] couple was going to live together when they do
not come back. The friends notice that. The following day the parents of the boyfriend have to go to
the house of the girlfriend to notify [the girlfriend's
parents] and to make the engagement more official.

En los bailes me divierto: tandas [Batches]

In the ranches and towns of Chihuahua, people dance by tandas (batch-
es) of music. Each tanda is made of approximately fifteen songs, with a
recess of fifteen minutes between each tanda. Dancers use the recesses to
clean up, have a drink, get fresh air, and prepare to choose their next dancing partner. Every dance has five tandas. Couples dance the entire tanda
with the same person unless a serious problem arises. If the couple like
each other, they agree that the girl won't accept an invitation to dance with
another person until the next tanda.

Porque tus padres están celosos y tienen miedo que yo te quiera: Legends Related to Dances

As a means of social control over the sexuality of young girls, many communities in northern Mexico have legends designed to keep women from
engaging in sexual activities before marriage. These same legends help
keep them safe and discourage them from trusting men too readily.
Dancing has been seen as a dangerous sexual expression for women.
According to Dallal (2000, 293), "The couples perceive the rhythm as a
coupling necessity. The bodies perceive each other simultaneously, they
integrate, adhere with the rhythm. . . . This identification is produced in an
instinctive manner that does not rely on discursive language."

The most well-known legend is about young women going to a dance
without the permission of their parents. These women are enticed by a
man who, according to the legend, is the devil. The devil disguises himself as a handsome man—a great dancer who takes the girls out of the
dance halls to make love to them. When the devil is leaving the dance

A man asking a lady to dance norteña music in El Sinaloense dance club in Ciudad Juárez (2004). Photo by Selfa Chew.

hall, he goes through a metamorphosis and his true personality is shown little by little. Of course this implies that every girl must be constantly on watch for signs that her male companion is the devil. (You'd be surprised how much the devil gets around.) If any such signs are found, the young girl must pray that he will leave her alone—and if she doesn't pray, the devil will take her with him. There are many versions of this story, and several study participants noted that girls do not believe in such legends anymore. Still, these stories are kept as part of the oral tradition in ranching towns. Almost all the musicians I interviewed knew about this legend, and they told me several versions. Domingo, from Los Misioneros de Chihuahua, said:

> There are many legends about dances. I think that
> they exist to prevent girls from trusting not-so-good
> men.... When I was a child, I was told that the devil
> appeared in a dance; people saw him with rooster
> feet. That happened before I was born.

Don Leandro Rodríguez had another version:

> I heard on one occasion that in Delicias, a young
> woman was dancing with a very handsome and well-
> dressed man. He was very charming. But she went to
> dance without the permission of her parents, and
> before she knew it, she saw that his feet had the
> shape of hooves and that he had the tail of the devil.
> She managed to say something to make him disap-
> pear. But nowadays young people do not get scared.
> That was a long time ago.

Vestida de color de rosa como flor hermosa: Clothing

Dressing to dance is an important element of the performance of música
norteña. Clothes are a way to preserve an identity that connects individuals to a meaningful heritage. Part of the creation and co-creation of clothing involves a recognition of the need to define the community.

The crystallization of symbols of collective identity and the reconstruction of tradition seem to be most important and most fully articu-
lated when the community has experienced a set of shared conflicts. One
of the distinctive features of transnational communities that follow the
route of central Chihuahua, crossing El Paso, Texas, then New Mexico and
northern Texas, is that they are part of the vaquero culture of this area,
which originated with the introduction of livestock by Don Juan de Oñate
in the sixteenth century. According to Herrera-Sobek (1993, 3), "The
Mexican and Texas vaquero who happens to be the cultural ancestor of the
Anglo-American cowboy is hardly acknowledged in textbooks discussing
cowboy lore and cowboy history.... Most of the things the cowboy was
wearing, using and even speaking were Mexican."

The cowboy (vaquero) culture is similar to that of the gauchos in
Argentina in that both cultures were formed in Spanish colonies and both
are based on open-range ranching in areas of abundant open grassland,
enough water for stock but not enough for crops, and abundant wild cattle that can be controlled only by men on horseback. The English colonists
who arrived from the northeastern United States were unfamiliar with handling wild and domestic cattle in open spaces and lacked the skills of horsemanship, roping, and riding that Mexican cowboys created and commanded.

Men getting ready to ask women to dance norteña music in El Sinaloense dance club in Ciudad Juárez (2004). Photo by Selfa Chew.

When English colonists arrived at the American frontier between 1820 and 1836, they learned and adapted from the Mexican cowboys the art of handling cattle on horseback, using their ranching techniques and equipment. The origin of the Anglo-American cowboy jargon has its roots mainly in Spanish and Mexican ranching culture.[6]

By the 1870s, the vaquero's saddle, chaps, bandana, hat, branding iron, lasso, spurs, and even the elements of his expertise were widespread in the southwestern United States, and the Mexican identity of the vaquero became simply "Texan." The vaquero was robbed of his prominent place in the history of the Southwest. There are many important differences between the vaqueros and the cowboys in terms of their philosophy and everyday life.[7] Regardless of whether U.S. mainstream society acknowledges that the cowboy outfit comes from Mexico, however, the participants in this study never doubted that the origin of the cowboy outfit was Mexican. In fact, they always referred to it as "typical Mexican."

The basic outfit for cowboys consists of two items that have endured over five centuries due to their functionality, safety, and style: boots and a

Vaqueros outside a dance hall in El Paso, Texas (2001). Photo by Selfa Chew.

cowboy hat or *sombrero vaquero*, which in Spanish means "shade maker for cowboys." The cowboy hat and the leather boots are designed for use by people who spend much time working under the sun on horseback. The cowboy outfit must be very tight because the cowboy's work, such as swinging and throwing the rope and making a catch, has to be done on horseback, and the horse itself is a very unstable platform that is constantly running, turning, stopping, stumbling, or bucking. The sombrero vaquero must stay on the vaquero's head regardless of weather conditions and intensity of movement, and it must be of such good quality and design that the brim does not interfere with the cowboy's vision.

Las botas vaqueras (the cowboy boots) are made to leave the stirrup when the vaquero leaves the saddle and to protect his ankles and legs. Cowboy boots first arrived on the continent as high bucket leather boots secured above the knee with leather thongs or tassels. The pointy-toed,

Sombreros vaqueros, or Tejanas, on display in Ciudad Juárez (2005). Photograph by Selfa Chew.

high-heeled, tight-fitting boots have been perfected from the original boots of the Moors in Andalusia. The jeans and shirts have to fit snugly so that the cowboy has free use of his arms and legs. The Spanish skill in manufacturing leather goods and making use of leather from both wild and domesticated animals proved to be very useful in the New World, since leather is superior to other natural materials in its water and wind resistance.

The cultural significance of the vaquero outfit emphasizes the idealization of the northern part of Mexico—of the rural communities to which many Mexican migrants are no longer connected. Clothes for dancing also express the cultural parameters for the behavior of men and women. In the case of música norteña, it seems that respectability in the way dancers dress is a fundamental element of both genders' reputation. The way vaqueros dress is almost a celebration of men's sensuality. The tight jeans emphasize the legs and rear, and the shirt emphasizes the shoulders. Together, the outfit and attitude make them look proud, self-confident, defiant, aggressive, and often arrogant.

For women, however, clothing incorporates a range of contradictory values: modesty and flamboyance, concealment and exposure,

Vaquerito (2004).
Photograph by Selfa Chew.

respectability, domesticity, and controlled sexuality. These elements of
dress are even more relevant if we consider that dances are the meeting
places for most couples and potential spouses. Very often, the woman's
way of dressing is the main criterion by which her marriageability is
assessed. Young men, too, must look respectable, but in different ways.
Men must give the impression that they are healthy and wealthy, hard
workers who can provide for a family. Some of the men's accessories for
dancing are therefore related to their work, or at least to the historical

work of the *vaqueros*. In the case of música norteña, most men wear a cowboy hat and bandana and carry a horse whip.

Pantalón vaquero, botas y sombrero, es como me visto yo: Outfit to Dance

The typical outfit for men to dance música norteña in is the outfit of the vaquero. The cowboy outfit helps to forge a regional identity within Mexico—that is, the identity of *norteños* (northerners) and also of rural Mexico. In northern Mexico, the cowboy identity is not necessarily associated with the poor or working class as it is in other regions of Mexico. The U.S. mainstream perception of the cowboy outfit used by Mexicans is strongly associated with rural Mexican migrants, with uneducated people, and with the working class.

The basic outfit for men includes cowboy boots, a *tejana* (felted Stetson hat), a white shirt, button-fly jeans, a fringed leather vest, and a belt (often gold) with the wearer's name on it. The outfit for men can be very expensive. (The cowboy boots alone can cost up to eight hundred dollars.) The shape of the boots has an influence on the posture of the dancers and the steps they can perform. For accessories, men often use a *cuarta* (a horse whip), a long wallet, and a bandana.

Women's outfits tend to be less expensive than men's. In Chihuahua State, perhaps with the exception of Ciudad Juárez, women normally dress in evening dresses and high heels. Young women may dress in tight-fitting jeans or western skirts, belts with big buckles, tight tops, and cowboy boots. In general, women make themselves attractive by using clothes that emphasize their breasts, waist, and hips. The tension between sensuality and restraint expected in women creates a powerful ambiguity in the dances.

According to some people, men often try to express their economic status through their cowboy clothing. Nicolás Hernández, who is from Chihuahua but lives in Albuquerque, explains that

> people wear expensive clothes to show off, to look
> elegant. I have, like, ten cowboy hats. I think we men
> put more money into the clothes because the clothes
> for us are more expensive. I mean, the buckles cost a
> lot. The ones you saw there can cost two hundred

dollars or even more. Sometimes, you see boys with
leather jackets that can cost about a thousand dollars. Here [in Albuquerque] there are many businesses that have made themselves rich selling clothes to
Mexicans. There are various reasons. One thing is
that...how should I explain it?...I know people
who in their towns or ranches were very poor and
using these clothes is a way of expressing that they
are better off. On the other hand, women do not have
something typical. The women from Chihuahua dress
very nicely, but when they come here, they do not
take much care of themselves.

In general, it seems to me that men's dancing clothes are more highly valued and more important than women's. People spoke very eloquently about the accessories of men's outfits, the different types of heels for
cowboy boots, the colors of the shirts, and the different styles of hats.
These items tend to be associated with masculinity, hard work, rural identity, northern identity, or simply a desire to be seen as "Mexican."
Likewise, many of the women explained in great detail how much they
like to see men dressed in the vaquero outfit. For instance, Iliana
Hernández proclaimed,

I like their cowboy hats. They make them look mag-
nificent. Among the cowboys you see their buckles
that are very flashy. I like their leather belts with their
names engraved on them. There are many types of
heels for their cowboy boots: with *tacón cubano* [short
heels], high heels.... The color of the boot is important so that it combines with their clothes. Clothes for
men in the U.S. tend to be very flashy. To be honest,
I like men with their cowboy clothes more sober,
restrained, with more clear colors, not strong ones.
Even the bandana is important, as well as their wallet. A man who is truly a cowboy will have a long
and big wallet. The bandana on their neck is more
from the borderlands.

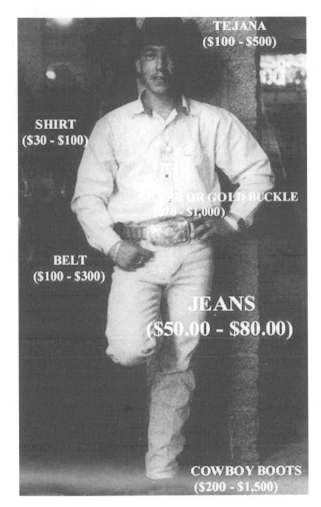

TEJANA
($100 - $500)

SHIRT
($30 - $100)

SILVER OR GOLD BUCKLE
($70 - $1,000)

BELT
($100 - $300)

JEANS
($50.00 - $80.00)

COWBOY BOOTS
($200 - $1,500)

A vaquero proudly posing in his outfit. Men's outfits define the norteño style and can often be quite expensive (2001). Photo by Selfa Chew.

Many people told me that their way of dressing for dances depends on the type of dance and the time of the dance. In the dances that take place in the afternoon (the *tardeadas*), young people can dress very informally. The tardeadas are attended chiefly by young people and are usually perceived as safer, healthier, and more desirable for young people, who might want to gather with less supervision from their parents. These perceptions are closely tied to the time of day, since the tardeadas take place during daylight hours. The dances that take place at night tend to be more formal. Because of that, attendees dress more elegantly. Some migrants pointed out that such a distinction is less clear in the United States. In general, they perceived mainstream youngsters in the United States as having a more casual attitude toward proper dress for dancing. As Ileana Hernández said,

> The way women dress has changed a lot; particularly if it is not a formal dance, we tend to have more liberties. Before, the fashion for us was more static. Like in Parral, I always went to the dances that took place in the dance halls. There you had to dress really elegant. In Mexico, if you do not have a proper evening dress or at least a skirt, they do not allow you to enter into the dance halls, I mean the formal ones. In Parral, men used to wear their suits. But if it was a tardeada [a dance that takes place in the afternoon or while the sun is still up, usually from 4 p.m. to 8 p.m.], then we had more liberty. Likewise, during the *tertulia* [a dance that normally takes from 8 p.m. to 10 p.m.] it was also a little bit informal. The *bailes de noche* [normally from 10 p.m. to 2 or 4 a.m.] were more elegant. Here in the United States people are more careless in the way they dress in dances. You can even go in flip-flops and nobody will tell you anything. I know that things have also changed in Mexico, but not that much; here [in the United States], *les vale* [they do not care]. I do not know if this is related to the fact that here they value individual freedom and everybody can behave as he/she pleases.

Mexican migrants frequently told me about the differences in the organization of dances in the United States and Mexico. At family events such as weddings, christenings, or quinceañeras, the dances are basically the same, with the same conjuntos norteños and the same type of food. The only real difference is that in the United States, the participants must rent the dance hall. Public dances are another matter, however. In the United States, there are no community dances in honor of the various

Boys with the typical
vaquero outfit chat-
ting after a norteño
music concert in El
Paso, Texas (2001).
Photo by Selfa Chew.

saints, and some of the major celebration days in migrants' hometowns go
unnoticed north of the border. Likewise, commercially sponsored dances
such as those organized by the promoters of conjuntos norteños are a
new concept for some Mexican emigrants. Armando Chavira, a Texas resident with family in Chihuahua, sees many differences in the way people
organize dances in the United States and in Mexico:

> People here [in Mexico] are very different. People
> here are more kind and polite. Here people know
> each other better, and they offer you food and every-
> thing. They make you feel at home...and there [in
> the United States], no, that is not the case. One has to

buy everything. Here people are more polite, they welcome you.... Here it is the custom to offer food to musicians and over there, no. Over there [in the U.S.], if you want to eat, you buy your stuff.... Here musicians have to eat first and then they play and also in their breaks they have to eat. Musicians know that is the custom. In the United States people pay to dance; there is not a particular festivity, except for weddings and christenings. But there is not so much in the celebration of a saint or for getting funding for the schools; no, that does not exist. The dances are for the bands to make money and for us to meet girls. In the U.S. young people go to dance every weekend. Here dances are more special; they are not so frequent. But it is okay because one listens to Mexican music. Regarding the weddings, here, in the ranches, they bake many bizcochos and the banquet is in the home of the bride. Over there, people there do not bake many bizcochos because it takes a lot of time...and people rent a dance hall and the wedding banquet and dance is held there. But the mass, the dance, and the type of food is exactly the same. Another difference is the frequency of dances In the U.S. there are dances almost every weekend. Not here.

The differences between events in Mexico and the United States can be seen in Amarillo and Dumas, Texas, where the immigrant community from Chihuahua State organizes coleaderos and horse races. People who participate in such events in the towns and ranches near Chihuahua City cross the border northward and southward in order to attend these events, just as conjunto norteño musicians do. However, these events cannot be exactly the same due to differences in the laws and regulations of the two countries. Armando Chavira discussed some of the differences:

Regarding the differences between coleaderos organized there [in the United States] and those organized here [in Mexico], here people arrive to the coleaderos

Men in the bar of a
conjunto norteño
dance hall watching
people dance (2004).
Photo by Selfa Chew.

walking, on their horses or their trucks. Very much
like the old-fashioned way. Over there, people always
arrive in their trucks, never on horses. Everything is
very well organized, regarding time...and also the
racetracks are quite well done, quite clean. They have
to be perfect, you see?...And here, no, everything
can be organized from one day to the next without
too much preparation...just like that...

Another thing is that we do not feel the same
freedom that we have here, you know, in the way
we behave....In Mexico if people want, they can
sing, scream, run, and over there, no. One cannot do

A norteño boy watching a rodeo with his sister in El Paso, Texas (2001). Photo by Selfa Chew.

anything because they send us *la ley* [the police], you see? And here, that is not a problem, we are not a threat, they know our limits, they know how to handle the situation. Over there, singing a little song or screaming means an excuse to put us in jail, and the situation would be worse if we have guns or if we want to have a beer.

Horse races are quite important among vaqueros, and they take place on both sides of the border. Homar Prieto explained the way horse races are organized in Chihuahua City and other towns of Chihuahua State:

The horses...are grouped in a *cuadra* [group]. The distance is in *varas*; a *vara* is eighty-four centimeters.

The varas vary from race to race, depending on the kind of horses that are run long distance. Those are horses that because of their breed, they can run long distance. There are different ways of betting. One is by a *faja*; that is when the whole rear of the horse is ahead of the other horse's rear. There is another way that is called *de pico a cola*, which is when the entire horse, including the tail, is ahead of the other horse. Another is *de a pico* [beak or mouth], which is when the mouth of the horse is ahead of the other horse.

There is a lot of money involved in the horse races.... Sometimes one horse race is about 250,000 U.S. dollars. The way you do it is that you get together with friends, just to have fun. We agree beforehand how much we are going to pay. It is really a very expensive pastime. There are *corredores*; they are the ones who give you a ticket and tell you, "There is a man who is betting on X horse, no?" and he asks you, "How much do you want to bet on him?" If you lose, he comes and asks you for the money and charges you a percentage, which is 10 percent, which goes to the company that organizes the horse races. They do not lose a thing because they do not risk anything. The *corredor* is paid for finding people to be 5 percent of the money.

You do not see many corredores because there is a *sindicato* [union] of corredores. Everything is controlled here. It is a *sindicato de corredores de apuesta*, where there are only fourteen corredores. Their job is to find people to bet. If there is a cockfight or any other race, you have to notify them so that they attend the event. They are the only ones who are allowed to be there....

There is a lottery game going on between the horse races. There are girls who sell fourteen numbers and each number costs twenty U.S. dollars. If you win, you get two hundred dollars, no? What does

Vaqueros watching two horses about to finish a horse race in Satevó, Chihuahua (1999).
Courtesy of Homar Prieto Barrera.

that mean?—that there are four ticket numbers that
are not given to the winner. Well, that money is given
to the company who organizes it. The company also
rents stalls for people to sell food and beer here. The
way the racehorses operate is like this: there are lanes,
and the owners of the lanes are the same owners of
this establishment. You buy that from the government
of the state of Chihuahua. You also have to get a
permit from the federal, state, and municipal authorities. If you do not have a permit, they do not give
you the one on the next level. It is a sequence to all
levels of authorities. The federal government charges
you one thousand pesos [one hundred U.S. dollars]
per race, the state 16,500 pesos [165 dollars], and the
municipal charge varies.

The government comes to the races and checks
everything before the races start. There are times
when there are fifteen races per day and others that
there are ten or twelve per day. It varies according to
what a cuadra decides to put together for a specific
day. Usually the races are set within a month or two

Vaqueros betting near mesquites before the horse race starts in Satevó, Chihuahua (1999). Courtesy of Homar Prieto Barrera.

of anticipation. Then what one does is to talk to the owner of a *carril* [lane], and you say, "Listen, write my name down for the racehorse on X day," and so other people do that as well. There is a moment when the program is full. For example, the program is full for next Sunday, and the permit from the Ministry of Interior should be ready fifteen days before the race. Sometimes people from other towns come to Chihuahua City or the other way around. Mainly from Aldama, Parral, and Jiménez.

At dances, Mexican migrants encounter countrymen and country-women from other parts of Mexico. When conjunto norteños play, the Mexicans who attend are often from the north. Dancers from other places also attend, however, often to meet their compatriots and to lessen the sense of isolation and marginalization that many of them feel. In some parts of the United States, such as Dumas, Texas, most Mexican immigrants are from the north—Chihuahua State in particular—so the dances reflect this composition of the population. These encounters among people from different regions of Mexico have resulted in the cross-fertilization of cultural expressions.

Madrinas (godmothers of the horse race event) holding the trophy of the winning team, team members posing with the winning horse, and people who supported them (2000). Courtesy of Homar Prieto Barrera.

Vaqueros waiting for a horse race to start in Chihuahua City (2002). Photo by the author.

Members of the winning team of a horse race posing with their horse in Satevó, Chihuahua (2000). Courtesy of Homar Prieto Barrera.

No pude cruzar la raya, se me atravezó el Río Bravo:
Some Differences between New and Old Mexican Music:
The Conjunto Norteño

Most Mexican immigrants and some New Mexicans perceive New Mexican music (a distinctive genre) as more sad and nostalgic than the conjunto norteño music played by Mexicans. Even if the lyrics and the musical notes are the same, they tend to sound sadder when performed by New Mexican bands. There are other differences as well. For example, typical New Mexican bands use the keyboard rather than the accordion, and New Mexican Spanish pronunciation is part of the identity of many New Mexican songs. Al Hurricane, the godfather of New Mexican music, told me some of the main differences between New Mexican music and conjunto norteño music:

> In New Mexico, the rhythm is more calm, more sad, more slow. The songs are played more slowly. The voice is lower and the rhythm is slower than that of música norteña, more *pausadito* [slow]. That is in New Mexico, because Texans who are Mexicans also

have a more lively music. In New Mexico our songs
are more sad....In Mexico they sing more emphati-
cally, with more *ganas* [passion]. Mexicans are more
dramatic...New Mexicans are sad. Even if these
songs are made to be happy, we make them sad. In
Mexico "música norteña" music means that it is from
the north of Mexico, but here [in New Mexico] it
means that it is from the north of New Mexico,
which is played more with guitars. We must not con-
fuse the two. The Mexican and the New Mexican
music performed by us [Mexicans or Mexican
Americans] is basically the same music but with different instruments. In New Mexico, we do not vibrate
the voice as high as the mariachis from Mexico do.
Let's see....On one extreme you have the mariachi,
on the other extreme, you have the norteño music
and we New Mexicans are in the middle in terms of
pitch. We sing mariachi and norteño with orchestra.
The songs are the same with different accompani-
ments. For example, Los Tigres del Norte do everything with accordion and bajo. The singers of Los
Tigres del Norte have a very high, vibrant and strong
voice. I perform these songs with different musical
arrangements. I use the keyboard. The conjunto
norteño has to have a guitar and a bass. But it is the
same, the same language. Sometimes the words are
not pronounced the same and sometimes we mix
Spanish with English.

Musicians of música norteña are cultural and social actors who re-cre-
ate and co-create the communities for which they perform. At least in
some sense, all musicians are part of the communities for which they
play, and so the interaction between musicians and their audiences tends
to be dialogical. Both elements are in a continuous intimate conversation—when dancers make requests for songs, when musicians send *dedicatorias* and greetings, and when they share the same rural, working-class
(migrant) identity.

Musicians' knowledge is part of the oral tradition that is enriched and consolidated during their transnational performances. The voices of norteño musicians, just like particular accents and regional idioms, seem to evoke the rural life of their homeland as well as the desires, dreams, and fantasies of people from rural northern Mexico. Their voices also reconfigure the spaces inhabited by Mexicans in the United States and in Mexico, in rural areas and in cities. One of the voices that, according to the musicians and DJs I talked to, evokes and reflects the aesthetic values of central Chihuahua is the voice of Antonio (Tony) Meléndez, vocalist of Conjunto Primavera. In the early stages Conjunto Primavera recorded classic corridos; its popularity started when their music mellowed and became more romantic. Their music has achieved an artistic and commercial peak in the last four years and has received important nominations for their commercial success. This conjunto, together with groups such as Los Tigres del Norte, Los Tucanes de Tijuana, and Conjunto Primavera, is now the staple of major dances that take place on both sides of this region. Although this conjunto was created in the border town of Ojinaga, Chihuahua, Tony Meléndez is from Ejido El Mendoceño in Satevó, Chihuahua.

Dancers are also an important part of the dynamics of the musical production and performance that in some senses reflect social norms and in others push the boundaries of such norms. According to Dallal (2000, 239), "In general, there is no dance without militancy. This process is as old as the myth, the linguistic code, the rites and religion. Once they are ready to perform certain dances, the young people from the community will be the owners of the choreographic secret received by the eldest and those youngsters in turn will transmit it to the new generations." The música norteña dance is taught informally; it is part of the embodied knowledge of the community in which the old generation teaches the new ones. Most participants learned to dance because their parents taught them and they dance with them at home and in public places. In many senses the private places where people learn to dance are not so different from the public ones. There seems to be a coherent continuum in which everyday movements express people's ideas, feelings, sensations, and views of the world. Such continuum is developed in people's specific social contexts and reflected in the way people move their bodies. In dances that are performed in the community, the body's dancistic movements reflect body movements that are

A norteña teenage couple
outside a dance hall in
El Paso, Texas (2001).
Photo by Selfa Chew.

carried out in people's everyday lives. The steps of música norteña
dance are a part of the process of elaboration through which the dance
is a stereotyped act of the movements and gestures that are carried out
in the everyday life of the community.

Cultural expressions are not isolated or individual phenomena independent of the social groups from which they arose. In fact, they are an
important part of the struggles for contested meanings among social
classes. In Mexico, the hegemonic culture is of predominantly European
origin and has achieved the most fully dominant status in south and central Mexico. In the United States, the hegemonic dance expressions are

chiefly European. In this context, norteño music can be seen as a subaltern culture with different forms of symbolic presentation. It incorporates certain elements of the hegemonic model but also represents a new aesthetic consistent with the values and traditions of those who have shaped its development. As illustrated in this chapter, Mexican immigrants seem to have gained control over their own artistic performances, especially in the context of live concerts and events. This control is based on friendship and informal networks. Norteño musical culture creates its own spaces of social recreation that serve as sites of collectivity and mutuality; of conflict, resentment, and all of the feelings that humans are capable of experiencing, positive and negative. In these spaces, individual coexistences and everyday experiences link people with similar backgrounds into a community. This might explain why norteño dance takes a symbolic dimension for people because they reflect their everyday life in their homeland. The symbolic dimension of the norteño dances is particularly important when dances are taken by migrants in new cultural contexts because dances are a way in which migrants can resonate and reconstruct their past in their present circumstances and therefore project or envision their future in the new cultural contexts they inhabit.

Transnational migrants from central Chihuahua, New Mexico, and northern Texas have created a network of mobility, both permanent and temporary, that crisscrosses the Rio Bravo/Rio Grande. These same migrants have persisted in maintaining their social and economic networks despite the many hardships they have endured. Their communities, linked by a common vaquero heritage, continue to weave transnational linkages wherever there is a persistent interaction of goods, capital, workers, and consumers. Workers and consumers are people, of course, and they carry with them a wide assortment of cultural expressions, including the música norteña, the conjunto norteño, corridos, *carrera de caballos* (race horse), quinceañeras, weddings, and other celebrations.

Conjuntos norteño musicians, promoters, writers of corridos, migrants who listen to corridos, and dancers of this genre are all drawn predominantly from the working classes of Mexico and the United States. They have all learned to be creators of cultural expressions of joy and resistance. Inheriting the cultural capital that was entrusted to

Girls after a norteña
music concert in El
Paso, Texas (2001).
Photo by Selfa Chew.

them by their families and communities, they, in turn, will pass it down
to subsequent generations. The cultural capital embodied in the corridos
and in música norteña music more generally has been treated in the
most delicate and respectful way by most of people involved in preserving it. One long-term strategy for preserving this cultural capital is to
keep it always within reach of the individuals and communities that dis-
seminate, enjoy, and inspire it.

Allá hay amor en la gente: Romanticization of Mexico

The Mexican homeland is highly romanticized in the narratives of the
corridos and in the remembrances of those who participated in this
study. The corridos reinforce the image of the idyllic rural life, an image
that helps many migrants cope with their everyday hardships while
allowing them to reconstruct and dignify their identity as migrants.
Many of the corridos express the migrants' desires to return to their

homeland, where they can spend their hard-earned money and appreciate the social and cultural advantages of their country of origin. The importance of the homeland can be seen most clearly in the return visits of expatriate Mexicans every Christmas season. Although these migrants know that their economic prospects are much better in the United States than in Mexico, their visits to their hometowns play a significant part in the re-creation of the idyllic rural life—not least because their families in Mexico look forward to their arrival. Just as many migrants feel incomplete when working in the United States, the families they leave behind may feel incomplete as long as their husbands, wives, and brothers are elsewhere. Family gatherings often provide a temporary sense of completion or respite. For this reason, most weddings and christening events take place during the Christmas season, the time of year when community members know that their expatriate friends and family members will be able to join them.

Family and community fiestas are only one expression, although a very important one, of solidarity and communion among people. Working-class people rely on other members of the family and the community to fulfill the vacuum created by the economic and political systems of Mexico and the United States. Self-reliance is a survival strategy for most migrant communities, a consequence of their political, economic, and social abandonment by the elites of both countries. One consequence of this self-reliance is a degree of control over who can or cannot be part of the community.

For outsiders, performances of conjuntos norteños at family and community events may not seem accessible or open. After all, these performances take place in the most intimate and secure places for immigrants—in the home of a family hosting a fiesta, for example, or in a community dance hall where people feel safe and *a gusto* (at ease). Immigrant communities maintain control over such events largely through the informal but reliable means of organizing such gatherings through personal contact and other high-context methods of communication.

Performances of corridos by conjuntos norteños often bring forth a sense of communion, creating a place where migrants gain the support they need to make sense of their positive and negative experiences. These performances incorporate many of the complexities and

A young couple and a
sister getting into a
norteño music concert in
El Paso, Texas (2001).
Photo by Selfa Chew.

contradictions of the migrant experience—an experience that often
includes violence and disruption as well as celebration and conviviality.

Chapter Five

De paisano a paisano:
NEGOTIATIONS AND RESISTANCE BETWEEN
MIGRANTS AND CULTURAL INDUSTRIES

> White folks who do not see black pain, never really understand
> the complexity of black pleasure.
> — bell hooks, *Black Looks: Race and Representation*, 1995

> South Americans and Caribbeans are experiencing the same problems we
> Mexicans have in the United States, but they are experiencing them in other
> parts of the world....This means that we not only sing for *la raza* [Mexicans and/
> or Mexican descendents]...so our songs are also meaningful to them.
> — Jorge Hernández, leader of Los Tigres del Norte, 2001

In December 2000, I visited a friend in El Torreón, in Satevó. Graciela explained to me that she had been saving money for over a year to buy stereo equipment just to enjoy Los Tigres del Norte songs. In the border region and elsewhere, people make references to Los Tigres del Norte and their songs in their everyday conversations. They talk about the great admiration and respect they have for Los Tigres del Norte, particularly because Los Tigres are perceived as voicing the experience of these transnational communities. Their corridos are fundamental in the understanding of one of the most important migration waves of Latin Americans in the 1980s. I myself was truly excited and nervous just to think about getting close to them to ask for an interview. At the time I was carrying out my fieldwork, their album *De paisano a paisano* [From a Countryman to a Countryman] was very popular. In fact, the album was nominated for the 2001 Latin Grammy Award for Best Norteño Album and Best Regional Mexican Album. About four of the songs strongly resemble corridos and may be regarded as corrido-canción.

The word *paisano* (countryman) is quite powerful in Mexico, and it is often associated with *el terruño* (the homeland), the attachment and love people have for their native landscape. It is used as a way of creating an intimate bond similar to a brotherhood when one is abroad. The corrido-canción "De paisano a paisano," by Enrique Valencia, is about an undocumented migrant who is talking with another about the injustices they have experienced and his plans to be buried in their native land:

> He pasado la vida explorando otras tierras para darle a mis hijos un mañana mejor...de paisano a paisano, del hermano al hermano, por querer trabajar, nos han hecho la guerra patrullando fronteras, no nos pueden domar...de paisano a paisano del hermano al hermano, es de hombres llorar. Como duele la patria cuando llora mi raza, llanto internacional." [I have been spending my life exploring other lands to give a better future to my children...from a countryman to a countryman, from a brother to a brother, they have declared war on us for wanting to work, they are patrolling the borders, but they cannot tame us...from a countryman to a countryman, from a brother to a brother, it is okay for men to cry. How much the nation hurts when my people cry; this is an international cry.]

The cover of the *De paisano a paisano* album has a mural called *La pared que habla, canta y grita* [The Wall That Speaks, Sings, and Screams]. The mural was painted by Paul Botello and was dedicated and installed at Rubén Salazar Park in East Los Angeles.[1] The main sponsors of the mural were Fonovisa and the Los Tigres de Norte Foundation. The cover of the

CD has a comprehensive and lengthy explanation of the mural written by
the painter:

> The mural starts with the conjunto norteño Los
> Tigres de Norte, the intermediaries between the
> urban realities of the streets and a world where their
> lyrics and music are transformed in images of social
> surrealisms.... There are drawings of men and
> women who have been heroes and who have fought
> for a change and always against injustice: John F.
> Kennedy, César Chávez, Martin Luther King Jr.,
> Benito Juárez, Miguel Hidalgo, Pancho Villa, Sor
> Juana Inés de la Cruz, Doña Josefa Ortíz de
> Domínguez.... The family in front is being lead by
> the matriarch, who is holding her granddaughter's
> hand with one hand and with the other is holding a
> computer with a screen that says from a countryman
> to a countryman.... There is a shawl over her heart
> embroidered with the map of the American conti-
> nent   showing   fraternity   among   all   the
> Americans.... The topic of migration is a continuous
> debate.... Behind the women, there is a man who is
> coming out of the depths and is looking for a bet-
> ter place where he can survive.... The family
> advances and the lovers dance and the musicians
> continue singing about the reality, hope and change
> (Botello 2000).

No me agradezcas hermano: Intertextuality and Advertising

One particular event led me to analyze the phenomenon of corridos about
migration with a different lens than that of a serious admirer. When I was
in Los Angeles doing my postdoctoral studies, Alberto, a friend, and I
went to a MoneyGram office to send some money to Mexico. As we
approached the desk to get the necessary forms, we saw on the wall a
MoneyGram ad in Spanish showing Los Tigres de Norte photographed in
front of the mural *The Wall That Speaks, Sings, and Screams*. To the left of the
photograph, the text in Spanish reads: *MoneyGram. International sending of*

Los Tigres del Norte in a MoneyGram ad with the mural of their album *De paisano a paisano* in the back (2001). Courtesy of MoneyGram.

money. The best exchange rate to Mexico. Better than ever. Send all the money you have with a fixed charge. From countryman to countryman, we recommend it to you. Los Tigres de Norte.

MoneyGram uses intertextuality to aid in the interpretation of their advertisements and to gain instant recognition of them. The use of intertextuality establishes associations between consumers and the product, and the allusions involving wordplay and puns create a community of people who wish to view themselves (or who already view themselves) in this light. The advertisement invites the audience to concentrate on how the services of the company relate to the "migrant story" and on what the audience already knows about the music and performance of Los Tigres de Norte. The notion of intertextuality was first formally introduced by Julia Kristeva (1986), who argued against the concept of the text as an isolated entity that operates in a self-contained manner. Roland Barthes explores the idea of intertextuality in a literary context, concluding that all texts are "a new tissue of past citations. Bits of code, formulae, rhythmic models, fragments of social language, etc., pass into the text and are redistributed within it" (Barthes 1981, 20).

Media intertextuality is certainly not new to advertising. A common form of intertextuality is the celebrity spokesperson whose presence summons forth the cultural value they have accumulated and attempts to transfer it to the product. For example, the MoneyGram ad relies on migrants' knowledge of the conjunto norteño to anchor the association of the commodity with the everyday life of the target audience. Advertising uses intertextuality because the attempt to persuade the audience to buy a product builds on beliefs and attitudes that the audience has already developed (Ulrike and Smith, 2001).

The MoneyGram ad exploits the family and comradeship metaphor to persuade the audience to commit themselves to a variety of principles: sending money back home to their families, using this particular money transfer company, and acquiring specific purchasing habits. The call for justice is erased from the MoneyGram ad while Los Tigres' leadership, their call for fraternity, and the need to care for relatives in Mexico is used to capture migrants' business and their money. Univisión, the largest U.S.-based Spanish-language media conglomerate, also broadcasts TV ads in which Los Tigres invoked "De paisano a paisano" when recommending that migrants send money to their mothers through Western Union. The TV ad was broadcast in May, the month of the "day of the mothers." According to the Latin American Institute (1997), this is the most important time for sending money to Mexico.

Music enhances the impact of the words that accompany it, whether these words are spoken or sung. People have a response to music that is associative: they imbue music with meaning by relating it to the contexts in which they hear it. Many other components of music also carry meaning as a result of their intertextual references.

The metaphor of the family is especially meaningful for undocumented Latin American migrants because neither the Mexican government nor the U.S. government provides them with a social safety net. Migrants know that they can rely only on their families in times of crisis; the family is a secure realm. It is not accidental that Los Tigres de Norte consists of four brothers and a cousin. They themselves overcame various obstacles by being together, and they now use that image to create a sense of a united group. The MoneyGram ad exploits the Latin American regard for family by reinforcing the idea that each migrant, regardless of his or her social and economic situation, is obliged to help support the family. In this way, the hopes, hardships, and ideals of migrant communities are translated into a demand for consumer products.

Studies of oppositional cultural expressions tend to employ a dichotomy: either total opposition to dominant ideologies or total reproduction of them. The corridos about migration do not fit squarely into either category, however. The musical experience tends to be anti-essentialist because it doesn't separate body and mind and also because it is a performance of a complex synergy between voice, language, gestures, desires, imaginative fantasies, bodily practices, aesthetics, values, and the community memory and their social organization. On the one hand, the performance, production, and distribution of corridos are commercial activities that support the dominant cultural industries. On the other hand, the corridos also play a fundamental role in resisting and negotiating the life experiences of migrants.

While cultures of resistance emerge within and are influenced by the "relations of cultural power and domination," they are also part of an "arena of consent and resistance" (Hall 1981, 239). These cultures of resistance are therefore capable of resisting and contradicting the very hegemony of which they are a part. Williams suggests that while literature, art, and music are part of the dominant hegemonic model and contribute to it, they are also capable of expressing "emergent practices and meanings" that the dominant culture will consistently seek to transform and absorb (Williams 2001, 159). In a similar vein, Hall (1981) points out that although popular culture might be embedded within and even contribute to the dominant hegemonic framework, it is still capable of resisting that framework.

Although the corridos tend to be engaging and spirited, they are nonetheless a form of oppositional culture, a glaring critique of the system. However, the fact that the corridos are an artifact of popular culture—a component of capitalist production and consumption—problematizes yet another aspect of the translation of popular culture into resistance.

Migrants' remittances are the largest and most reliable source of income for many Mexican families. (Migrants send approximately $912 million to Mexico each year.) Moreover, their economic contributions to the U.S. economy are substantial. The "Latino" market, of which over 50 percent is Mexican, has a purchasing power of about $490.7 billion (Robles 2003). This purchasing power has resulted in aggressive marketing strategies targeted at the "Latino" market. The Latino market is especially desirable because it is relatively young and predominantly urban. Latinos buy high-quality products, their brand loyalty is the greatest of all ethnic groups, and even though their incomes are relatively low, they spend most of their money on consumer goods and services. Latinos in the United States spend over 70 percent of their income on transportation, housing, clothing, food at home, and education (Robles 2003).

One factor that partly explains the popularity (and the economic success) of conjunto norteños is that the emergence of corridos about migration coincided with a major wave of migration from Mexico and Central America to the United States. The migration of the 1980s was caused by neoliberal economic and political reforms that exacerbated the already poor living conditions of people in Latin American countries. Another outcome of these economic reforms was an intensive process of deregulation, the acquisition of new technologies, and the privatization of government media. The deregulation of the cultural industries led to an increase in the broadcasting of conjunto norteño. Conjunto norteño music has since enjoyed unprecedented success and popularity. This can be attributed to transnational interactions, marketing, and the incorporation, movement, and intermingling of the best elements from both sides of the border in terms of musicians, equipment, and promotional techniques.

Los Tigres del Norte record their music with Fonovisa, which is part of Televisa. Televisa is the world's most profitable producer, exporter, and distributor of Spanish-speaking television broadcasting, film, publishing, and music recording. Televisa sells programming to 350 million Spanish speakers worldwide, not including those in Mexico (Corvi-Drueta 1999). The globalization of the economy produces a strong impact on popular culture. The new economic order creates a need for the production of standardized products targeted to the largest-possible market.

Currently, 85 percent of Hispanics watch Univisión (Fernández and Paxman 2000). Although most programs are targeted to the general audience, prime-time programming is targeted to youths, who have a tendency to spend more on purchases for themselves. Fonovisa and Univisión play a substantial role in the construction of a Mexican market in the United States and Mexico because in order to maximize profits, they control all levels and every aspect of production, distribution, and transmission.

According to *El Universal* (2004), a leading newspaper in Mexico, Los Tigres del Norte, Inc., generates $150 million in revenues each year. They have two hundred annual presentations and charge a fixed rate of $300,000 per concert. The main sources of income for Los Tigres are the royalties on their music and the ticket sales for their concert performances. Los Tigres del Norte seem to capitalize on, and construct a story or myth around, the migrant experience of "Latinos." This story is then transmitted through many voices and means: murals, songs, TV programs, radio programs, concerts, and other public performances. According to Barthes (1972, 31), "What allows the reader to consume myth innocently is that he does not see it as a semiological system but as an inductive one. Where there is only an equivalence, he sees a kind of causal process: the signifier and the signified have, in his eyes, a natural relationship." However, the naturalization proves that the myth or story that has been constructed around Los Tigres del Norte as the "voice of the migrants" introduces and maintains the hold of consumerism on the Latino market. As part of this myth, the performances, lyrics, and advertisements provide possibilities of living out and enacting the myths and stories of the migrant communities. The stories and myths associated with the products play a central role in the reconfiguration of the Latino market. The mythologizing and remythologizing pop culture is grounded in the process of intertextual circularity.

Los Tigres del Norte offer spaces of empathy and validation of the migrant experience, in contrast to the rejection and invisibilization of migrant groups in the U.S. mainstream arena. Audience participation in these stories is quite important in the reinforcement of the "migrant" story and therefore in the economic success of Los Tigres del Norte. As Jorge Hernández has stated in several interviews with me, part of the group's success is the open communication they have with their audiences. At the same time, the ads and products that Los Tigres endorse reinforce the idea that material gains and consumerism are a central part of success.

Un saludo cordial a nuestros amigos que nos escuchan:
Radio Stations in the United States

One of the ironies of the "boom" of the Latino market is that although this market is substantial, the Spanish-language media still face great barriers in gaining the sponsorship of major corporations. Abel Valenzuela, a professor at UCLA's Chicano Studies Research Center, told me that Spanish-language media workers are quite underpaid. For instance, in Los Angeles,

Spanish-language television broadcasters earn 70 percent less on average than those at English-language stations, with fewer comprehensive health and retirement benefits than their English-language counterparts.

Most of the radio broadcasters I talked to told me that they struggle to convince retail owners of the value of the Mexican market—that "all of us spend the same dollar regardless of our color." The idea that Mexican immigrants have been granted full participation and visibility in American society is merely an illusion arising from the fact that migrants have been targeted as consumers. Their representation within the population and their purchasing power have not been translated into political and social participation.

Radio stations play an important role in the dissemination of música norteña, especially in northern Mexico and in those parts of the United States with large populations of Mexican migrants. For instance, the Albuquerque radio station La Super X, which plays música norteña on a regular basis and devotes a full hour to corridos played by conjuntos norteños, is one of the most popular radio stations among Spanish-speaking people in New Mexico. According to Alfredo Baca, CEO of the radio stations La Super X and XABQ La Mariachi, Spanish-language radio stations have to struggle to get advertising from private companies. Mr. Baca mentioned that although the Spanish-speaking community is well established in New Mexico, large car and retail companies do not want to advertise their merchandise on Spanish-language radio stations for fear that they will not have enough Spanish-speaking personnel to handle such clients.

According to a sales representative at a local radio station in Albuquerque, the task of convincing national retail companies to announce their business in commercial spots on Spanish-language radio stations is a very challenging job because many such companies openly express their unwillingness to have Spanish-speaking clients in their stores. The businesses that have commercial spots in Spanish-language radios stations are mostly owned by Mexicans or people of Mexican descent. Mr. Baca often referred to the growing purchasing power of Mexican immigrants and their purchasing habits as proof that they are buying and that retail and car companies can profit from placing spots on Spanish-language radio stations. Mr. Baca explained some of the problems that Spanish-language radio stations face:

Mexicans and New Mexicans like variety. The marketing research shows that Hispanics are always tuned to at least one radio station in Spanish. La Super X is the number-two radio station in the market. Every day, from 4 p.m. to 5 p.m., there is a program with only corridos, called "La hora de los corridos." Actually, the Hispanic market is always growing. In fact, La Super X is sometimes number one; we rate them differently depending on the time. KABQ is the first station in Spanish and has never changed its acronym. La Super X is mainly for Mexicans from Mexico who have migrated to Albuquerque. The New Mexican and Mexican music is basically the same; the differences are very subtle. The New Mexican [music] has the keyboard more like an orchestra, and also they mix more English in the New Mexican music. People from Mexico like more the música norteña, even though they may sing the very same songs as the mariachi.

The sponsors of the radio station, such as Coca-Cola, will finance us if we target young people, and so we go for mariachi, cumbias, merengues but more than anything conjunto norteño and corridos. If it was not for the migratory influx of Mexican people, I think people would stop liking Mexican music. People start realizing that the Hispanic market is growing. Some companies ignore the Mexican market....Many companies do not want to advertise their merchandise. They ignore it because they are afraid of that market. They do not want to be announced in the radio because they think their stores are going to be full of Mexicans, and they cannot speak Spanish. But this fear should not exist because Mexicans can communicate very well when they want to buy something.

Many people are afraid because they do not know how to create announcements for Hispanics or in Spanish. They do not have a talent for that. This happens because they are confused. They follow the advice of people who do not know our culture and newly arrived Mexicans. If you go to a dance, you will see the Mexicans wearing very elegant clothes and beautiful cowboy hats. Mexican people like to spend even if the merchandise is not targeted at them. The Mexicans like to buy big trucks even though truck agencies ignore them. It is crazy.... It is a struggle for me to convince them. You have to educate them, although there is an increasing number of companies that are putting their eyes on the Mexican market. They know that Mexicans drive and that they are buying houses. I have met real estate agents that think that Mexicans do not buy houses! You have to educate them. In reality, it is the same dollar, whether spent or earned by a Mexican or by an Anglo. They have that attitude because they do not know the market.

Let me tell you something. I am from Las Vegas, New Mexico. My family has been here for generations, for really a long time. The original surname was Cabeza de Baca; later it changed into C. de Baca, then to Baca. Anyway, I was not allowed to speak Spanish at school. Teachers used to punish us for speaking Spanish, and they hit us frequently with a ruler. I did not like that very much. I used to say to myself: "They are not going to tell me what to speak." From there, I started liking more Spanish and I took Spanish and theater classes. I have lived in Mexico and in Spain. So, I have managed to keep my language alive. I was in the air force during the Vietnam War, then I went to Spain and Germany. When I came back, I studied for my bachelor's in Spanish at Highlands University, New Mexico. At that time I extended the time schedule to really very late in the evening. I have worked as a sales manager, radio station manager, in various

shifts. I have worked as a cameraman in Univisión and
started a live program. Thanks to my language, I have
worked in fascinating places and I have done fascinating work.

Mr. Baca talked in great detail about the role of Mexican migrants
from Chihuahua State in shaping the programming of the radio stations
and even the style of Texan and New Mexican bands. New Mexican and
Texan musicians are finding themselves reconfiguring their musical styles
in order to meet the demands of this market.

The situation of radio stations in Mexico is different from that of the
Spanish-language radio stations in the United States. Radio is the most
important medium in Mexico for several reasons: there is not as high pen-
etration of cable and other media alternatives to radio; radio is much less
expensive to produce than newspapers or TV programs; many regions in
the country still have no newspaper circulation; and a strong tradition of
oral culture exists, which creates a powerful medium for discussing social
issues as well as for entertainment. Radio stations provide a vital messen-
ger service between rural communities and are also an important link
between Mexicans in the United States and in Mexico. Many radio stations
have whole programs dedicated to finding people or reading messages
back and forth, providing a real public service.

XEBU, La Norteñita radio station in Chihuahua City, has real and
symbolic importance for corridos and conjunto norteño music in
Chihuahua State. For a very long time, this radio station served as the
only rapid mean of communication among remote communities. The station is quite important to the survival of rural Chihuahua. People know the
schedule of the programs by heart. It is through La Norteñita that people
know about dances, deaths, christenings, and commerce. I went to the
radio station in downtown Chihuahua with a friend of mine from a town
near Chihuahua City. He said to me, "Who would imagine that this very
small building is a radio station that has been so important for us?" As we
entered the building, I saw two vaqueros at the front desk filling in a form
to broadcast a death announcement. These men traveled from their ranch
to Chihuahua City to inform their relatives about the death.

The office of Manuel Pineda, a DJ at the radio station, was close to
the front desk, where people would pay for announcements concerning

the community. Manuel was waiting for me. He was very generous with his time, and my friend was even happier to be in the radio room to see how things worked. It was very interesting to hear after every announcement, "Recados a la Sierra [message to the Sierra], se les suplica hagan extensivo este mensaje." (We ask you to inform others about this message.) That is, people who happen to hear the announcement have a duty to inform others. It is very common to hear people recalling the death of a beloved one and saying, "I heard about it on the radio." Other announcements may be more practical, such as "Para el compadre Baltazar Chacón, del Rancho El Mendozeño, que tenga listas las vacas que las vamos a recoger mañana temprano." (For the compadre Baltazar Cacho, from El Mendozeño ranch: Have the cattle ready because we are going to pick them up tomorrow morning.)

Está usted escuchando: Radio and Transnational Relations

Radio stations in Mexico are heard in the United States, just as radio stations in the United States are heard in Mexico. According to some DJs from radio stations in Mexico, very often their programming reflects the needs of the Mexican market in the United States more than the needs of the market in Mexico, particularly in border cities between the United States and Mexico. For example, since most Mexicans in the United States do not have health insurance, the main commercial spots of Radio Cañón, in Ciudad Juárez, Chihuahua, are from a natural-medicine company based in California.

Mexican radio stations also play an important role in providing guidance and social services to migrants—contacting relatives on both sides of the border, for example. One way of doing this is by broadcasting phone calls from prison inmates in the United States. The executive of the radio station Radio Cañón stated that DJs become witnesses of the hardships migrants go through. DJs notify people that a relative has died, or send messages about deportations, or give information about missing people. The following conversation with Manuel Pineda, the DJ at radio station XEBU, La Norteñita, explains some of the transnational interactions that take place through radio stations:

> Very often people who live in the United States call
> us to request a song or tell us that they are visiting

the city because they are on holidays. Sometimes they call us directly from the U.S. to send regards to their relatives who live in the state of Chihuahua. They call in specific dates, for instance, the day of the mother, the children's day, or during their relatives' birthdays. People call us from different places. They have called us from California, from different parts of the state of Texas, from New Mexico, and from Arizona. On one occasion, I had the opportunity to receive a call from Washington from people who work there but wanted to send regards to their family who live over here. You can hear this radio station in some border areas of the United States.

People also call us to send messages in our section *recados a la sierra* [messages to the sierra]. Every morning, from nine to nine thirty there, we send the messages but often send them between programs and when there are emergencies. People from all the state of Chihuahua know that the messages are going to be sent out in the morning, and they pay attention. It is like a very established ritual. For example, right now we have this case of somebody who passed away and we are going to send it, because it is something important. Most of the messages are about deaths, but there are also invitations to quinceañeras and weddings that are going to take place in the ranches. We also have announcements from different businesses like dentists, buses that go to the United States. It varies. For example, "Please have the animals ready because we are going to pick them up to take them to another ranch," you know, that kind of message.

Spanish-language radio stations in the border region devote much of their time to playing songs specifically requested by listeners. However, many radio stations also have a section called a *pronóstico* (forecast) group in which the radio station will play new songs and select those that the audience requests most often through phone calls. On the surface, it seems that radio stations will only broadcast conjunto norteño music that the audience requests, but the radio stations play an important role in shaping the taste of the audience by familiarizing their audiences with certain conjuntos norteños. Normally those conjuntos norteños are the ones that have been recorded with important recording companies such as Fonovisa or Sony. However, many conjuntos norteños in the United States have been recorded with small companies, often owned by Mexicans or Mexican Americans themselves, and they have managed to somehow succeed. As Pineda states:

> Regarding the content of the programs, most of the programs are based on petitions. For instance, the whole radio program is divided in groups. Group number one is the one in which we play the music that is most requested and popular and group number four are the least requested. We have *canciones de catálogo* [catalog songs]. Those are the classics, the old but liked by every generation. We also have two segments *de pronóstico* [forecasts], which is the music that record companies bring to us. For instance, what is brought to us from La Banda del Recodo we accommodate into the whole programming, little by little. The pronósticos are songs that are left to the consideration of the public. For example, in the case of the La Banda del Recodo song "Pena tras pena," we placed it first in the pronóstico section. Then, if people ask for it a lot, then we start to put it into group one. We have around fifteen songs that are there, rotating in between the sections, that are the ones that have been requested. We receive petitions from different places. There are slightly more phone calls from Chihuahua City, but people who come from the ranches and live in Chihuahua to work or to visit also call. We have received calls from all over the state: Cuauhutémoc, Ojinaga, Delicias, Anahuac, Satevó, Parral, and other places. It is very nice to

know that the conjuntos that we broadcast in this radio station are also broadcast in the U.S. I am very happy about that because many of those artists are from ranches nearby Chihuahua and we know them pretty well. They are popular now because they had the support of Fonovisa. This company understood the market. People who migrate like to keep their music and that is what they record and broadcast in both sides of the border.

A leguas se les notaba que andaban en malos pasos: Representation of Narcocorridos

In English-speaking countries, the interpretation and perception of conjunto norteño tends to take a different form than in Spanish-speaking countries. Most non-Spanish-speaking people who are aware of corridos have a very strong perception that the main corpus of this genre is narcocorridos, or corridos about drug smuggling. This perception has been confirmed at almost every conference that I have attended on corridos, popular culture, or discourse analysis. Last October, I attended a conference in China about discourse analysis and was approached by some scholars from England and Malaysia. Knowing that I am Mexican, they wanted to have a conversation about corridos and made references to newspapers articles about narcocorridos. I was surprised that people were so familiar with narcocorridos in the Far East. The English-language media has covered narcocorridos mostly in the last three years. Usually the coverage of narcocorridos reinforces and fixes the idea of Mexico as a bizarre and corrupt place with consequently bizarre cultural expressions such as the narcocorridos.

The corridos performed by conjuntos norteños, the upbeat música norteña, and in general cultural expressions of Mexican and Latino American migrants have often been decontextualized and exoticized. As bell hooks (1995) states in reference to Madonna's appropriation of Black cultural expression, pain and pleasure are intertwined, and we cannot understand one without the other. Discourses on multiculturalism are often permeated by selective appropriation of cultural expressions that will not cause discomfort to the tacit and implicit role of white people in supporting and reinventing ideologies of domination. As explained in the narrative analysis of the corridos about migration, migrants express in the corridos many losses and hardships as well as dreams and a sense of hope. Corridos, like other elements of Mexican culture, help migrants negotiate their survival in an often hostile environment. They provide a framework for making sense of the displacement and violent realities that migrants encounter. Unfortunately the music, dance, and rituals of transnational communities are often treated as chic performances of culture by the cultural industries and by Western academe. This appropriation and exotization of Mexican music and dance does nothing to lessen the asymmetries enacted by patriarchy, white supremacy, and capitalism.

People often told me about the transformations and changes that corridos have undergone in recent years. The topic of narcocorridos, or corridos about drug smuggling, is particularly controversial. Corridos about smuggling practices are not a recent phenomenon. Smugglers have thrived in all the border regions of the world, since smugglers have a clear understanding that nations are not self-contained and sealed—that border communities are interdependent. Borders offer many loopholes for dynamic surreptitious trade, and these networks are often global in scope. Contraband activities were present on the Spanish frontier. Nueva Vizcaya and New Mexico were so neglected by the Spanish crown that smuggling was the only way to acquire needed goods and to avoid starvation. Opium smuggling also occurred at an early stage in Mexican history, and corridos about bootleggers (e.g., "Los tequileros") were common during the years of Prohibition in the United States. Many of the narcocorridos provide moral advice and warnings about the impact of smuggling on the smugglers' families. As stated before, Los Tigres have twice created new trends, first with their narcocorridos and later with their corridos about migration. Given the complexities of both genres, it is impossible to analyze narcocorridos thoroughly here. My intention is to engage in only a brief discussion of the perceptions of narcocorridos.

I found out during my fieldwork that perceptions of the narcocorridos varied according to the social class and the urban or rural upbringing of the participants. In general, the higher the social class and the more urban people were, the more negatively they perceived narcocorridos. Most people expressed ambivalent feelings regarding narcocorridos. Some of the most appealing elements of the narcocorridos are the acts of transgressions the main characters use in order to deceive the political and judicial systems through their craftiness and bravery. The main characters of the narcocorridos were perceived by some participants as similar to the social bandits who cross social and economic barriers through their delinquency. Narcocorridos are seen as different from corridos of the Mexican Revolution or any other social revolution in the sense that there is more emphasis on individualism and/or on personal social promotion. This social promotion is perceived by many as decentering the rigid classism of Mexico. Some participants insisted that the narcocorridos denounce the socioeconomic factors that push ordinary people to engage in drug-smuggling activities.

In his book *Poetry and Violence: The Ballad Tradition of Mexico's Costa Chica*, McDowell (2000) provides an academically useful model to understand allusions to violence in a Mexican ballad community. McDowell presents three main uses of violence in corridos about the Costa Chica: to celebrate it, to regulate it, and to heal it. The three can coexist with one another (149). McDowell also states that the content of most corridos is neither sentimental nor moralizing nor especially critical of the events they describe. Corridos have a very important healing effect, particularly in times of public trauma; the corridos of the coast articulate the "stories" underlying these disruptive events as a prelude to constructing a consensual interpretation of their meaning. Along with celebratory and regulatory motifs, Costa Chica corridos contain therapeutic elements seeking revalidation of the social bond (196–97).

Most of the narcocorridos listeners I spoke with told me that the main goal of the narcocorridos is not to promote delinquency, but to show how delinquency has become one of the relatively few options for the poor, a means of survival within an undemocratic system that offers only limited opportunities for economic success. Mexican labor on both sides of the border has helped to reinforce advanced capitalism, yet Mexicans have never been paid living wages.

Although there are some stories of success at the individual level, the worsening of the economy collectively affects racial minorities more than anyone else. Drug smuggling therefore appears attractive because it does not discriminate; it gives "equal opportunity" to all men. (I say "men" because the crime "industry," like many others, is based on a set of patriarchal, capitalist, sexist ideologies.) Drug smuggling is seductive to men because it promises what white American men have enjoyed and denied to men of color: manhood based on domination and money. Men of color are rewarded for acting in accordance with the ideologies of domination that exist within patriarchal societies. The few women who are part of drug-smuggling networks are admired because they embrace and reinforce patri-archal values and lifestyles. Drug smugglers do not offer a critique of capitalism. Instead, they are active players in a market where only those with money matter. As a friend of mine told me, "Drug smuggling is the Viagra for many, because it helps men to cover their insecurities with new cars, M-16s, and buying the company of young docile women."

It is surprising that some male academics, often white, whose privi-lege frees them from involvement in the day-to-day experiences of peo-ple who are blamed for drug consumption, have a tendency to focus their work on corridos about drug smuggling. The common portrayal of nar-cocorridos has simplified and decontextualized the harsh economic, social, and cultural processes that are taking place in transnational communities. At the same time, it liberates drug consumers from any responsibility for these processes. Most representations and studies of narcocorridos still depict Mexican men, especially working-class men, as irrational, cruel, playful, and childish. The study of narcocorridos seems to mirror the very male bonding in their content: a bonding in looking for the bizarre in the "other." Narcocorridos are studied in much the same way as rap music: they are the topic of choice of researchers who are fascinated with the "strange" behavior of the "other" but who simultaneously estab-lish solidarity with male violence, regardless of who produces such cul-tural expressions. Such studies are not really interested in changing unequal gender, classist, and racial dynamics. On the contrary, their cri-tique of Mexican working-class masculinity has served as an excuse to focus on the "problems" of people of color and not on the gender imbal-ances that occur within their own groups.

Repletas de hierba mala: Censorship in the Broadcasting of Corridos

Corridos about drug smuggling offer a rich narrative archive of the drug world: the governments that are involved, the hierarchies that have been established, the places where smugglers operate, their codes and values, the ways they smuggle, their love affairs and personal stories, and their social critique of consumers. Drug smuggling is an activity that affects the everyday life and culture of people wherever it happens. For example, many economic and leisure activities—restaurants, hotels, bars, and real estate—are directly or indirectly tied to the drug-smuggling business.

The socioeconomic and political elites who often indirectly take part in drug smuggling have continuously prohibited the broadcasting of narcocorridos because, according to these elites, narcocorridos promote violence and drug smuggling. The academic discussion of narcocorridos has hardly included an analysis of the economic system that places people in systemic poverty and closes most other avenues to economic success. According to Jorge Hernández, the corrido has been an important cultural element that expresses the everyday lives of ordinary people. In Hernandez's opinion, it is not a contradiction that although Los Tigres del Norte send peaceful messages to their audiences at the end of their concerts, they also sing stories about drug smuggling. Drug smuggling is a very real phenomenon, and the corridistas have addressed it.

Narcocorridos describe a version of the drug-smuggling phenomenon that is often misrepresented or omitted in the official version of events. These corridos document and maintain a collective memory of the social, economic, and political effects of narcotraffic on communities in Mexico, Colombia, and the United States. Hernández stated in an interview that narcocorridos do not necessarily glorify or judge drug smuggling but document the different ways it affects people:

> We sing true stories that have happened in any part of the Mexican Republic or in the United States. We work on corridos that are like a film and have all the ingredients of a story. We think that while people continue singing and writing corridos in a dignified way, the public will continue liking corridos. In our corridos, we do not abuse anybody or use bad words. We simply sing the reality, with respect. It all depends on the language. If some corridos use swearwords, then I agree that they should be prohibited because in order to sing corridos, it is important to do it with decency and justification, to contribute to our language, to our songs, to our culture, to our culture that is the Mexican music that has persisted for so

many years. We record stories of real life. All we sing are real stories; our songs are like editorials. We do not make up things or sing fictitious stories and that it [drug smuggling] is part of people's experience (April 2001).

Manuel Pineda, from La Norteñita radio station, expressed a different view. He acknowledged that narcocorridos are well liked by the public but reported that his station does not broadcast them even though he thereby loses money. His station broadcasts with five thousand watts of power and covers all of Chihuahua State—the largest in Mexico. Most of La Norteñita's audience can be found in rural areas, specifically in *la sierra*, the mountainous part of the state. Pineda stated that although narcocorridos are the most popular genre, his station does not play them

because we think that the smugglers have enough publicity and it is just not right to make people listen to this kind of problematic [song]. We do not think it is okay that many musical bands portray smugglers as heroes and glorify the fact that they deceive the police or that they managed to pass I do not know how many kilos of drugs. We think it is absurd to broadcast them. We play corridos like "El corrido de los Mendoza" about people who live in la sierra, more local, more traditional, from the state of Chihuahua.

Radio Cañón XEROK (AM), the oldest radio station in Ciudad Juárez, Chihuahua, broadcasts across the entire American continent with 150,000 watts of power. The executive manager of the station reported the existence of unofficial censorship regarding narcocorridos; that is, the chamber of commerce and other official institutions put indirect pressure on the radio stations not to broadcast narcocorridos. The prohibition of narcocorridos in Chihuahua became official, however, when Francisco Barrio became governor of Chihuahua for the PAN (Partido de Acción Nacional) political party. Although narcocorridos are not being broadcast by radio stations, people still listen to them in concerts, on tapes, and on CDs. In fact, narcocorridos are so popular that the largest profits of the conjuntos norteños come from narcocorridos. Narcocorridos are also disseminated through "informal means that avoid the Mexican music industry's normal promotion routes. They get produced directly to the public without having to rely on advertising, big distributors, credit lines, or, especially, Mexican radio" (Quiñones 2001, 15).

Regardless of what radio stations managers or governors think of the narcocorridos and the controversies they generate, they are the market leaders of corridos. In fact, they are the most commercially successful genre among men. Some of the newest conjuntos norteños started their careers with this genre and rely heavily on cursing in order to attract young consumers. These same groups tend to become more formal and sophisticated once their careers are better established, however. A street vendor of pirate CDs told me that teenagers often ask him for the conjunto music that has the most *groserías* (bad words). Corridos cannot survive the test of time unless they reflect the complexities of culture and community.

¿*Porqué no ayudar a los pobres?*: Corridos as Part of Social Struggles

As Quiñones (2001) states, certain corridos topics are still not part of the cultural industries or are taking a long time to be appropriated by them. This was the case of the corrido about Tierra Amarilla that Roberto Martínez wrote during the land grant movement. In general, "El corrido de Tierra Amarilla" brought attention to the plight of the Hispanos of northern New Mexico, people who live in one of the most impoverished areas of the United States. For those reasons, it was censored by almost all radio stations in New Mexico. As Roberto Martínez explained to me,

> "El corrido de Tierra Amarilla" was a success, and it was very much liked by the public, but since most of the owners of the radio stations were Anglos, they did not accept it. The corrido was so liked that it went underground. You know, the corrido was played more in California than here because here there was a lot of division, and Fullerman from KABQ was the owner. So people started to put a lot of pressure, and Roberto Mondragón told Fullerman, "I want you to tell me the real reason why you do

not want this corrido to be broadcasted in the radio,"
and he replied, "Because Roberto [Roberto Martínez]
is going to get rich." Roberto Mondragón replied,
"And so what? Gallegos has written corridos...and if
you do not broadcast this one, we are going to see
each other in court." Corridos always find their way
to be broadcasted regardless of whether they are
censured or not.

During Christmas 2004, I went with my family to Oaxaca State. When
we were on the coast of Oaxaca, a duet of musicians *taloneando* (pound the
pavement singing, day and night) were performing. It was my friend's
birthday, and we asked them to sing him "Las mañanitas" (a traditional
Mexican song to serenade someone with on a birthday). As they were
singing, it occurred to me to ask them for "El corrido de Lucio Cabañas,"
the corrido that I listened to when I was quite small and through which I
learned Lucio Cabañas was killed. I had the opportunity to listen it thoroughly. The duet sang it with great enthusiasm and asked me if I wanted
to listen to "El corrido del Chango," the nickname of another guerrilla
leader who fought with Lucio Cabañas. The musicians told me that during the 1970s, it was quite common to put musicians in jail who sang corridos about the guerrilla leaders. They told me that inevitably, every time
they sing those corridos, they remember the attempts of the government
to silence people and of the harsh consequences for musicians.

Para los pueblo de América les canto mi canción: Changes in Conjunto Norteño Music

Within the cultural industries, there seems to be an intense dialogue
between the performance of conjunto norteño music and *rock en español*.
Some incorporation of rock rhythms into música norteña has occurred,
most notably in the Los Tigres hit "América," and rock en español is incor-
porating some elements of corridos and norteña music as well. The most
famous rock en español bands, such as Los Fabulosos Cadillacs, Todos tus
Muertos, and Caifanes, have often given credit to Los Tigres del Norte for
their musical influence, particularly in regard to the creation of historical-
musical archives of important events in the communities. For a long time,
the division between the two genres was irreconcilable and obvious. Rock

artists regarded música norteña as the music of the unsophisticated rural poor, while most conjunto norteño performers regarded rock as an imitation of American music by well-off kids. However, young Mexican fans of conjunto norteño were also followers of rock en español in the United States and Mexico. It is not a coincidence that *El más grande homenaje a Los Tigres del Norte* (Greatest Homage to Los Tigres del Norte) is an album in which the most popular rock bands from Mexico (Maldita Vecindad, El Gran Silencio, Julieta Venegas, Café Tacuba, Molotov, El Haragán, and Compañía) pay tribute to Los Tigres del Norte and the norteña music by playing a creolized version of rock.

The cultural and political forms fostered by migrations are glimpses along the imagery of cultural expressions such as corridos, corridos-canciones performed by conjunto norteños, and often música norteña with very strong rock, cumbia, and mariachi overtones. Jorge Hernández states that although norteño music has evolved, it is a very stable music in the sense that people always buy it. Los Tigres del Norte was the first conjunto norteño to introduce electric bass and full drum. They have also infused boleros, cumbias, rock rhythms, waltzes, and special effects (sirens, cars, and machine guns) into their performances.

Donde me la pinten brinco y en cualquier metate tiendo: Opening Doors

On November 8, 2001, I was invited to attend a fund-raising event in which Los Tigres del Norte performed in West Hollywood, California, at the House of Blues. At the time, I was doing postdoctoral work at UCLA at the Chicano Studies Research Center, and some students were given tickets to attend the event. One of the organizers of the event asked one of the curators of the center to choose students to recognize Los Tigres for their financial contribution to carry out research on music in Spanish recorded in the United States. I prepared a short speech for the event.

This was the first time I was in the House of Blues, and the euphoria over the expected arrival of Los Tigres del Norte was immediately evident. There were bodyguards, cameramen from different TV stations, and a long line to get inside. The five students who had been asked to give a plaque to Los Tigres were outside the main entrance of the House of Blues. We were all Mexicans and Mexican Americans, mostly undergraduate students, and we began to talk about our hometowns and the places where we had lived or had relatives in Mexico and the United States. Every single student felt proud to be present at this event because Los Tigres were highly valued *acompañantes* (companions) of migrants in their joys and hardships. The girls dressed up quite elegantly for this occasion and took their task very seriously.

When we entered the House of Blues, I was quite surprised to see many music scholars and professors of Chicano studies and American studies from various universities in Los Angeles. Most of them were Mexican Americans, but not all. After a while, we were called backstage. There I saw Los Tigres del Norte; Alfonso de Alba, their manager; Martha Lara from the Mexican embassy; and California lieutenant governor Cruz Bustamante. Los Tigres and their manager remembered me from previous interviews. I was very nervous because I was about to speak in an unfamiliar place. But I had written my short speech, and I intended to read it. Los Tigres reassured me that I was going to be all right, and Alfonso de Alba said to me: "Calm down, Martha. Listen, if you can study to get a Ph.D., I do not see why you cannot talk about Los Tigres in front of people."

We all were in high spirits, and due to my nervousness I forgot their status and told them, as I would have a friend, about Manny Márquez, the musician from Dumas, Texas, who named his son, Hernán, after one of the members of Los Tigres del Norte. Hernán liked that very much. He introduced me to his eldest son in a very respectful way. The boy was being taught how to be polite to elders in accordance with the Mexican custom. I informed the group about the progress of my Ph.D. work, and we enjoyed nice moments of camaraderie. Soon the technical assistants told us to be ready to go onstage—and for the students to be brief.

Los Tigres played for over three hours as the young people danced and sang along with the corridos. Even though I had seen them in five concerts, I was as touched and engaged by their beautiful performance as I was on previous occasions. However, the audience was slightly different than before. First, fewer people attended than at most of their concerts, perhaps because the place was quite small. Second, many scholars of corridos, American studies, Chicano studies, and ethnic studies had come. About a month later I was watching Univisión when I saw a commercial spot announcing a TV program based on the performance of Los Tigres in the House of Blues and an interview with Eduardo, the youngest brother. This fund-raising event was covered by Univisión and Televisa and gave more promotion to Los Tigres del Norte.

Within the U.S. cultural industries, the conjunto has been the subject of major battles. Despite the fact that Mexican music constitutes over two-thirds of the music in Spanish that is listened to and sold in the United States, it took a very long time for the Latin Grammys to make room for Mexican musicians. Thanks to the insistence of Los Tigres and other popular Mexican musicians and recording companies, the event that was once dominated by Sony artists and Caribbean genres is slowly acknowledging the presence of Mexican music.

Los Tigres del Norte has carried the cultural torch of the norteño music that has been stigmatized in Mexico and in the United States. They have found a space and a voice in international arts festivals, museums, and exhibitions at institutions of the stature of El Festival Cervantino, the Smithsonian Museum, and many universities in the United States, thanks to their popularity, vision, and financial support to many of these educational institutions. The dialogue between cultural industries, audiences, and corridos sung by conjuntos norteños has gone beyond utilitarian goals. Los Tigres del Norte have the ability to articulate common desires, feelings, and experiences of migrants through corridos, corridos-canción, and música norteña. Their "authenticity" relies on their musical interaction with their listeners. Their directness appeals to emotional, aesthetic, and cultural triggers that give their audiences the humanity and visibility that has been denied in mainstream culture. The commodification of corridos has not deterred the group's calls for human rights to migrants, which has gone beyond the Mexican experience. Although Los Tigres del Norte have been fundamental in mobilizing "traditional" corridos with more fluid soundscapes and media outlets, they have given continuity to the corrido by appealing to new generations without compromising their social critique.

Afterword

I n April 2001, during my last spring break in Albuquerque, I went to the border and saw my father near El Puente Santa Fé. This is an international bridge that connects or divides the border community. My father was walking down Juárez Street. It was a Saturday, and he was coming from the El Paso library, as he did most Saturdays. We had not seen each other for a while, and we went to have lunch together. My father chose the Chinese restaurant called Har-Har, which is in front of the Tecnológico de Ciudad Juárez. The owner of the restaurant is Francisco Yepo, a son of Chinese migrants whose family became very well-known merchants in Juárez and who was a longtime friend of my father. Most of the cooks in that restaurant are Chinese. Enrique, who still has a heavy Chinese accent, was my dad's neighbor for a long time, and he used to spoil us with his great food when we were kids. My dad liked to go to that restaurant because it had long been one of the meeting points for Chinese people in Juárez.

My father always wanted me to keep him updated on my life plans and my studies. As we were talking, I was thinking of his extensive library and one of his favorite subjects—the Mexican Revolution. He also had a very good collection of books about corridos, and I started to ask him questions related to my work on corridos. He always chose books for us to read. Every time I saw him, he had a pile of books that he thought were appropriate to my studies or interests. So, he was preparing a selection of studies of corridos for me. He used to collect stamps, and I have vivid memories of him organizing his stamps and listening to corridos or classical music. In trying to answer my questions, my father drew on both his knowledge of corridos and his personal life.

My grandfather emigrated from China and lived in various parts of Mexico—especially in Chihuahua and Tamaulipas. All my uncles and aunts were born in different cities in northern Mexico. My grandfather lived in various cities along El Camino Real, mainly in Santa Bárbara, San Francisco del Oro, Parral, and Ciudad Juárez, but he also lived in other mining towns that were part of this Royal Road: Zacatecas, Torreón, Coahuila, Nueva Rosita, Coahuila, and Chihuahua City. My grandfather, like so many, followed the path between the two sierras that was a symbol of the search for a better life due to the trade and mining towns that could be found along the way. My father's family knew the Chihuahuan part of El Camino Real by heart. My grandfather made a living by running a small restaurant or coffee shop and by working as a cook along the trail that was constantly braided by people, droughts, inundations, and local commerce. My father once told me that some of the sections of El Camino Real were often abandoned or branched out as it suited the local needs.

It was in those cities and restaurants that my father told me he had became familiar with corridos and música norteña. The conversation struck me as so fascinating that I said to my father I wanted to record his narrative, good ethnographer that I am. This is what he told me:

> ¿Sabes? Allá afuera en la Plaza o en el Mercado, se ponía uno a cantar y a veces había un duo o a veces, como siempre, había una muchacha guapa, o a veces el hijo y decía: "el corrido de..." y luego sacaba su hojita...nunca era blanca, era amarilla, verde, azul y la vendía a diez centavos o cinco centavos. Eso era común. Pero ya no se ve. En Santa Bárbara a veces lanzaban propaganda, entonces pasaba un avión, y decia uno "tira papel" porque era un espectáculo, pero pues ya no hay eso. Pero pues a mi si me tocó. Pues lo hacían con dibujitos muy bonitos...la hojas de colores. Rojos no, pero si verde, amarillo, rosa....Y entonces iban a Parral, a Jiménez, y Santa Bárbara....Mi papá tenía una rocola en el negocio y así fue como yo siempre escuché los corridos...en cierto sentido yo era privilegiado porque yo iba a Parral. Mi papá me llevaba. Además, Parral tiene

mucho dinero por las minas. Mira, muy sencillo,
donde anduvo mi papá siempre hubo lana. Y sí, me
acuerdo que en los pueblos siempre preguntaban, ¿y
qué no hay café de Chinos en este pueblo? y si no
había, la gente decía "pues para que no haya un café
de chinos aquí es señal de que no hay dinero en el
pueblo."...Bueno, los corridos son tan importantes,
que déjame te digo, un escritor de Jalisco, de la talla
de Juan Rulfo, cuando estaba enfermo le preguntaron
"¿qué quieres que te hagamos? ¿un monumento? ¿un
nombre de calle?" y él dijo "no, no y le preguntaron."
"¿qué quieres?" "pues que me hagan un corrido."...A
mí me gustan mucho los corridos, los de López Tarso,
"El Gato Lobo Bateado," porque habla como el hacen
dado, y luego le cambia las voces....Yo conocí de
lejos a uno de un corrido. Se llamaba Santiago Reyes
Quezada, era un matón...también Rafael Varela, que
lo mencionaban en los corridos solo indirectamente.
[You know? Over there in the main square or in the
market, a person would sing, or sometimes there was
a duet, or, as always happens, there was a pretty girl
or her son, and the singer would say: "The corrido
about..." and then he or she would take the little
sheet, which normally was...it was never white; it
was yellow, green, blue...and it was sold for five or
ten cents. This was quite common. But you don't see
that anymore. In Santa Bárbara sometimes an airplane
would drop ads and we used to say, "Drop the paper,"
because it was a spectacle. There is no more of
that...but it was part of my experience. They use to
print them [the corridos] with quite nice draw-
ings...on colored paper...not red, but green, yellow,
pink...and they would go to Parral, to Jiménez and
Santa Bárbara....In a way, I was privileged because I
used to go to Parral, Chihuahua. My dad used to take
me there. Parral had a lot of money because of the
mines. Look, it's very simple, where my dad was,

there was always money. And I always remember that in the towns people used to ask: "Are there any Chinese coffee shops in this town?" and if there weren't, people used to say: "If there isn't a Chinese coffee shop here, it's a sign that there is no money in this town." My dad used to have a jukebox in his business, and that was how I always listened to corridos. Well, the corridos were so important that...let me tell you, a writer from Jalisco, someone of the stature of Juan Rulfo, was asked when he was sick: "What do you want us to do for you? Build a monument? Name a street after you?" He said: "No, no," and they asked him: "What do you want?" and he said: "Write a corrido after me." I love corridos very much. The one of López Tarso, like "El Gato Lobo Bateado," because he used to talk like the landlord and then he used to change the voices....I met a guy, you know from far away, who was mentioned in a corrido. He was a bandit. His name was Santiago Reyes Quezada. I also saw Rafael Varela, who appeared indirectly in one corrido.]

My father recited parts of the various corridos. He knew "El Corrido de Felipe Ángeles, the Great Villista General" by heart: "Preparen muy bien sus armas, y apúntenme al corazón. Apúntenme al corazón, no me demuestren tristeza, a los hombres como yo, no se les dá en la cabeza." [Get arms ready and point toward my heart. Point toward my heart and do not show me sadness. Men like me are not meant to be shot in the head.] He also told me with great enthusiasm the different versions of el corrido of the battle of Celaya, which marked the downfall of Francisco Villa.

Over a year after this conversation, I was in my first job as a professor at a liberal arts college in northern New York State. It was the beginning of October, the weather was changing, and I was getting to know my students and developing friendships with my colleagues. I got a phone call and an e-mail message from my sister telling me that my dad had passed away. A few hours later I was in the Ottawa airport catching a plane to El Paso. When I arrived at the El Paso airport, my brother, sisters, nephew, and nieces were waiting for me, and we went to Ciudad Juárez to my father's funeral. I was so far away from home. A few months earlier, I had told my father that I was going to a job interview at a university near the U.S.-Canadian border, and he told me in a very decisive and enthusiastic tone: "You should go there, *m'ija*. It's always fun to know new places and new people. The only bad thing is that *hace un frío de los mil demonios* [it's cold as hell]." My father, like my grandfather, had a very adventurous spirit. He liked the idea of my living in upstate New York and immediately told me of the places I should visit. He would be always ready to travel, to try new foods, and to meet new people.

I remember a photograph of my father when he was in primary school in Ciudad Juárez. He stands out in that photograph, which was taken in a classroom where the students were sitting at their work tables and *la maestra* Catita was standing, supervising her students. He looks very different from the rest because he is the only Chinese student among all the Mexicans. He also looks minuscule beside them. He was the youngest student, due to his academic achievement. The school, named Guadalupe J. Viuda de Bermúdez, still exists. The Bermúdez family gave him a scholarship for his academic excellence. I studied my second year of primary school at the same school, and this very photograph was still in the principal's office. My father's family and my own nuclear family were always the different ones, the eternal nomads who kept moving. They were subjected to the rampant and well-developed Orientalism that has long been pervasive in Mexico, particularly during the first half of the twentieth century. In those years, it was common to say that the Chinese had tails like mice or that they used to cook children (as well as their Mexican waitresses or cooks who didn't behave). As a son of immigrants, my father rarely felt entitled to his space and place in Mexico. He was always seen as a foreigner. My father negotiated his migrant identity, trying to excel as a student and as a worker, but he never quite achieved full acceptance. He could not travel around Mexico without his passport, since his citizenship was often in question.

One of his biggest joys was when he got his Mexican birth certificate with his right name and the right date of birth. I remember his persistence in trying to get his birth certificate right. Since I was very small, I remember his numerous trips to his hometown and the visits he paid to the people he thought might help him get it. He never lost hope and always kept us updated on this process: *"Ya platiqué m'ija que hablé con este licenciado? El me va a ayudar."* [Have I told you, my daughter, that I have talked to this lawyer? He will help me.] My sisters, my brother, and I knew the whole procedure concerning this matter by heart. We would normally listen to my father's plans and hopes without much reply, just nodding. What could we have said to him after decades of unsuccessful attempts? Not having a proper birth certificate made him feel a stateless person for almost all his life. My brother, Pedro, was so sorry about my dad's anxiety and pain that getting the certificate for my dad became one of my brother's missions in life. My dad finally got his corrected birth certificate two years before he passed away. Although at the time his sickness did not allow him to be the independent and free traveler he always wanted to be, having his birth certificate right was probably one of the most important achievements of his life. It was almost like having finally resolved the tension of not "officially" belonging and therefore of being mistrusted in the country he knew very well and loved very much.

The Chinese Mexican identity of my brother and sisters was often constructed in a favorable way by my mother and her brothers. My mother, who is from Chilapa de Díaz, a pueblo of the Mixteca Alta region in Oaxaca State, was in love with my father. My mother and her family sheltered us and worked hard to make us feel proud of being mixed-race people. However, we had conflicting experiences once we stepped out of our home. Colleagues used to imitate the way Chinese people spoke Spanish. I was told many "jokes" about the mysterious and sadistic personalities of Chinese people. I am often called "Chew" (that is my surname) de *cariño* (out of love) or "China" (Chinese) in Mexico. I often liked that because they would always say it with love and tenderness. My attitude is due in part to the fact that I feel entitled to be in Mexico. My mother is from Mexico, I was raised there, and my family is there. While in Mexico, my situation was quite different from my father's earlier experiences. However, my experiences in England, Austria, and the United States have pushed me to intense negotiations of spaces mainly because of my racialized status and other markers of "third worldliness."

I found that the corridos about migration meant more to me once I began to live outside Mexico. This project on the corridos did not really start while I was a Ph.D. student but rather, as is the case for many Mexicans, was a powerful spiritual and historical framework that has been reshaped along the centuries by people. In very real ways, this project began before we were even born.

The process of carrying out a narrative analysis was very draining for me. I had always heard corridos and I have danced them, but I cried often when I was writing the analysis. I was touched by the artists' performance as much as their sung interpretation of the lyrics that analyze migrants' social conditions. Like my grandfather and my father, I started to become familiar with the unfamiliar. A radical change in my life began when I moved to northern New York, where winters can be extremely cold and where there is no visible, "legal" Mexican community. (Many dairy farms in the area do employ undocumented workers from Mexico and Central America, however.) The fact that I am now the only Mexican professor at this university (with only three "Latino" colleagues) has forced me to reshape certain elements of my identity. As the corrido "Tres veces mojado" states, I have to say that I have experienced fortunate opportunities to know people and to grow at a personal and professional level by moving here.

When I first arrived in Canton, New York, I kept remembering the song that "El Piporro" sang during the bracero program, "Chulas fronteras del norte" (Beautiful Border Cities of the North), a song that describes the love a migrant has for the U.S.-Mexican border cities and his experiences in crossing back and forth. A friend of mine told me, "Listen to batanga.com. It's a radio station that has all the genres in Spanish." Sitting in my office in Canton, I went to the section called Norteños, Bandas, and Corridos. When I found the radio station, I told myself, "Now I can survive in the north country, and I can even face the winter." When I called friends by phone during the first weeks and tried to explain to them where I was, I always made reference to El Piporro and Vicente Fernández and told them I was living in the borderland like all the Mexican migrants that are described in their songs. This reference was always powerful to us and caused a lot of laughter. I never imagined that I was going to experience, under somewhat different conditions, some of the loneliness of the migrant workers described in the corridos.

In August 2002, on my way to my new job, I flew from El Paso to the Syracuse airport. I took a Greyhound bus to Canton. Along the way, several people asked if I was from Japan. I smiled and answered, "No, I am from Mexico." On the bus, an Amish boy of about ten sat next to me.

He was quite shy but managed to keep looking at me often. He asked me, in a very naive way, "Where are you from? I have never seen people like you." I also kept looking at him, probably because I had never seen people like him. Neither of us belonged to mainstream America, and neither had a frame of reference that would have allowed us to be familiar with each other. I was looking at the landscape full of maples and scattered small villages, and I decided that this bus trip was going to be a metaphor for my life in Canton. I had to take a chance, even if that meant traveling to upstate New York, a place that was so different from where I had been before. It was quite comforting to think that the town was close to the border with Canada. Somehow, border places have become places of comfort to me.

Like any migrant, I experience these losses and also attempt to resolve them in various ways. I read Mexican newspapers every day, I listen to radio stations in Spanish through the Internet, I call my friends and family often, I get together with colleagues with whom I have various points of identification and those who are familiar with the migrant experience, and I go to Mexico as often as I can. Perhaps my life, like that of so many others, resembles the metaphors of the corridos that my father used to love, but I feel that I need to continue searching for the resolution and moral messages in the open and unfinished corrido that is my life.

Appendix:
CORRIDOS

"EL MOJADO ACAUDALADO"	THE RICH WETBACK

Enrique Franco (1988). Performed by Los Tigres del Norte.

Me está esperando México lindo	Beautiful Mexico is waiting for me
por eso mismo me voy a ir	that is exactly why I am leaving
soy el mojado acaudalado	I am the rich wetback
pero en mi tierra quiero morir	but in my country I want to die
Adiós, adiós, California	Goodbye, goodbye, California
Texas, Chicago, Illinois	Texas, Chicago, Illinois
Me llevaré su recuerdo	I will remember you when I leave
porque a mi tierra me voy	because I am leaving for my country
pues aunque tengo dinero	although I have money
no soy feliz donde estoy	I am not happy where I am living
Adiós, adiós, Colorado	Goodbye, goodbye, Colorado
Nevada y Oregon	Nevada and Oregon
adiós les dice el mojado	the wetback says to you goodbye
que se empapó de sudor	covered with sweat from the hard work
en los campos de Arizona	in the Arizona fields
fábricas de Nueva York	and in the factories of New York
Me está esperando México lindo	Beautiful Mexico is waiting for me
por eso mismo me voy a ir	that is exactly why I am leaving
soy el mojado acaudalado	I am the rich wetback
pero en mi tierra quiero morir	but in my country I want to die

Aventurero y mojado	Adventurer and wetback
hablando muy buen inglés	speaking very good English
ya me pasié por Atlanta	I have already traveled through Atlanta
por Oklahoma también	as well as through Oklahoma
decia una guera en Florida	a blond lady from Florida told me,
"I love you all Mexican men"	"I love you all Mexican men"
De los Estados Unidos	I won't forget the United States
yo no me voy a olvidar	I wanted to earn good money
quise tener buen dinero	and I came to earn it
y me lo vine a ganar	but in my beloved country
pero en mi tierra querida	I want to enjoy it
yo me lo pienso gastar	

"LA TUMBA DEL MOJADO"　　THE TOMB OF THE WETBACK

Paulino Vargas (1998). Performed by Los Tigres de Norte.

No pude cruzar la raya	I could not cross the line
se me atrevezó el Río Bravo	the Rio Grande got in my way
me aprendieron malamente	I was detained unfairly
cuando vivía en el otro lado	when I was living on the other side
los dólares son bonitos	the dollars are beautiful
pero yo soy mexicano	but I am Mexican
No tenía tarjeta verde	I did not have the green card
Cuando trabajé en Luisiana	when I worked in Louisiana
en un sótano viví	I lived in a basement
porque era espalda mojada	because I was a wetback
tuve que inclinar la frente	I had to work very hard
para cobrar la semana	to earn money for the week
La rosa de Mexicali	The rose of Mexicali
y la sangre en el Río Bravo	and the blood of the Rio Grande
son dos cosas diferentes	are two different things
pero en color son hermanos	but they are brothers by color
y la linea divisoria	and the political line
es la tumba del mojado	is the tomb of the wetback

La cerca de la tortilla	The tortilla wall
es ofensa para el pueblo	is an offense to the people
en México se pasean	in Mexico people go and travel
franceses, chinos y griegos	Frenchmen, Chinese, and Greeks
y algunos americanos	and some Americans
son caciques de los pueblos	are even landlords of the Mexican towns
La rosa de Mexicali	The rose of Mexicali
y la sangre en el Rio Bravo	and the blood of the Rio Grande
son dos cosas diferentes	are two different things
pero en color son hermanos	but they are brothers by color
y la linea divisoria	and the political line
es la tumba del mojado	is the tomb of the wetback

"A QUIEN CORRESPONDA" TO WHOM IT MAY CONCERN

Luis Torres (2000). Performed by Los Tigres del Norte.

Vamos despierten señores	Come on, wake up, gentlemen
encargados del gobierno	in charge of the government
porque ya el odio racial	because the racial hate
va despertando un infierno	is making hell
y esto no lo va a parar	this is not going to be stopped
ningún presidente tierno	by a tender president
Se invita por internet	There is an invitation via Internet
en los Estados Unidos	in the United States
a unirse para matar	to get united to kill
a nuestros paisas sufridos	our suffered countrymen
pues su pecado es pasar	because their sin is to cross
por donde no son queridos	through places where they are not loved
A esos racistas cobardes	Those coward racists
se les tiene que parar	have to be stopped
Joaquín Murrieta es ejemplo	Joaquín Murrieta is an example
y ahora lo vamos a honrar	we should honor him
cuando se enciende la sangre	when the blood boils
nada la puede apagar	nothing can stop it

A quienes les corresponda,	To whom it may concern
abran los ojos ya ahorita	open your eyes now
este es un asunto serio	this is a serious matter
no se tiren la bolita	do not pass the ball
es por los cuernos al toro	fight the bull from the horns
no por las redonditas	not from the sides
Dice el anuncio maldito	The wicked message
que me tiene tan dañado	that has left me damaged says,
"vamos a cazar mojados	"Let's go hunt wetbacks
que crucen para este lado"	who cross to this side,"
muchos hermanos latinos	many Latino brothers
han sido ya asesinados	have been assassinated
Un demoniaco sujeto	A devil man who is a
de la guerra excombaneinte	war veteran
con ramos ocultó unos pozos	with tree branches; he hid wells
donde se ahogó mucha gente	and many people got drowned
niños, mujeres y hombres	children, women, and men
qué racismo tan demente!	what an insane racism!
Pero que poca memoria	But what a small memory
la que tiene esas gente	those people have
ellos pisotean pueblos	they tread down countries
con sus guerras indecentes	with their indecent wars
ahora agreden dentro y fuera	they attack our people inside and outside
de nuestra patria a mi gente	our country
A quienes les corresponda	To whom it may concern
la solución es urgente	the solution is urgent

"EL OTRO MÉXICO"   THE OTHER MEXICO

Enrique Franco (1998). Performed by Los Tigres del Norte.

No me critquen	Do not criticize me
porque vivo al otro lado	because I am living on the other side
no soy un desarraigado	I am not an uprooted one

vine por necesidad	I came here out of necessity
Ya muchos años	It has been many years
que me vine de mojado	since I came as a wetback
mis construmbres	my customs
no han cambiado	have not changed
ni mi nacionalidad	nor my nationality
Soy como tantos	I am like so many,
otros muchos mexicanos	many other Mexicans
que la vida nos ganamos	who earn our living
trabajando bajo el sol	working under the sun
Reconocidos	Renowned
por buenos trabjadores	as good workers
que hasta los mismos patrones	so that even the employers themselves
nos hablan en español	speak to us in Spanish
Cuando han sabido	When have you known
que un doctor un ingeniero	that a doctor or an engineer
se ha cruzado de bracero	has crossed as a bracero
Por que quieran progresar	because they want to progress
O que un cacique	Or that a landlord would
deje tierras y ganado	leave land and cattle
por cruzar el Río Bravo	to cross the Rio Bravo
eso nunca lo verán	that you will never see
El otro México	The other Mexico
que aqui hemos construido	that we have constructed here
en este suelo que ha sido	on this soil that has been
teritorio nacional	national territory
Es el esfuerzo	It is the effort
de todos nuestros hermanos	of all our brothers
y Latinoamericanos	and Latin Americans
que han sabido progresar	who have known how to progress

Mientras los ricos,	While the rich
se van para el extranjero	go abroad
para esconder su dinero	to hide their money
y por europa pasear	and tour Europe

Los campesinos	We peasants
que venimos de mojados	who come as wetbacks
casi todos se lo enviamos	we send almost all our money
a los que quedan allá	to those who remain back there

"CARRERA CONTRA LA MUERTE" — RACE AGAINST DEATH

Enrique Valencia (2003). Performed by Los Tigres del Norte.

Quiso ganarle a la muerte	He wanted to beat death
quiso ganar la carrera	he wanted to beat the race
tres años sin verla	three years without seeing her
y no la alcanzó	and he could not arrive on time to see her again

En una cruz de Madera	On a wooden cross
colgó los zapatos	he placed a pair of shoes
que el día de la boda	that the day of their wedding
el le prometió	he promised to her

Alzó los ojos al cielo	He looked at the sky
y le gritaba te quiero	and he screamed, "I love you"
soy el extranjero	I am the foreigner
que al fin regresó	who came back at last

Te traigo mucho dinero	I brought you a lot of money
dice la gente del pueblo	people from town say
que de tanto quererlo	that she died because
ella se murió	she loved him so much

Debajo de su retrato	Below her picture
tendió su vestido blanco	he placed her white dress
y ahogado en el llanto	and drowned in tears
su voz se escuchó.	his voice was heard saying

"Si cuando pedí tu mano
llegamos casi desnudos
hasta el altar de la iglesia
y yo arrastrando mi orgullo"

"When I asked for your hand in marriage
we looked so poor
when we were in the church altar
and I was dragging along my pride"

En la noche de mi boda,
no pudimos tener fiesta
tu querías vestido blanco
y yo te lo prometí

The night of our wedding
we could not have a feast
you wanted to wear a wedding dress
and I promised it to you

Ojalá que en la otra vida
el mundo sea más parejo
porque yo sin tu cariño
no me moriré de viejo

Hopefully in the other life
the world will be more fair
because without your love
I will not die old

Otro día por la mañana
se levantó el extranjero
su niño y su perro
y se despidió

The next day in the morning
the foreigner woke up
his child and his dog
and left

Con gran dolor vió la tierra
donde vivió su misera
y por culpa de ella
su amada murió

With great pain he saw the land
where he lived in poverty
and because of it
his beloved wife died

Al paso de su caballo
iba rezando un rosario
por el novenario
de la que adoró

While he was riding his horse
he was praying a rosary
a novena
for the woman he adored

En la ladera del cerro
se oyó cantar un jilguero
dicen que del cielo
ella les cantó

At the foothills
a goldfinch was heard singing
people say that from the sky
she sang for him

Quiso ganarle a la muerte
quiso ganar la carrera

He wanted to defeat death
he wanted to win the race

tres años sin verla	three years without seeing her
y no la alcanzó	and he did not arrive on time to see her

"MI DISTRITO FEDERAL" ## MY FEDERAL DISTRICT

Enrique Franco (1998). Performed by Los Tigres del Norte.

Con el corazón herido	With my hurt heart
Mexico lindo y querido	beautiful and beloved Mexico
aqui te vengo a cantar	I came to sing to you
Que mi voz se lleve el viento	I hope that my voice, which
con un sentido lamento	has a deeply felt lament,
llegue hasta tu capital	is taken by the wind to the capital city
Se lo sabe tu grandeza	Your greatness is known
la madre naturaleza	but Mother Nature
te ha querido doblegar	wants to make you give in
Pero Diós no lo ha querido	But God has not wanted it
solamente has sido herido	you have only been hurt
pero no es de gravedad	but it is not serious
Diecinueve de septiembre	September nineteenth
nunca se podrá olvidar	I will never forget it
ha llenado para siempre	that date has filled for good
de luto nuestra gran ciudad	this great city of sorrow
Unidos en sentimiento	We are united in feelings
con los que hoy llorando están	with those who are now crying
haremos un monumento	we are going to build a monument
de esta gran Tenochtitlan	out of this great Tenochtitlán
El destino te ha hecho daño	Destiny has hurt you
dos veces un mismo año	twice in the same year
te hizo sangre derramar	it made you shed blood
Pero solo ha conseguido	But that has made

ver tus hijos mas unidos	your children more united
en una fraternindad	in a fraternity
Los latinoamericanos	Latin Americans
nos sentimos como hermanos	feel like brothers
contra de la adversidad	and fight against adversity
Y aunque de la parte ausente	Although they are not in their home country
se saben hacer presentes cuando	they know how to make their presence felt
hay la necesidad	when it is required
Será el descubrimiento	It will be the discovery
de otra más linda ciudad	of another more beautiful city
será la sangre cemento	the blood will act as cement
que paredes unirá	to unite walls
Como el águila su vuelo	Like the eagle's flight
otra vez levantará	it will take off again
con sus torres hasta el cielo	with its towers up to the sky
mi Distrito Federal	my Federal District

"PEDRO Y PABLO"   PEDRO AND PABLO

Enrique Franco (1998). Performed by Los Tigres del Norte.

Pedro y Pablo eran hermanos	Pedro and Pablo were brothers
y amigos inseparables	and inseparable friends
quedaron abandonados	they were left abandoned
cuando murieron sus padres	when their parents died
Pedro, el mayor se decía	Pedro, the eldest, used to say to himself,
"que a Pablo nada le falte"	"I wish Pablo will never lack what he needs"
Pedro habló con entereza	Pedro talked with strength of mind
"tienes que seguir la escuela	"You have to keep studying
tienes muy buena cabeza	you are intelligent
yo me voy aunque nos duela	I will leave although it will hurt us
yo trabajo y tu estudias	I will work and you will study
al cabo que el tiempo vuela"	since time flies, our separation will be short"

Pedro se fué para el Norte
y cruzó para el otro lado
dijo a su novia Leticia
"Ahí te lo dejo encargado"
Y al transcurso de los años
Pablo se hizo licenciado

Pedro left for the North
and crossed to the other side
he said to his girlfriend Leticia,
"Take care of my brother"
When the years passed
Pablo became a lawyer

"Pedro que gusto de verte"
"Supe que eras licenciado"
"No sé como agradecerte"
"No me agradezcas, hermano"

"Pedro, what a pleasure to see you"
"I learned that you are now a lawyer"
"I do not know how to express my gratefulness"
"There is nothing to be grateful for, brother"

"Quiero decirte una cosa"
"Habla te estoy escuchando"
"Conocerás a mi esposa"
"Es lo que estoy esperando"

"I want to tell you something"
"Tell me, I am waiting"
"You will meet my wife"
"That is what I am waiting for"

(Hablado)
"Gracias señor que has permitido
realizar su vida a mi hermano querido
hoy se que mi esfuerzo no fué en vano
ya podré ser feliz con la mujer que tanto amo"
woman that I love so much"

(spoken)
"Thanks to God for having allowed me to
to help my dear brother to fulfill his aims in life
Today I know that my effort was worthwhile
Now I will be able to be happy with the

"Esta es mi esposa Leticia"
"Creo que ya nos conocemos"
"Se te borró la sonrisa"
"Es que me vino un recuerdo"

"This is my wife, Leticia"
"I believe we already know each other"
"Your smile disappeared"
"It is because I suddenly remembered something"

"Vas a quedarte en la casa"
"Eso yo nunca podría"
"Pedro ¿qué es lo que te pasa?"
"Es que lloro de alegría"

"You will stay at home"
"I could never do that"
"Pedro, what is happening to you?"
"I am crying out of happiness"

No es que Pablo fuera malo
o que no supo apreciar
el sacrifico de hermano

It is not that Pablo was a bad person
or that he did not appreciate
the sacrifice of brother

que Pedro supo brindar	that Pedro knew how to provide
de Leticia mejor ni hablo	for Leticia; I better not talk about her
ella si se portó mal	she was the one who behaved badly

"BAJO EL CIELO DE MORELIA" UNDER THE SKY OF MORELIA

Rubén López (2003). Performed by Los Tigres del Norte.

Una mañana de marzo	One morning in March
en la central de Morelia	in the bus station of Morelia
rompí el boleto a lo macho	I tore up the ticket without hesitation
que saqué para la frontera	that I bought to the border
nomás de ver tan precioso	because I saw the beautiful
al cielo azul de mi tierra	sky of my hometown
Después oí una campana	Afterward I heard the bells tolling
que estaba llamando a misa	calling for mass
la Catedral Moreliana	in the Morelian cathedral
joya Tarasca y Castiza	which is a Tarascan and Castillian jewel
veo que una mujer rezaba	I saw a woman praying
sin consuelo en su carita	whose face looked distressed
Era mi Juare Maria	She was my Juare Maria
que por mi rezaba un credo	who was praying a creed for me
hasta lloró de alegría	she even cried out of happiness
cuando le dije me quedo	when I told her, "I am going to stay
en esta tierra, mi vida	in this land, my love,
bajo su precioso cielo	under its beautiful sky"
Me miraban sus ojitos	Her little eyes looked at me
mi Juare creía un milagro	my Juare thought it was a miracle
después nos fuímos camino	later we took a walk
a dar una vuelta al lago	to the lake
y cuando andaba en Janitzio	and when I was in Janitzio
se me olvidó el otro lado	I forgot the other side
Bajo el cielo del Morelia	Under the sky of Morelia
ninguno se ha muerto de hambre	nobody has died of hunger
aqui me quedo en mi tierra	I will stay in my land

muy cerquita de mi madre
y de mi Juare Maria
nunca vuelvo a separarme

Adiós, lindo San Francisco
Los Angeles y Chicago
me quedo en el paraiso
que tanto habia despreciado
alcabo no me hice rico
cuando anduve de mojado

very close to my mother
and I will never separate again
from my Juare Maria

Goodbye, beautiful San Francisco
Los Angeles and Chicago
I will stay in the paradise
that I despise so much
I did not become rich anyway
when I was working as a wetback

Notes

Preface

1. There are various definitions of *música norteña*. In Mexico, it means the music played in the northern part of the country, mainly by conjunto norteños but not exclusively. In New Mexico, it means music played in northern New Mexico with guitar accompaniment. Not all música norteña involves ballads, a common misperception.

Introduction

1. El Camino Real de Tierra Adentro, the Royal Highway of the Interior Lands, was the road used by Native Americans and colonists, merchants, and ranchers traveling between New Mexico and Mexico. El Camino Real served as the only commercial route linking the territories north of the Rio Grande with the outside world. The route had fostered trade and cultural exchanges among the Pueblo and more southern indigenous peoples since well before the Spanish invasion.

2. *Cowboy* is a fairly literal translation of the Spanish word *vaquero* ("cow" + "-er," masculine gender) into English. This new breed of worker had his origin in the northern frontier of New Spain, which later became northern Mexico and the U.S. Southwest.

3. Very broadly, *mestizo* means a person of mixed blood. In Latin American contexts, the term normally refers to the descendants of mixed Native American and European ancestry. The concept has various and contradictory social and cultural connotations in different Latin American contexts.

4. A *conjunto norteño* ("northern band") is a musical group from northern Mexico with accordion as the main instrument, twelve-string Mexican guitar (slightly larger than the six-string guitar and with steel strings, called *bajo sexto*), drums, saxophone, and bass (Reyna 1996).

5. *El México de afuera* is a term coined by one of the pioneers of Chicano studies, Américo Paredes, referring to social spaces where there are Mexicans and Mexican cultural and economic practices. This term is in essence the very well worn Andersonian notion of "imagined communities" that transgress the

arbitrary boundaries that help to maintain systems of domination, exploitation, and imperialism.

6. Approximately four hundred people died crossing the border between 1985 and 2000. From 2001 on, the average has been about five hundred people (Marossi 2005). Seventy people died attempting to escape over the Berlin Wall between 1961 and 1989.

7. One of these routes is located on the western side of the Sierra Madre Occidental and includes the Mexican states of Baja California, Baja California Sur, Sonora, Sinaloa, Nayarit, Colima, Nayarit, Michoacán, Guerrero, and Oaxaca. The central corridor lies between the Sierra Madre Occidental and the Sierra Madre Oriental and includes the states of Chihuahua, Durango, San Luis Potosí, Aguascalientes, Guanajuato, and Querétaro. The third lies to the east of the Sierra Madre Oriental. It includes the states of Tamaulipas, Nuevo León, Veracruz, and Tabasco. The mountain ranges (sierras) are quite high and rugged, with deep, steep-sided canyons (*barrancas*). They have long been a barrier to east-west movement. The Caribbean region of Mexico is connected to the United States mainly by sea.

Chapter Two

1. A hybrid of a corrido and a lyric song that has some but not all of the elements present in the narrative of corridos.

2. The cumbia is the most typical and popular Colombian form of dance and fuses Andean Indian, African, and European musical styles. It is quite popular in Latin America, especially in Mexico. It is played in 4/4 time with a heavy beat one and accentuated beats three and four. The bolero is a very romantic popular song that is midpaced and has Spanish roots, but Latin American musicians make it international with the *acompañamiento* of string trios. Currently, it is usually sung by one person and is quite slow and very sentimental. The music is usually arranged with Spanish vocals and a subtle percussion effect. Baladas románticas are songs that narrate painful and joyful aspects of love affairs and are played very slowly.

3. Another dimension of the space mentioned in the corridos is cyberspace. This is most obvious in "A quien corresponda" (see the appendix), which tells of xenophobic nativists who call for the hunting of Mexicans in the Arizona desert. It is interesting to note that while cyberspace has been lauded for its potential to overcome and transcend political boundaries, it is incapable (at least in this case) of dismantling the ethnic, cultural, and political barriers that come between Anglo Americans and Mexican immigrants. In fact, cyberspace has sometimes been an arena of mobilization for those who hope to maintain and reinforce current racial, ethnic, and economic hierarchies based on fundamentalist notions of the nation-state.

Corridos about immigration are prone to be pessimistic. They tend to express a profound bitterness, perhaps because they emerge during periods of strong social crisis, moments in which popular concerns are more repressed. Mexican migrants, particularly undocumented ones, are subjected to racial and cultural terror and do not have the economic means to respond to such symbolic and physical harassment. Consequently, the corridos about immigrants' experiences tend to portray their frustrations with intensity. The tone of the participants' voices, and their silence, is often more telling and rich than the answers themselves.

For instance, the two surnames most often cited on the Wall of the Vietnam Memorial in Washington, DC, are Johnson and Rodríguez (Rosales 1997).

Chapter Three

1. This objective became particularly important since I started to witness academic discussions that tended to monitorize changes of this genre without taking into account the point of view of those who are active creators, performers, and listeners of corridos. Dr. Manuel Arroyo from the Universidad Autónoma de Ciudad Juárez also helped me in carrying out focus groups with students about their perceptions of corridos.

2. People talked in great detail about the reasons why corridos are important to their everyday lives. What appeared to matter most was the social and moral values that the corrido privileges in its narrative. People liked the ability of the writers to simultaneously transmit information about events that are important to the community and offer social, political, and economic analysis of the context of the events.

3. In 1980 thirty-three inmates were killed by National Guardsmen in an inmate rebellion. The prison was overcrowded, poorly managed (enforcing physical abuse and mixing predatory inmates with minimum-security prisoners), and had poor government funding for rehabilitation programs such as education. The Santa Fe riot is seen in New Mexico as a shameful event in the prison system.

4. Reies López Tijerina, leader of the Alianza Federal de Mercedes (Federal Alliance of Land Grants), is also one of the major leaders of the Mexican American civil rights movement of the 1960s and has fought for retention of the lands, the language, and the culture of the native people of the Southwest. Tijerina founded La Alianza in 1963 as a vehicle for bringing action to enforce the Treaty of Guadalupe Hidalgo regarding the land grants that the United States has not honored. When the U.S. Senate ratified the Treaty of Guadalupe Hidalgo in 1848 and took the territories of New Mexico and northern California from the defeated Republic of Mexico, land grants in the area totaled an estimated thirty-three million acres. The treaty promised to protect the property rights of Mexican landowners living on the land grant properties. The property-owning system in New Mexico was based on Spanish land law that created self-sustaining communities. When the United States took over, the land law system was changed and most of

the lands owned by Mexican Americans became "public domain." In a few years Nuevo Mexicanos lost what their forefathers had held since the sixteenth and seventeenth centuries. The takeover of the land became more aggressive during the time of the Santa Fe Ring: with the coming of the railroad and the need to ship cattle and mutton to midwestern markets, the grant land was needed for grazing. The dispossession of the land in New Mexico created endemic poverty and also deep-felt resentment. As Rosales told me: "Tijerina did not introduce militancy to the villagers; they introduced it to him," because resistance movements had continued among Nuevo Mexicanos since their land was occupied.

In 1967, La Alianza took over the country courthouse in Tierra Amarilla, New Mexico, and held law officers as hostages for several hours. The *aliancistas* arrested the district attorney, who they thought should enforce the 1848 Treaty of Guadalupe Hidalgo and restore property rights to the heirs of those who had lived on Mexican territory at the end of the Mexican-American War. The raid on the courthouse ended with a jailer and a state policeman shot and wounded. The New Mexico National Guard and state police were called, and almost all Nuevo Mexicanos were considered enemies of the country. Tijerina was captured in 1969 and served almost three years in federal prison; he was released contingent on his not associating with the militant parts of La Alianza. Martin Luther King, Jr., invited Tijerina and the aliancistas to be part of the "Poor People's March." Although few mainstream U.S. citizens know about Tijerina's role in the civil rights movement, many Nuevo Mexicanos consider him a hero, and every Chicano studies program devotes space to his contribution to the Chicano movement.

5. In general, the more educated individuals and those with higher incomes tend to have a purist position toward corridos. For them, the true corridos are the ones that were created during or before the Mexican Revolution. The Mexican elite and middle class still looks down on contemporary corridos performed by conjunto norteños and still trace "true" corridos in the archives of the Mexican Revolution. According to these people, contemporary corridos lack the older corridos' emphasis on the concerns of the people.

The evidence from both personal interviews and focus groups suggests that corridos continue to be popular for several reasons: the resonance they have with the community, their ability to narrate a story in a very clear and short manner using the vocabulary of the region, and the moral messages embedded in the narration.

In regard to corridos about immigration, both migrant and nonmigrant participants perceived this genre as an important means of expressing migrants' experiences in the United States. One of the most salient characteristics was the music's propensity to portray feelings of pessimism and sadness. Migrants often mentioned similarities between their own experiences and those portrayed in the corridos.

In general, nonmigrants with higher formal education and income tended to express more eloquently their perceptions, positions, and attitudes toward the phenomenon of Mexican migration to the United States.

6.   In Chihuahua and New Mexico matanza (butchering) is a family and community-gathering event, with friends and neighbors helping in a labor-intensive job of processing a large pig, goat, or sheep. Taking an entire day, the process goes from the slaughtering and butchering to cooking the various meat products and preparing what is left over for distribution or storage. The women in the families make extensive preparations of food to feed the helpers and themselves. A matanza lasts an entire day, from four o'clock in the morning to very late in the evening. Often musicians are brought to the house where the matanza is taking place and play when the men are done with their part of the work.

Chapter Four

1.   Música banda is a brass-based form of music that originated in Sinaloa, a state in northern Mexico on the Pacific coast. Música banda has had a very strong influence on Central European and U.S. band music. It has been quite popular since the late 1990s throughout Mexico and in el México de afuera. Bandas play a wide variety of songs, including rancheras, corridos, cumbias, and boleros.

2.   According to Herrera-Sobek (1993), Corrido de Kiansis (Kansas) developed during the 1860s during the establishment of the major cattle trails from Texas to the newly created railhead in Kansas. This type of corrido is also known as the "Corrido de los quinientos novillos" (The Five Hundred Steers), which has been identified as the earliest complete corrido text that describes the rivalry between tejano vaqueros and American cowboys rivalry in their vaquero skills.

3.   The literal translation of *la quebradita* is "little break." Female dancers "break" their hips with their movements. This dancing genre is the backbone of the modern música banda, which originated in the early 1990s in el México de afuera and northern Mexico as part of the youth culture of Mexican transnational communities. It has a very accelerated tempo and is based on a two-step pattern where dancers rock back and forth between the left and right foot in time with the bass and percussion beats. La quebradita is a very challenging dance that requires athletic abilities to perform the variety of combinations of springs, breaks, and turns.

4.   Tents that were used for variety shows in working-class neighborhoods.

5.   El vallenato is one of the most popular musical genres of Colombia and is becoming increasingly popular in Latin America and the United States. It has strong African roots and is played mainly on the Atlantic coast. The distinctive instruments of el vallento are *la caja* (a small drum held between the knees and played with bare hands); the *guacharaca*, a wooden scraper about

eighteen inches long; and the button accordion.

6. Including words such as *buckaroo* (*vaquero*), *rodeo, lariat, mesteño, canyon, stampede, quirt,* and *lasso*.

7. According to Ramírez (1971, 59), the image of the white cowboy epitomizes the American construction of masculinity based on individuality, desire to conquer men, and nature, ruggedness, and toughness, whereas the vaquero tended to stay as permanently as he could with his employer, work his own small spread while he was also a vaquero, and help his neighbors as they needed. Loyalty to the employer and other vaqueros was important. Rather than moving around different ranches, a vaquero tend to develop a "string of good mounts that he hated to leave for the untried horses he might find elsewhere."

Chapter Five

1. It is significant that Los Tigers del Norte chose to place the mural in this park because Rubén Salazar was born in Ciudad Juárez, Chihuahua, and then moved to El Paso, Texas, where he studied journalism. He was one of the few reporters who covered extensively the Chicano anti–Vietnam War movement and was very critical of the recruitment of Chicanos in the army and the disproportionate number of Chicano casualties during the war. He was a reporter and columnist at the *Los Angeles Times* and the news director of Spanish-language television station KMEX in Los Angeles. In 1970 he was shot by the Los Angeles Police Department shortly after he covered the Chicano antiwar moratorium rally in East Los Angeles. Salazar's violent death has been a subject of Chicano art and academic work.

References

Acuña, R. 2000. *Occupied America: A history of Chicanos*, 4th ed. New York: Longman.

Anderson, B. 1991. *Imagined communities: Reflections on the origin and spread of nationalism*. London: Verso.

Anzaldúa, G. 1987, 1999. *Borderlands/La frontera: The new mestiza*. San Francisco: Aunt Lute Books.

Barthes, R. 1972. *Mythologies*. New York: Hill and Wang.

———. 1981. The theory of the text. In *Untying the text*, ed. Robert Young. Boston: Routledge, 31–47.

Botello, J. 2000. La pared que habla, canta y grita. In *De paisano a paisano*. CD cover SDCD 6092. Van Nuys, CA: Fonovisa.

Chew Sánchez, M., J. M. Cramer, and L. Prieto. 2003. *Sábado Gigante* (Giant Saturday) and the cultural homogenization of Spanish-speaking people. In *The Globalization of corporate media hegemony*, ed. L. Artz and Y. Kamalipour. Suny Series in Global Media Studies. Albany: State University of New York Press.

Crovi-Drueta, D. 1999. Inequidades del NAFTA/TLCAN: Un análisis del sector audiovisual Mexicano. In *Globalización y monopolios en la comunicación en América Latina, Colección Comunicación y Medios de Cultura*, vol. 1. Buenos Aires: Editorial Biblos, 151–70.

Dallal, A. 2000. *El dancing mexicano*. Mexico, D.F.: Universidad Nacional Autónoma de México, Instituto de Investigaciones Estéticas.

Fanon, F. 1968. *The wretched of the earth*. New York: Grove Press.

Fernández, C., and A. Paxman. 2000. *El Tigre Emilio Azcárraga y su imperio televisa*. Mexico, D.F.: Editorial Grijalbo.

Fiske, G. 1991. Popular discrimination. In *Modernity and mass culture*, ed. J. Naremore and P. Brantlinger. Bloomington: Indiana University Press.

Fiske, J. 1987. *Television culture*. London: Metheun.

Foucault, M. 1980. *Power/knowledge: Selected interviews and other writings, 1972–1977*. New York: Pantheon.

Fregoso, R. 1999. Recycling colonialist fantasies on the Texas borderlands. In *Home, exile, homelands: Film, media and the politics of place*, ed. H. Naficy. New York: Routledge, 169–92.

Frith, S. 1996. *Performing rites: On the value of popular music.* Cambridge, MA: Harvard University Press.

———. 1990. Towards an aesthetic of popular music. In *Music and society: The politics of composition performance and reception,* ed. R. Leppert and S. McClarey. Cambridge [Cambridgeshire], NY: Cambridge University Press.

Geijerstam, C. 1976. *Popular music in Mexico.* Albuquerque. University of New Mexico Press.

Gilroy, P. 1993. *The Black Atlantic: Modernity and double consciousness.* London: Verso.

Gómez-Quiñones, J., and D. R. Maciel. 1998. What goes around, comes around: Political practice and cultural response in the internationalization of Mexican labor, 1890–1997. In *Culture across borders: Mexican immigration & popular culture,* ed. D. R. Maciel and M. Herrera-Sobek. Tucson: University of Arizona Press, 27–66.

Halbwachs, H. 1980. *The collective memory.* New York: Harper and Row.

Hall, S. 1980. Encoding/decoding. In *Culture, media, languages,* ed. S. Hall, D. Hobson, A. Lowe, and P. Willis. London: Hutchinson, 128–38.

———. 1981. Notes on deconstructing the popular. In *People's history and socialist theory,* ed. S. Samuel. London: Routledge.

———. 1997. The spectacle of the "other." In *Representation: Cultural representation and signifying practices,* ed. Stuart Hall. Milton Keynes, U.K.: Open University Press, 229–91.

Harding, S. 2004. How standpoint methodology informs philosophy of science. In *Approaches to qualitative research: A reader on theory and practice,* ed. S. Nagy Hesse-Bibber and P. Leavy. New York: Oxford University Press, 62–80.

Hernández, G. E. 1999. What is a *corrido*? Thematic representation and narrative discourse. *Studies in Latin American Popular Culture* 18:69–93.

Herrera-Sobek, M. H. 1979. *The bracero experience: Elitelore versus folklore.* Los Angeles: University of California Press.

———. 1993. *Northward bound: The Mexican immigrant experience in ballad and song.* Bloomington and Indianapolis: Indiana University Press.

———. 1996. Toward the promised land: *La frontera* as myth and reality in ballad and song. *Aztlán: Journal of Chicano Studies* 21 (1–2): 228–61.

———. 1998. The *corrido* as hypertext. In *Culture across borders: Mexican immigration & popular culture.* Tucson: University of Arizona Press, 227–58.

Hetcher, M. I. 1975. *Internal colonialism: The Celtic fringe in British national development, 1536–1966.* Berkeley: University of California Press.

———. 1978. Group formation and cultural division of labor. *American Journal of Sociology* 84:293–318.

Hoffman, A. 1974. *Unwanted Mexican Americans in the Great Depression: Repatriation pressures, 1929–1939.* Tucson: University of Arizona Press.

Hondagneu-Sotelo, P. 1994. *Gendered transitions: Mexican experiences of immigration.* Los Angeles: University of California Press.

hooks, b. 1995. Madonna: Plantation mistress or soul sister? In *Gender, race and class in media*, ed. Gail Dines and Jean M. Humez. Thousand Oaks, CA: Sage, 28–32.

———. 2002. *Black looks: Race and representation*. Boston: South England Press.

———. 2004. Culture to culture: Ethnography and cultural studies as critical intervention. In *Approaches to qualitative research: A reader on theory and practice*, ed. S. Nagy Heese-Bibber and P. Leavy. New York: Oxford University Press, 149–58.

Jhally, S. (producer/director). 1998. *Edward Said on Orientalism* (video recording). Northampton, MA: Media Education Foundation.

Kristeve, J., and T. Moi. 1986. *The Kristeva reader*. New York: Columbia University Press.

Langellier, K. M., and E. E. Peterson. 2004. *Storytelling in daily life: Performing narrative*. Philadelphia: Temple University Press.

Latin American Institute. 1997. *Latin America data base 8* (8). Albuquerque: Latin American Institute, University of New Mexico.

Lefebvre, H. 1991. *The production of space*. London: Basil Blackwell.

Lorde, A. 1984. The master's tools will never dismantle the master's house. In *Sister outsider: Essays and speeches*, ed. A. Lorde. Santa Cruz, CA: Crossing Press.

Lull, J. 1992. *Popular music and communication*. Newbury Park, CA: Sage.

Maciel, D. R., and M. Herrera-Sobek. 1998. *Culture across borders: Mexican immigration and popular culture*. Tucson: University of Arizona Press.

Manuel, P. 1988. *Popular music of the non-western world*. New York: Oxford University Press.

Mariscal, J. 2004. Counter-recruiting the "Hispanic market." *Draf Notices*, March–April 2003, http://www.comdsd.org/article_archive/Counter RecruitingtheHispanicMarket.htm.

Marosi, R. 2005. Border crossing deaths set a 12-month record. *Los Angeles Times*, part A, October 1, 2005, 1.

Martínez, O. J. 2001. *Mexican-origin people in the United States: A topical history*. Tucson: University of Arizona Press.

McDowell, J. H. 2000. *Poetry and violence: The ballad tradition of Mexico's Costa Chica*. Urbana: University of Illinois Press.

———. 1981. The *corrido* of greater Mexico as discourse, music, event. In *And other neighborly names: Social process and cultural image in Texas folklore*, ed. Richard D. Bauman and Roger D. Abrahams. Austin: University of Texas Press, 44–75.

———. 1972. The Mexican *corrido*: Formula and theme in a ballad tradition. *Journal of American Folklore* 85 (337): 205–20.

Meinhof, U., and Jonathon Smith. 2002. *Intertextuality and the Media: From genre to everyday life*. Manchester, U.K.: Manchester University Press.

Mendoza, V. T. 1939. *El romance español y el corrido mexicano*. Mexico, D.F.: Universidad Nacional Autónoma de México, Instituto de Investigaciones Estéticas.

———. 1964. *Lírica narrativa de México: El corrido*. Mexico, D.F.: Universidad Nacional Autónoma de México, Instituto de Investigaciones Estéticas.

———. 1974. *El corrido mexicano: Antología*. Mexico, D.F.: Fondo de Cultura Económica.

———. 1961; repr., 1998). *La canción Mexicana: Ensayo de clasificación y antología*.

Mexico, D.F.: Fondo de Cultura Económica.

Mohanty, C. T. 1991. Under Western eyes: Feminist scholarship and colonial discourse. In *Third world women and the politics of feminism*, ed. C. T. Mohanty, A. Russo, and L. Torres. Bloomington and Indianapolis: Indiana University Press, 51–80.

Muñoz, C. 2000. *The Latino challenge.* http://news.bbc.co.uk/hi/english/in_depth/americas/2000/us_elections/hispanic_vote/newsid_1003000/1003642.stm.

Paredes, A. 1958; repr., 1990. *With his pistol in his hand: A border ballad and its hero.* Austin: University of Texas Press.

Peña, M. H. 2001. From ranchero to Jaitón: Ethnicity and class in Texas-Mexican music. In *Puro conjunto: An album in words and pictures*, ed. Juan Tejada and Avelardo Valdez. Austin: Center for Mexican American Studies, University of Texas at Austin, 31–60.

———. 1999. *Música tejana: The cultural economy of artistic transformation.* College Station: Texas A&M University Press.

———. 1996. Musica fronteriza/border music. *Aztlán: Journal of Chicano Studies* 21 (1–2): 191–225.

———. 1985. *The Texas-Mexican conjunto: History of a working class music.* Austin: University of Texas Press.

———. 1982. Folksong and social change: Two *corridos* as interpretative sources. *Aztlán: Journal of Chicano Studies* 13:13–42.

Pérez, E. 1999. *The decolonial imaginary: Writing Chicanas into history.* Bloomington and Indianapolis: Indiana University Press.

Potter, W. J. 1996. *An analysis of thinking research about qualitative methods.* Mahwah, NJ: Lawrence Erlbaum.

Quiñones, S. 2001. *True tales from Another Mexico: The lynch mob, the Popsicle kings, chalino, and the Bronx.* Albuquerque: University of New Mexico Press.

Ramírez, N. E. 1979. The *vaquero* and ranching in the Southwestern United States, 1600–1970. Indiana University, 0093. *Dissertation Abstracts International, 40* (02A): 1033.

Reyna, J. 1996. Notes on Tejano music. *Aztlán: Journal of Chicano Studies* 13:120–37.

Robles, B. J. July 2003. Latino families: Consumption and purchasing power. Working paper, LBJ School of Public Affairs, University of Texas; Institute for Latino Studies, University of Notre Dame.

Rooney, E. 1990. Discipline and vanish: Feminism, the resistance to theory, and the politics of cultural studies. *Differences* 2 (3): 14–28.

Rosales, F. A. 1997. *Chicano! The history of the Mexican American civil rights movement.* Houston: University of Houston Press.

Rosaldo, R. 1989. *Culture and truth: The remaking of social analysis.* Boston: Beacon Press.

Roy, A. 2004. Peace and the New Corporate Liberation Theology. 2004 City of Sydney Peace Prize Lecture. Sydney Peace Foundation, Occasional Papers series, no. 4/2.

Ruíz, V. 1998. *From out of the shadows: Mexican women in twentieth-century America.*

New York: Oxford University Press.

Said, E. 1979. *Orientalism.* New York: Vintage.

Sassen, S. 1998. *Globalization and its discontents: Essays on the new mobility of people and money.* New York: New Press.

Scott, J. C. 1990. *Domination and the arts of resistance: Hidden transcripts.* New Haven, CT: Yale University Press.

Stokes, M. 1994. *Ethnicity, identity, and music: The musical construction of place.* Oxford, U.K; Providence, RI: Berg.

Talpade Mohanty, C. 1997. Women workers and capitalist scripts: Ideologies of domination, common interests and the politics of solidarity. In *Feminist genealogies, colonial legacies, democratic futures,* ed. M. Jacqui Alexander and Chandra Talpade Mohanty. New York: Routledge, 3–29.

Tigres del Norte genera 150 mdd al año (October 25, 2004). *El Universal.* Espectáculos, 2. Mexico, D.F.

Van Dijk, T. 1995. *Elite discourse and the reproduction of racism.* In *Hate speech,* ed. R. K. Whillock and D. Slayden. Thousand Oaks, CA: Sage.

Williams, R. 2001. Base and superstructure in Marxist cultural theory. In *Media and cultural studies: keyworks,* ed. M. G. Durham and D. M. Kellner. Malden, MA: Blackwell, 152–76.

Index

Page numbers in italic text indicate illustrations.